Penguin Books
Philby

Patrick Seale, journalist, literary agent and art dealer, was educated at Balliol College and St Antony's College, Oxford. He spent five years with Reuter's and another decade with the *Observer*. He first met Kim Philby in Beirut in 1960, when he was writing his first book, *The Struggle for Syria*, a study of Arab politics, and Philby, nearing the end of his espionage career, was Middle East correspondent for the *Economist* and the *Observer* – appointments which Patrick Seale took over when Philby fled to Moscow in 1963.

Maureen McConville, a graduate of London University, began her career in provincial newspapers and joined the *Observer* in 1964. She now works as a book editor, and has collaborated with such authors as Yehudi Menuhin and Bernadette Devlin in the preparation of their autobiographies.

Apart from their biography of Philby, joint books by Patrick Seale and Maureen McConville include *French Revolution 1968* and *The Hilton Assignment* (1973).

PHILBY:

The Long Road to Moscow

Patrick Seale and
Maureen McConville

Penguin Books

Penguin Books Ltd, Harmondsworth,
Middlesex, England
Penguin Books, 625 Madison Avenue,
New York, New York 10022, U.S.A.
Penguin Books Australia Ltd, Ringwood,
Victoria, Australia
Penguin Books Canada Ltd, 2801 John Street,
Markham, Ontario, Canada L3R 1B4
Penguin Books (N.Z.) Ltd, 182–190 Wairau Road,
Auckland 10, New Zealand

First published by Hamish Hamilton Ltd 1973
This revised edition published in Penguin Books 1978

Made and printed in Great Britain by
Richard Clay (The Chaucer Press) Ltd, Bungay, Suffolk
Set in Linotype Times

Contents

Illustrations

Acknowledgements

Since we first began following the trail of Kim Philby, our debt to the many people who helped us has grown to the point where only a general statement of gratitude can be attempted. To all the sources mentioned below, and to the others, our warmest thanks. We hope they will feel that their information has been used fairly and honestly in the sole cause of truth.

H. B. Alexander, W. E. D. Allen, F. Armesto, Neal Ascherson, the Hon. David Astor, Salvo Baker, Mrs Ilsa Barea, Mrs Franziska Becker, Nicholas Bentley, Andrew Berding, Anthony Blake, Denis Blakeley, Mrs H. B. Blunden, Sam Pope Brewer, the late Sir Reader Bullard, John D. Carleton, Sir Roger Chance, the late Sir Richard Clarke, the late Douglas Collins, Mrs Patricia Collins, Colonel Bruce Abd al-Rahman Condé, Mrs Geraldine Cooper-Key, Edward Crankshaw, Mr and Mrs F. W. D. Deakin, the late Paul Dehn, Robin Denniston, J. K. Dick, Maurice H. Dobb, the late Admiral Sir Barry Domvile, the late Allen Dulles, Nicholas Elliot, W. N. Ewer, Mrs Margaret Finch, Mrs Marion Fitzgibbon, David Footman, William Forest, Mark Frankland, Baroness Gaitskell, the late G. E. R. Gedye, Alan Hare, Mrs Eilanna B. Hindle, Miss Clare Hollingworth, Mrs Molly Izzard, Professor Marie Jahoda, Admiral Sir William M. James, Mrs Melanie Learoyd, Mrs Joyce Leather, Jim Lees, John Lehmann, the late Sir Basil Liddell Hart, the late Lady Lindsay-Hogg, Sir William Lindsay-Hogg, Marcus Lipton, Baroness Llewellyn-Davies, James McCargar, G. McIntosh Whyte, Mr McKenzie, the late Donald McLachlan, Anthony McLean, Lieutenant-Colonel Neil McLean, Professor Charles Madge, Dr Wilfrid Mann, Neil Marten, Paul and Olga Matthews, John Midgley, Naomi Mitchison, Miss Elizabeth Monroe, Homer Mueller,

Acknowledgements

K. P. Obank, Professor Roy Pascal, the late Mrs Eleanor Philby, John Philby, Sir Edward Playfair, V. S. Pritchett, Goronwy Rees, Sir Patrick Reilly, George Rentz, Archie Roosevelt, Stewart Samuels, Dr Frederick Scheu, Dr R. B. Serjeant, Miss Evelyn Sinclair, H. Peter Smolka, Mrs Hazel Sporel, Robert Stephens, G. R. Storry, Tom Streithorst, William C. Sullivan, Bickham Sweet-Escott, the late Randall Swingler, Fred Tomlinson, J. Kenneth Thompson, Philip Toynbee, Professor Hugh Trevor-Roper, Donald Tyerman, the late Colonel Valentine Vivian, Sir John Wedgwood, Miss Esther Whitfield, Peter Wilby, Arthur Wittall, George Young, the late Right Hon. Kenneth Younger.

PATRICK SEALE
MAUREEN McCONVILLE
London, 1977

For which will exhibit a true love of his country, the Englishman who follows blindly where his present rulers are leading; who follows them until they have taken his country to certain destruction, or he who joins with that advance guard of the British working class which has already realized that the only possible future for Britain is as a free Republic of an at first European, and later world-wide, Union of Soviet Republics?

John Strachey,
THE COMING STRUGGLE FOR POWER 1932

Foreword

Kim Philby now has his place in Western demonology. His name has become a byword of reproach, a symbol of a peculiarly odious treachery. He is seen as a favourite son who lived only to destroy his family, a viper whose deadly cunning kept him concealed for thirty years in the trusting bosom of his country.

Much is wrong with this caricature, even down to the facts it is based on. Fifteen years after his flight to Russia it is time to take Philby out of his niche in the rogues' gallery and attempt a dispassionate reappraisal of his character and his career. Praise and blame come into the story of any man's life, but this book is more concerned with understanding what Philby did and why he did it than with passing judgement. Not only is it a fuller and more detailed account of his clandestine activities than any yet published, but it also tries to present him in the round, showing how Philby the man struggled and suffered under the burden of Philby the secret agent. In demythologizing the super-spy, this book suggests that he was essentially an ordinary man in an extraordinary situation.

His has been a life much battered by the politics of the twentieth century, and it is to these violent events that he must be related. A spy of his kind, ideologically motivated and politically sensitive, becomes comprehensible only if his exploits are projected against the background of the contemporary history which shaped him and which he, in turn, hoped to shape. Thus the secret agent becomes a man of politics for whom the great issues of international affairs transcend the technical aspects of espionage. Philby's concern for politics was genuine. With great seriousness he travelled from the anti-fascism of the thirties through the struggle against Hitler to the global tensions of the Cold War. In this journey lies the substance of his claim to moral stature. For Philby sees himself as a moral man. He demands that we reconsider the snap judgement of cynical treachery and the charge that he was a blind instrument of Soviet power.

So, if we are to understand him, we must examine both the political background of his story and the moral dilemmas he faced. Was it always my country right or wrong? Could an international ideal, such as Communism for his generation, command a loyalty above that owed to the nation-state? Could Stalin's tyranny be forgiven, even forgotten, because Hitler was the greater evil? Was it not in the interests of humanity to share out America's atomic secrets – even if it meant stealing them? Beyond the narrative, beyond the emotional counterpoint of Philby's loves and marriages, it is the more ambitious aim of this book to lay out the spy on the political and moral dissection table. But, regrettably, it is a fact of espionage that its practice blunts morality and restricts political choice: Philby's tragedy is that, once embarked – with the most generous of motives – on his career as a Soviet agent, he found himself trapped in a situation where he could not do otherwise than he did and where his undoubted moral and political sensibilities had little scope. He is perhaps the principal victim of his own career.

So much for the clever villain of popular myth. There remains the appraisal of his professional achievements in the Soviet service. Both East and West have built him up as the man who made monkeys of the British not once but twice, penetrated to the heart of their secret service, lived a double life for three decades – only to escape in the nick of time to comfortable retirement in Moscow. This summary needs as much correction as the popular estimate of his character. There are some grounds for believing that Philby was pawn as well as player, exploited as well as exploiter in his silent war, and that in the end he was allowed to 'escape' to Russia – a poisoned gift sent by Britain to the KGB in an eleventh-hour attempt to limit the damage of his long betrayal. The question of who won and who lost in any intelligence operation is always a ticklish one, and not less so in drawing up the balance sheet of the Philby dossier.

1 The Mistake of Being Right

> From the earliest times I have ever had a
> comfortable feeling of adequate intellectual,
> physical and spiritual equipment and a definite
> consciousness of my individual right to think
> for myself and to act or speak accordingly.
>
> H. ST JOHN B. PHILBY

Kim Philby grew up in a climate of moral arrogance which armour-plated him for life against the assaults of doubt. In the circumstances it was a valuable asset. The donor of this benefaction was his father, a man who lived for seventy-five years in the passionate conviction that he was right. Harry St John Bridger Philby was a born nonconformist whose belief in his own judgement rocketed him out of British government service in the 1920s to become a freebooting explorer, courtier and adviser to kings in Arabia. This confident, eccentric, domineering father cast a bold shadow over the childhood of his gentle-natured son, and it is questionable whether Kim ever fully emerged from it.

Most grown men have difficulty in recognizing to what extent they have been shaped by their fathers' influence; they prefer to believe that they have outgrown uncritical admiration and now see their parents in an objective, if sympathetic, light. Once out of his teens, no doubt Kim achieved a measure of detachment from St John and assumed responsibility for his own lonely decisions; but the very fact that they were lonely – as well as stubbornly and self-righteously held to – betrays the imprint of the father. Willy-nilly, Kim inherited tastes, interests, habits, values, and notably a scepticism about the wisdom of British rulers and institutions, which were to be decisive in his life.

St John started life conventionally enough. The second of four sons of a tea-planter, he was born in 1885 at Badulla in Ceylon, and was christened St John (a name he embarrassedly suppressed in youth) not for religious or family reasons but merely because it was the name of the bungalow on a neighbouring tea estate where his mother was delivered. Later in life he used to explain his dark, exotic looks, not to mention his rebellious nature, by a joking reference to a family legend: apparently when his parents were travelling in Ceylon, St John, then still an infant, was accidentally left behind at one of the halts. Servants were sent back to look for him but, at the rest house where his parents had spent the night, they found a gypsy woman nursing two babies of similar age and appearance – St John and her own child. Which was which? Identification was difficult as St John's clothes had been shared out between the two babies. The servants recovered a child, but was it the right one?

In the course of time St John won a scholarship to Westminster school where he spent 'six years of real happiness'; and another in 1904 to Trinity College, Cambridge; institutions of which he remained intensely proud to the end of his days. He was a normal, fairly liberal-minded undergraduate who gave little sign of his later nonconformity. A contemporary recalls him reading a paper entitled 'The convenience of convention' to Trinity's Sunday Essay Society, and on another occasion delivering a scathing attack in the Cambridge Union on Wilfred Scawen Blunt, the late-nineteenth-century poet and traveller, for his advocacy of Egyptian nationalist aspirations.

When he came down from the university in 1908 St John, in spite of stirrings of doubt about the whole imperialist package with its ingredients of British supremacy and Christian dogma, was still enough of a straightforward imperialist to enter the Indian Civil Service *con amore*, and to request a posting to the Punjab, which in those days had something of the appeal of a Guards' regiment in that only certain families and their connections were sent there. To his delight his request was approved. He had made some conscious preparation for the job. After three years of classics and modern languages, he had stayed on at Cambridge a fourth year to take a probationary course in Hindustani, Persian and elementary Arabic, and had sat at the feet of the great Persian scholar, Professor E. G. Browne.

But exposure to the facts of imperial rule in India soon brought out the dissenter in St John. As a raw assistant commissioner, whose duties included serving as a magistrate, he early discovered that the ill-paid police took bribes. He loudly declared they should be given a rise on the grounds that they could not be expected to be both poor and honest. He also clamoured against what he considered inequities in the administration of justice, claiming that there was one law for the rich and one for the poor. In the summer months when senior officers were on leave, young men such as St John often took over their jobs with a welcome addition to their own meagre pay. It was during one such interval that occurred the incident which is thought to have snapped his inner loyalty to the Raj. With a contemptuous disregard for Indian caste distinctions, he committed for trial a doctor and a road-sweeper, jointly charged with perjury. Refusing them bail, he had the Brahmin and the Untouchable handcuffed together for their journey to the Sessions court. This high-handed treatment caused a public outcry and much official embarrassment. The young magistrate was reprimanded and deprived of acting promotion by a British establishment that no doubt felt his advanced ideas threatened the foundation of the social order. This was a blow to, among other things, his finances, as by now he had dependants, and so, to supplement his income, he threw himself with characteristic energy into the further study of Oriental languages which had already attracted him at Cambridge. So able did he prove that shortly after the outbreak of war in 1914 he managed to double his salary by securing the appointment of Secretary to the ICS's Board of Examiners in Oriental Languages at Calcutta. The following year, when linguists were needed to accompany the expeditionary force sent from India to drive the Turks out of Mesopotamia at the head of the Persian Gulf, St John was detached for service there – an event that launched him at the age of thirty on his life's work with the Arabs.

Five years earlier, in September 1910, in the little hill-station of Murree, he had married Dora, the tall, striking, red-headed daughter of Adrian Johnston, a municipal engineer in the Indian Public Works Department. Although Eurasians, Dora Philby's parents were fully accepted in the British community both in Murree and in Rawalpindi where they used to go in the winter.

On New Year's Day, 1912, St John and Dora Philby's first child and only son was born in Ambala, a military canton-ment at the eastern extremity of the Punjab, where St John had been appointed Revenue Assistant a few months earlier. The child was named – though not christened – Harold Adrian Russell Philby. Learning that his first-born's initials would spell HARP St John is said to have joked, 'What are you trying to do? Make the boy a bloody lyre?' In any event the child was soon nicknamed Kim, after Rudyard Kipling's young hero; fluent in Urdu and in the constant care of an Indian ayah, this 'little spy' was forever running to his mother with tales from the servants' quarters. The appropriateness of the Kipling reference went further: like Kipling, St John was conditioned by the Anglo-Indian world, largely accepting its narrow social conventions in spite of his feeling for the natives. He was restive with British officialdom, but he re-mained in many ways an upper-middle-class élitist. When it came, his revolt was not against his country, or even the English social structure, but against the little men in positions of power who so often failed to live up to his expectations of what Britons should be. Unfortunately these noble ideals were only too often expressed in his inability to get on with his sup-eriors. But in November 1915, on his posting to Mesopotamia, his break with government service was still nearly ten years away.

He arrived in the Arab world in time to witness the collapse of Turkish rule and to take part himself, as one of a handful of British officials, in deciding how this enormous tract of territory should be governed. The lowly Indian civil servant found himself in the company of kingmakers, a heady experi-ence. It gave him a taste for Arab politics and statecraft at the highest level. But his first tasks were hardly exalted: sorting out the accounts of the civil administration established at Basra on the Shatt al-Arab in the wake of the advancing army, purchasing supplies for the troops fighting up-river, and of course learning to speak Arabic with pungent fluency. On his own initiative he set about the arduous business of drawing up a new land register in the date groves of southern Iraq to replace the chaotic Turkish records of ownership – a labour of Sisyphus which won him a reputation for volunteering for tiring and tiresome jobs. When the Turks were driven out of Baghdad in March 1917 St John became one of the principal aides of the Civil Commissioner, Sir Percy Cox.

But with St John, disputes about policy always tended to become disputes with people, and usually ended with his marching defeated but defiant from the field. So it was in the great debate then raging about what to do with the newly conquered Arab territories. On the conquest of Basra and southern Iraq, some British officials, like the Political Officer, Arnold Wilson, automatically expected the country to be annexed to the Indian Empire. This St John, with his finer sense of what the Iraqis could be led to accept, opposed – with the result that he lost to Wilson his role as deputy to Sir Percy Cox. More seriously, he was to cross swords with T. E. Lawrence, on the crucial question of which Arab dynasty Britain should back as rulers not only of Iraq, but of much of Arab Asia (for simple annexation was early recognized to be unworkable).

The British attack on the Turkish presence in the Arab territories was two-pronged: the one mounted from India against Basra, with which St John was associated; the other mounted from Egypt, developed into the 'Arab Revolt' in which Lawrence, with British arms and gold, assisted the Sharif Husain of Mecca to rise against his Turkish overlords and drive them north through Sinai and Syria. So successful was the revolt that the Sharif's son, Faisal, was acclaimed king in Damascus in 1920, leading Lawrence (and the British government) to envisage establishing other Sharifian princes of the House of Hashim on newly created thrones in Iraq and

Transjordan – more or less as British puppets. St John was utterly convinced that this whole grandiose scheme of Hashemite supremacy was a tragic error. He had seen a new power rising in Arabia and made himself its prophet.

In the autumn of 1917 when St John's quarrel with Arnold Wilson was at its height, his boss, Sir Percy Cox, sent him on a mission to Abd al-Aziz ibn Saud, the ruler of Najd in Central Arabia and chieftain of the Wahhabi, a sect of fundamentalist Muslims whose influence was spreading across the Peninsula and eroding the power of Lawrence's Hashemites in the Hijaz on the western coast. St John's diplomatic mission was to persuade Ibn Saud to stop making war on the Sharif Husain and to turn his guns instead on another tribal chieftain who had sided with the Turks.

What happened to St John on that visit to the heart of Arabia was an emotional experience so intense it amounted to a mystical conversion. He fell violently and for good under the spell of a man and his setting. Ibn Saud was then thirty-seven years old against St John's thirty-two, and six foot four inches tall against St John's five foot eight and a half. The Arab incarnated for his English disciple the noblest of bedouin virtues: great dignity of bearing, courage, a highly developed sense of honour, princely hospitality but austere personal habits. It was to St John's credit that, right from the start, he recognized in this still indigent and uninfluential tribal chief a leader who would wrest from the Hashemites the overlordship of Arabia. With all the extravagance of a convert he trumpeted his hero's claims, to the growing irritation of the British government and its local representatives in whose scheme of things Ibn Saud had little place.

As important as his friendship with the man whom he was to call 'the greatest of all Arabs since the Prophet Muhammad' was his discovery of the Arabian desert. He tasted for the first time the unsurpassed excitements of the explorer, crossing the Peninsula on camel-back from Uqair to Jidda, from the Persian Gulf to the Red Sea, a journey of forty-four days. Only one European, Captain Sadlier in 1818, had made the crossing before him. This experience provided him with material enough for his first book, *The Heart of Arabia*, published in 1922. Once he had glimpsed the vast uncharted wastes, he could not rest until he had gone to chart them.

In August 1920 St John returned to Iraq from his Arabian adventure and a long leave in England, but his independent views made him an unwelcome colleague. The British were then engaged in rescuing Faisal whom the French had kicked off the throne of Syria (where Lawrence had put him), to install him as King of Iraq in August 1921. When Faisal arrived at Basra aboard a British warship, St John, unable to accept this turn of events, resigned. With puckish humour Lawrence recommended him for the job of Chief British Representative in Transjordan, a country carved out of the desert eight months earlier as a fief for yet another Hashemite prince, Faisal's brother, Abdullah. He held this last official position for two and a half years, doing his best to protect Abdullah's independence from the pressures of the French in Syria and the Palestine government across the Jordan. In April 1924 he decided the task was thankless and once more resigned, this time for good. After sixteen years in its service, he severed his links with the British government, and returned to London aged thirty-nine, a free man on a pension. But his passion was Arabia, and he dreamed only of exploring it. The *Daily Telegraph* put up money for him to mount an expedition with Rosita Forbes to the 'Empty Quarter', the great unmapped wilderness in south-eastern Arabia; but they were foiled by the war then raging in the Peninsula between the Wahhabis and the Hashemites. St John tried his hand at peacemaking between the Arab rivals, but when, as he had long prophesied, his friend, Ibn Saud, finally triumphed, he seized the opportunity to leave England and settle in Arabia in 1926, establishing his headquarters in Jidda where he launched Sharqieh Limited, a small trading company, to keep him in funds and to act as a front for his real enthusiasms: high politics and the empty desert.

What was this father to his son? What was it like to grow up in the aura of this unrepentant individualist? In fact, although he heard much about his father, Kim saw little of St John for the first seven years of his life. Even in India, from 1912 to 1915, the household was often deprived of St John's dominant presence when Dora with her baby and nanny retired to the hills for the hot season – to Kasauli, Fort Munro, or Darjeeling – while her husband sweated it out in the plains of the Punjab or in Calcutta. When St John went off with the invading army to Mesopotamia in 1915, Kim, not quite four years old, was shipped to England with his mother – not to see his father for another three wartime years.

His real home in this period was at Camberley in Surrey, where St John's adored mother, the widow of the Ceylon tea planter, lived in modest but respectable circumstances. For the whole of his childhood and indeed for long after, this house was Kim's only haven and his grandmother the one stable presence. She figured larger in his young life than his own mother because Dora was often abroad on the trail of her restless husband. The bond between St John and old Mrs Philby was unusually close and loving. With the same strong, heavy features and stocky build, mother and son looked alike, and shared the same sturdy self-reliance, the same disregard for officialdom. She gave him total approval and admiration, and in return he put her second only to himself in his private scale of importance (with Ibn Saud coming eventually third). His first volume of autobiography, *Arabian Days* (1948), was dedicated 'to my oldest friend, my mother'. This vital, sinuous relationship between them no doubt allowed St John the emotional leeway to treat his own wife with something like cavalier indifference. In the important turning-points of his life Dora appears not to have been consulted, and, in fact, was often left to her own devices while he pursued some private enthusiasm in Persia, Turkey, not to mention Arabia. She was a dutiful wife, letting him come and go as he pleased, but her lively, straightforward, sociable nature hid a lot of hurt and confusion.

In later life Kim too was to sacrifice his women to the imperatives of his career, and it is likely that this pattern owed something to his father's example and much to the sustaining attachment which he shared with St John for the family's matriarch. Old Mrs Philby travelled to India for Kim's birth, and if anybody can be said to have brought him up, it was she. As St John's son and heir, he was drawn into the exclusive relationship and taught to worship with her at the altar of the great man. He learned to blow his nose much earlier than his sisters – three daughters were born to Dora after Kim – because he wanted to make the same noise as his admired father.

Kim was seven when, on the ending of the First World War, St John arrived in London in January 1919 to enjoy his first leave in ten years, and to gather his family together in a rented house in St Petersburg Place. Fresh from his destiny-shaping encounter with Ibn Saud in the Arabian desert, he was already spreading the Saudi gospel on stony ground in Whitehall, already playing John the Baptist to the Wahhabi messiah. But for Kim the visit was memorable less for this obscure talk about desert wars than for the search for a preparatory school where he was to be enrolled. In May 1919 the family moved to Eastbourne for a month to comb the temperate south coast for a suitable establishment. In due course St John settled on Aldro School in Eastbourne itself, where Kim was confined for the next five years, save of course for holidays with his grandmother at Camberley. This conventional upbringing was dramatically interrupted in August 1923 by a summons from the East ordering Kim, then aged eleven, and his grandmother to proceed by ship to Port Said for a summer visit to His Majesty's chief representative in Amman. They were met by St John off the boat and after a brief halt in Transjordan set off almost immediately with their knowledgeable (and opinionated) guide on a grand tour of the area – Damascus, Baalbek, Beirut, Sidon, Tyre, Tiberias, Nazareth, Acre, Haifa, and last but not least Jerusalem. This was Kim's first contact with the Middle East, the first time he met his father's other, un-English persona, the man at home in the Arab world, on easy terms with everyone from King Abdullah to the bootblack. Perhaps for an English schoolboy there were aspects of this Arabic-speaking foreign-sounding personage which took some getting over; but the reassuring imperialist in his father re-emerged back in Transjordan before the end of Kim's visit. A rebellious tribe threatened to march on Amman and depose Abdullah. St John, with Kim in tow, climbed on board a bomb-laden RAF biplane to circle over the mutineer bedouin horsemen and frighten them into submission – an exploit to brag about in placid Eastbourne.

It is not too much to say that 1924 was the year which marked Kim's entry into adult life. He was a precocious twelve-year-old in whom much was well formed, including his exquisitely neat handwriting. Already in embryo was the disciplined, hardworking, tidy, obedient fellow who was to make such a good impression in early manhood. St John took this promising child and pumped him full of his special brand of self-righteousness; and in this way all these socially useful gifts came in time to be put to the service of a private ideal. It was a summer of intense indoctrination. St John had arrived in England in late spring after throwing up public service for good and, free of the last official restraint, was giving tongue more clamorously than ever about the follies of British policy and the need for right-thinking men resolutely to follow the dictates of their mind and conscience. There was no doubt a touch of aggressive apologia in his mood, seeing that his future – and that of his wife and children – was uncertain. When his leave expired he would be reduced to a pension of £700 a year, slashed to a mere £350 once he had traded in half his rights for a lump sum with which to buy a family house. This was a rambling Victorian dwelling in Acol Road, off Finchley Road, West Hampstead, which remained his London base for many years. But all this was secondary. Arabia filled his vision, and his real preoccupation was how to finance a return there in the style and manner of the independent explorer he longed to be.

Kim pulled his weight that summer. He won a scholarship to Westminster, St John's old school, and thus fulfilled a task set him by his father five years earlier. St John pronounced himself 'duly gratified' and as a reward carried Kim off on a tour of Spain, with a special emphasis, of course, on Andalusia, so powerfully marked by the Moors. Back at home Dora was giving birth to her youngest child, Helena, the only one of the children to be born in England. While the baby and her sisters, Diana and Patricia, spent their days in West Hampstead, Kim was trundling across the Iberian Peninsula by train and being lectured on the need to polish up his intellectual equipment and follow his own lonely path, heedless of the jeers of the vulgar herd. Inevitably time was set aside each night for writing up an account of the day's activities. The boy had to be taught to observe with accuracy and record faithfully. Evidence of Kim's efforts survives in a narrative of that journey, remarkable for a child of twelve. It shows high literacy, but little spontaneity – no doubt the price of such formal skills; and it is touched with the moral condescension of a well-bred Englishman travelling among inferior peoples – a curious blend of prep school snobbery and Philby arrogance. This is how Kim's essay opens:

After a tedious journey through that extraordinarily dull, flat country which some misguided people call 'la belle France', with a fat Frenchman in each corner, snoring loudly, and keeping every particle of air out of the compartment by shutting every ventilator and window, we crossed the western limits of the Pyrenees and exchanged the ceaseless bustle of the Frenchman for the calm gravity and noble bearing of the Spaniard.

The customs official is a stout bronzed individual who, in the intervals of puffing out his 'fair, round, belly' chalks hieroglyphics on the packages, with the calm deliberation that exasperates the traveller in a hurry ...

A month later, on 18 September 1924, this judicious child, clad in gown, mortar-board and white tie – the preposterous rig of a King's Scholar – joined the fourth form of Westminster School. Soon the visions of his father, majestic in Arab robes, traversing the sandy wastes on camel-back, winning a king's ransom from a grateful Arabian monarch, faded from his head, overlaid by his own privileged status. He arrived at Westminster with some advantages. Prodded by St John he had distinguished himself in 'the Challenge', a competitive entrance examination, and been elected one of the forty pupils, who have been called King's or Queen's Scholars according to the sex of the reigning sovereign ever since Queen Elizabeth I's new foundation in 1560. The Scholars were the élite of the school. Kim had a further boost in that his father was not only an old boy of Westminster but had been head of the school some twenty years earlier. That, after all, was why Kim was here: romantic and irreverent rebel though St John was, he was also a dutiful child of the British establishment. His revolt was mounted from an impeccably respectable base, and was all the more effective for it. Even had Kim wanted to, there was no escaping his father's ambiguous influence.

Unlike most of the great English public schools, Westminster still stands where at some unrecorded date in the early Middle Ages it was founded, in the shadow of Westminster Abbey. Engulfed by London, across the road from the Houses of Parliament, the school feels itself in touch with the affairs of state. Whenever the House of Commons is sitting, six seats in the Strangers' Gallery are reserved for the Scholars who also have a role in the elaborate ritual of a Coronation. In the seventeenth century Westminster was noted for producing bishops and poets, in the eighteenth statesmen, in the nineteenth soldiers. Ben Jonson was a pupil there, and Christopher Wren, John Locke and Gibbon, Warren Hastings and Jeremy Bentham. John Dryden carved his name on a school bench which is still preserved in the assembly hall. Because the school has grown haphazardly over the centuries, by accretion rather than plan, it has little of the regimented atmosphere of an institution, although it is sheltered from the roar of the traffic by the soaring walls of the Abbey and by the Abbey garden, the oldest garden in London.

As a King's Scholar, Kim lived in an eighteenth-century building, known as 'College', destroyed by German bombs in the Second World War. Upstairs was a dormitory, divided into forty tiny cubicles called 'houses', while on the ground floor the Scholars did their swotting in 'boxes', each equipped with a chair, table and bookcase. Confinement to one's 'box' except for meals, bed and games, was a standard punishment, known as 'desking'. Electric light was brought into general use only in 1923, the year before Kim arrived, but there were few other concessions to comfort: not until the boys complained of chilblains and numb joints, well on into the winter, would fires be lit in the open grates. Meals were served in a fourteenth-century dining hall, modernized in the sixteenth century, where the wooden tables smelled of generations of spilt milk.

The pattern of Kim's school career was that of a slow start quickly made good. In the fifth form, he started off seventeenth in the class and ended up second; the next year he began fifteenth and finished third; in the sixth form, where he specialized in history, he climbed from the bottom of his group to end his career at the top, proud holder of the Marshall Memorial Prize. By that year, 1928, his academic eminence meant that he could no longer be left out of the Latin play which Westminster scholars staged annually (preceded by a prologue in Latin verse written by the headmaster, reviewing the school year, and followed by an epilogue, also in Latin, burlesquing the national scene). But Kim, perhaps because of his stutter, was given only two remarks to make. Nor did he distinguish himself at team games, choosing instead the most solitary sport of all, gymnastics – a voluntary activity at which he was well above average. Each year Westminster sends three prize-winning boys to Trinity College, Cambridge, and another three to Christ Church, Oxford. Early in 1929, when Kim was just seventeen, he was first of the three Westminster boys elected to Trinity, a fitting culmination to his years at school – St John expected no less of him. The story has it that Kim first won a scholarship to Oxford, but on his father's irate intervention switched in time to St John's old Cambridge college.

No doubt one or two incidents interrupted the smooth and studious course of his five years at school. Like many boys growing up in a boarding school he first learned about sex in a homosexual context. Later, in a moment of adult vulgarity, he claimed that at Westminster he had 'buggered and been buggered', an experience which appears to have been emotionally disturbing at the time but which left no permanent mark on him. His stammer was falsely attributed to it, but as he had stammered since the age of four his fear of an over-dominant father was probably to blame. He was not at any stage of his life a homosexual, although he never passed judgement on those who were. Religion, in the compulsory, twice-daily variety doled out at Westminster, was more troublesome than sex. St John, himself a sceptic since his Cambridge days, had impressed on Kim not only freethinking but even a touch of contemptuous anticlericalism. But such attitudes are difficult to fit into the regimented observance of public-school religion, which as a matter of course herds boys through the ceremony of confirmation. So it was for Kim. Confirmation (and perhaps even delayed baptism) were urged upon him – and his was an obedient spirit. But his father's heritage was doubt, and his obedience pulled in two directions. Authority won in the end, but in the struggle Kim was badly mauled. Talking about it later, he said he suffered something like a nervous breakdown. Perhaps his lifelong hostility to religion can be traced back to his adolescent experience. At such moments of unhappiness, it was no doubt his grandmother at Camberley who provided re-assurance and comfort, rather than his mother, Dora, who was only fitfully in the family house at Acol Road. When he was about sixteen Kim began to break free from both women, and in the holidays travel alone in Europe. Before going up to Cambridge, he returned to Spain, the country his father had introduced him to and which was so greatly to mark his future. There he learned to ride a motorcycle, boasting later to his friends that he had reached speeds of eighty miles an hour.

Westminster had proved a pleasant and civilized place and Kim was not unhappy there. The boy was bright but not bril-liant. He had won his honours by diligence and discipline, by an ability to concentrate his energies rather than squander them, by a finely-tuned literacy rather than any great origin-ality or insight. Here was no powerful mind breaking out un-expectedly, but a well-behaved, well-drilled product of an ex-tremely efficient system. The curious thing about him was that even though he won school prizes and ended up first of his class, he made no impact to speak of. He was not forceful or flamboyant, not a leader. He was neither popular nor unpopular, but he made a few close friends who appreciated his quiet, stubborn individuality. He was an honest, decent boy, with a well-entrenched view of right and wrong. In sum he was unassuming, but by no means unsure.

Before the Second World War Jidda was a very unhealthy place. When St John established himself there in 1926, drinking water (from the Nile) was still shipped across the Red Sea by the Khedival Mail Line. Mosquitoes bred in the stagnant salt water of the lagoon and in the fresh water of the wells. Malaria was endemic, and everyone caught it – including St John, although he would never admit it, insisting that his complaint was no more than 'Hijaz fever'. The town, the port where most pilgrims to Mecca disembark, had never known the modernizing hand of a European occupation, but remained a mediaeval city, its narrow streets of beaten earth and its buildings of mud-brick ringed by crumbling fortifications. There was no urban life, no smoking in public, no cinema. Alcohol was strictly prohibited, but boot-legging was rife: whisky cost four times as much as in Egypt across the sea. The foreign community, numbering a score or so altogether, were not allowed to travel inland, while the European women, Dora among them, spent the winter with their husbands but escaped home from the great summer heat, when the men left behind grew beards.

St John was not really cut out to be a businessman. He was too impatient, too prone to take risks, too tolerant of verbal contracting. His control of costs and overheads was uncertain. Routine commercial transactions had little glamour for him, and he ran his company, Sharqieh Limited, as though there were always a bag of sovereigns to be fought for somewhere. Sharqieh was essentially a wholesale business, importing and selling on the local market anything from a handkerchief to a traction engine or a cargo of British coal. At various times over the years St John held the agency for Marconi, the Socony Vacuum Oil Company, Unilever, and – perhaps most important of all – the Ford Motor Company, whose cars and trucks before and during the war were needed to transport the annual flood of pilgrims (earning St John the nickname, 'the commercial pilgrim'). Crates would arrive by sea to be dragged across the sand to the workshops where the vehicles were assembled by a curious band of fitters and engineers of many different origins: Arabs and Javanese, as well as a Scot whom Ford sent from Egypt each year when the fresh intake arrived. One summer St John asked for an extra engineer, an Egyptian, who duly arrived with his young wife. As the European women were away, she was greeted by a party of bearded, wild-looking men – her husband's colleagues. Brought up in urban Cairo, she could not take it and had to be sent home.

Eventually St John established his headquarters in a vast house called the Green Palace, originally built for Ibn Saud to live in on his visits to Jidda. St John rented it as both offices and residence. There, late into the night, he would type away at his manuscripts, dressed as an Arab and squatting Arab-fashion on the floor. But he kept his medals and other relics of his government service in a locked box under his bed. The house was in the care of an old Yemeni door-keeper who lived in a hut at the bottom of the garden, where at night his oil-lamp could be seen flickering among the scrub. When addressing St John, his Arab servants would stand a little way off in case his temper flared up. Although he had a soft voice and enunciated very quietly, he managed to convey a rather frightening impression. He spoke, as Charles Doughty, his great predecessor in Arabian exploration, used to say, 'with the beard on the shoulder'. But if difficult to live with, he could be charming to meet, and cut a lively, if unconventional, figure at what few Western parties Jidda could offer. He liked to shock with such sallies, delivered with a little laugh, as, 'The only difference between me and Lawrence is that I was right,' and, after the Second World War, 'I don't believe in Jesus Christ or Winston Churchill.' Always healthy, he had a strong appetite for strong food (horrifying guests fresh from England by stuffing a handful of green chillies into his mouth) and for strong drink, although, sensitive to Muslim custom, he never drank outside Jidda, and then only in Western households. He always tried to be out of Arabia during the fast of Ramadan. Cricket was perhaps the only obsession he had brought from England. When

British warships called at Jidda, cricket matches were played on the sand. St John claimed a world record stumping four batsmen with consecutive balls. He was sometimes to be seen crouching over a radio in a corner of his office – listening to a Test match.

From the start St John's patchy business career took second place to his love for politics and exploration. He had come to Arabia on a political hunch: it was his judgement that Abd al-Aziz ibn Saud was one of the great figures of the twentieth century who would emerge as the dominant figure in the Middle East, sweeping away his Hashemite and other rivals. As his chief champion and foreign adviser, St John no doubt anticipated a role of the first importance for himself at the centre of Arab affairs. His great admiration for Ibn Saud was equalled only by the intensity of his exasperation with British policy, which on every Middle Eastern issue – particularly its encouragement for Zionist colonization in Palestine and its missed oil opportunities in Arabia – struck him as profoundly wrong-headed. A Foreign Office official once summed up his uncomplicated creed as 'a simple dualism in which the spirit of darkness is represented by H M G'. Not that he was anti-British: for all his years in Arabia he never abandoned his British nationality; rather he was convinced that the British government was damaging British national interests. Right at the start of his independent career he had tried to influence policy-making in London by seeking adoption as a Labour parliamentary candidate for Cambridge in 1926; but the General Strike was on, no trains were running, and he could not appear before the selection board. His distaste for the Raj and his own rebellion against authority had led him to put his hopes in the Labour Party. He became a Fabian (and lectured on Arabia to Fabian summer schools). But his grasp of British domestic issues was as wobbly as the British Left's concern for his own precious Arabs. Disillusion was mutual, and St John plumped once and for all for the desert.

In a way the desert let him down too. Ibn Saud largely united the Arabian Peninsula but political triumph in the rest of the Arab world eluded him. He never had the resources to exert real influence much beyond his own frontiers and in any event, despite the King's own stature, his country was to lag far behind such established centres of Arab power as Baghdad and Damascus, not to mention Cairo. Only when Saudi Arabia's gigantic oil reserves began to be exploited in bulk in the 1950s did St John's prophecies of its importance start to take on substance. The broad trend of his predictions may have been correct, but his timing was hopelessly optimistic. However, in the small pool of Saudi politics there is no doubt that St John was a frog of considerable size. From the beginning he was an intimate of the King's, bringing a Western judgement and a steady stream of information (culled from assiduous listening to radio broadcasts) to the court's counsels. When in 1930 Britain appointed Sir Andrew Ryan as Minister in Jidda, St John played a useful role as intermediary. Far more important, he was the go-between in 1933 who eased the way into Arabia for American oil interests, with momentous repercussions for the future prosperity of the country. But he never achieved his real ambitions. Nothing he did managed to shake the Middle East ground plan laid down after the First World War, and when change did come it was powered by radical ideas very different from those of his beloved Wahhabis. Arabia itself disappointed him, and he lived to become a bitter critic of Saudi incompetence and corruption. Admittedly the obstinate, egotistical, awkwardly clear-sighted St John was not an easy man to get on with. With the Saudis as with the British he made the bad mistake of always being right.

Fortunately for him, exploration was a passion equal to politics, and into it he was able to channel his frustrated ambitions. He had broken out of the strait-jacket of government service, abandoning its rewards of pomp and power, because he wanted to lead a free life without a master. From 1926 onwards, Ibn Saud was probably the only man he deferred to as his boss. In return he gained unique access to the Peninsula and the backing of the most powerful man in Arabia. His greatest joy was to roam about the desert in a Ford V8 station wagon, mapping, recording, collecting geological samples, archaeological remains, rare flora and fauna – and indulging in the local sport of shooting desert hare from a moving car. When the oil men came to Arabia they had a high regard for St John's topographical descriptions (although it has been said that his bedouin companions, wary of his fiery temper, would sometimes make up names for features of the landscape, rather than admit to ignorance). He knew his own merits as a geographer. When Britain used force to dispute the Saudi claim to the Buraimi oasis, he declared, 'Of course it belongs to Saudi Arabia. I drew the map and I should know.' Over the years he criss-crossed the immense country many times, scoring many 'firsts', although to his intense vexation he was beaten by Bertram Thomas to the 'Empty Quarter', that austere El Dorado of Arabian explorers. Pushing south, with an armed guard, he crossed into the Yemen and the Aden Protectorate, causing a minor international incident, which prompted the Imam of the Yemen earnestly to request Britain 'who is aware of every single thing that happens to inquire carefully into the matter ... and to inflict a suitable punishment on Mr Philby'. Unpunished, St John returned to his home base. His intentions were no more sinister than to be the first European to cross an unexplored route or to visit a site of historical interest.

This compulsion secretly to penetrate virgin territory was only one of the occupational traits of the explorer in St John. Like so many others, he displayed the characteristic mix of secretiveness and its opposite, a desire for publicity. Like other explorers, too, he was something of a masochist, priding himself on travelling without camping paraphernalia and even when sedentary on needing no more than a table, chair, typewriter and kerosene lamp. His adoption of Arab dress hinted at a love of disguise. And like those for whom the forest, the Antarctic, or the top of Everest are alone 'pure' and 'good', so he showed the same fundamentally anti-society attitude in his worship of the desert. The first judgement made by one explorer about another is, 'He's a liar and out for publicity'; so too St John tended to dismiss as 'trespassers' other visitors to 'his' territory, and to resent the fact that Lawrence had pinched Arabia in the public imagination. Even rival birdwatchers he accused of watching the wrong birds; and at

dinner at the Green Palace an argument between 'experts'
would lead to a carcass on its way to Kew being brought out
of the refrigerator and passed round the table.

It seems likely that within a very few years of settling in
Arabia St John saw clearly the limitations which this backward tribal society must necessarily impose on his restless, ambitious spirit. Certainly as early as 1929 he was finding Jidda
cramping. But he did not retreat as he could so easily have
done – he was then still only forty-four. Instead he deepened
his commitment, he stuck to his moral guns; he had chosen Ibn
Saud and Arabia, and he was damned if he was going to throw
them over – even if there was no fortune to be made, no
political crown to be gained, but much tedium to be suffered in
Saudi company. Morally self-approving, but having also carefully weighed social and political reasons, this apostle of the
lonely will decided to 'go all the way with the Arabs'. In
August 1930 he cast off his Western background and embraced Islam.

By this time Kim had been a year at Cambridge. From infancy he had learned much from his father but of all St John's
lessons perhaps the most enduring was that virtue in life lay in
making one's own choices, and then, in fair weather or foul, in
sticking to them.

2 Loss of Innocence

> We're the Trinity Soviet-ski
> You bet-ski!
> Just let-ski
> Us sing u our little song-i-vitch
> Not long-i-vitch
> But strong-i-vitch.
>
> Down with the law and order-ski;
> Represented by the Porter-ski;
> 'Tis our intent to shoot-i-vitch
> Don, Fellow, Dean and Tutor-vitch.
>
> *The Trinity Magazine*, February 1930

Had Kim gone up to Oxford he might never have become a Russian spy. His father's intervention sent him instead at one of the most impressionable moments of his life to Cambridge, and to Trinity – the very college which was to become the power-house of intellectual Marxism in Britain.

Trinity men considered themselves an élite, recognizing few others worthy of attention except perhaps a small counter-élite at Kings. They were members of a rich and powerful institution, and they lived and worked in noble buildings. Kim used to sit in Wren's great library where a statue of Byron, a former Trinity man (declined by Westminster Abbey on the grounds that the poet was immoral) dominates the room. Above the statue is a window, depicting Fame presenting Newton to George III, and Bacon taking a note of the proceedings. Kim, too, took notes, in his precise and microscopic hand.

Among the lordly, pranking, indolent nabobs who gave the college its tone, he was altogether unremarkable. Trinity contained 'most of the very rich young men who hunt, go to New-market, ride in the Cottenham point-to-point and are, very sensibly, determined to aim at nothing higher than a pass degree'.[1] In no college was there a greater acreage of check

1. John Steegman, *Cambridge: As it was and as it is today* (London, 1940), p. 95.

caps and dirty moustaches. As Kim's contemporary at Trinity, Nicholas Monsarrat, wrote in his autobiography, 'We rowed a little, ran a little, even played football a little ... We played poker as often as possible ... We had lazy lunches on the river ... We were there to play and grow up.'[1] But this frivolous hedonism was by no means universal. It did not at all matter if one was not in the smart set, or did not join the Pitt Club or the Hawks. Unlike the smaller colleges, which encouraged 'college spirit', Trinity was big enough to tolerate nonconformists. Effectively no one noticed what pattern one followed, and Kim had no reason to feel left out.

He was still only seventeen when he arrived at Cambridge to read history in October 1929. With nothing showy or aggressive in his nature, and sustained by a quiet self-respect that he owed to St John, he spent a rather reserved and solitary first year, bringing no close friends from school and seeming to make none. Very likely his stutter was a barrier to easy sociability. His best friend at Westminster, Tim Milne, went up to Oxford that October (but they continued to meet in the holidays, and their lives were to cross many times in the years to come). Joining no club, playing no sport, lacking a wide acquaintance, Kim spent his hours of lonely leisure obsessively listening to the music of Beethoven, often with tears in his eyes. With characteristic orderliness he learned to refer to each work by its opus number. His room on Jesus Lane (where the rents were stiff) was dominated by a photograph of the then famous French concert pianist, Alfred Cortot. He tried to play the French horn but made little progress. Ibsen, Turgenev and Dostoevsky filled his bookshelves, for in literature as in music Kim was fastidiously restrictive, maintaining there were only two or three authors worth reading. He read them repeatedly and knew them very well. One of his first acquaintances at Cambridge, Anthony McLean, recalls lending him Tolstoy's *Resurrection* in the Maude translation (and never getting it back) in exchange for Turgenev's *A Nest of Gentlefolk* in the

1. *Life is Four-Letter Word*, Vol. 1 (London, 1966), pp. 325–8.

Constance Garnett translation. Another contemporary, John Midgley (now Washington correspondent of *The Economist*) remembers Kim then as 'earnest, modest and rather "good" '.

Neither Kim nor Cambridge at large had much time for formal politics. By the time he arrived the older men who had come up to the university from service in the First World War had gone down, taking their political consciousness with them; the world crisis of the early thirties had not yet forced public affairs on a new generation. In the late twenties there was a brief interlude when the contradiction between the pursuit of knowledge and pleasure for their own sakes and a world recurrently threatened by war and barbarism could be ignored.

Of course the forums for political debate existed at Cambridge, as they had always done, but politics as practised in the Union or the clubs was little more than an occasion for oratorical display. Serious issues interested only a tiny minority, were poorly understood and aroused no passion. Insofar as views were expressed at all they were reactionary and uncritical. If Union debates may be taken as a guide to the climate of the time, undergraduates were confident that the soaring unemployment could be conquered, and were in no hurry to end British rule in India where Gandhi had started his campaign of civil disobedience. According to *Granta* of 24 October 1930, the Liberal Club was dead, the Conservative Club was recruited from the nearest boathouse, while the Labour Club 'with its thirty-nine officials and at least four ordinary members' met three or four times a term in Matthew's Café, in an atmosphere bristling with points of order. It was still poetry, rather than politics, which captured the minds and filled the conversations of young men of intellectual aspirations who sneered both at the hearties and at the wealthy philistines. But there were signs that this escapism was already being questioned. The university was just beginning to be aware that some nasty, possibly even dangerous, events were happening out there in the world. There was a hint of a loss of innocence, of the beginning of guilt, in *The University News* leader of June 1930: 'We are worried because we are not really worried about the League of Nations, another war, India, the Government, and politics in general. We think we should do better to work ourselves up into a frenzy about these things, and we shall try to do it.'

Kim's generation were babies during the Great War. They remembered nothing of it at first hand, nor of the European order which had led to it – but what they learned they didn't like. The prevalent mood was iconoclastic, disenchanted. Nearly everyone had read Lytton Strachey (very much a Trinity product himself) and Victorian high-mindedness was out, dismissed, although not always justly, as hypocrisy and pompous self-esteem. In the union, on the stage, at the 'flicks', the rhetorical or the high-flown were always greeted with derisive laughter. Perhaps the first enemy was the edifice of stuffy bourgeois proprieties and traditions that governed the lives of middle-class England. It is difficult today to realize just how exclusive class barriers were, and how uncomfortable many young people felt at being penned in behind them. Their whole moral and social landscape was in disorder as the Church, the monarchy, marriage and the family, class, rank and uniforms – indeed, anything that seemed to smack of the old smug pre-1914 system – came under attack.

There were, then, some things about which young men were prepared to be serious. If they had a political idea at all, it was pacifism. The better informed would have read G. Lowes Dickinson's *The International Anarchy*, Norman Angell's *The Great Illusion*, Arthur Ponsonby's *Falsehood in Wartime*. The war and all that it had involved was regarded with contempt, and particularly the frame of mind which could tolerate such senseless slaughter. At a packed Remembrance Day meeting staged by the League of Nations Union in Cambridge Town Hall in November 1929, the principal speaker, Laurence Housman, bitterly flayed the war leaders, the 'secret treaties', the long-drawn-out agony. The mayor of Cambridge in the chair dissociated himself from these unpatriotic criticisms, but it was Housman's anti-war sentiments that were applauded. Rupert Brooke was out of fashion, and many undergraduates read Remarque's *All Quiet on the Western Front*; huge crowds went to see the film which was fulsomely reviewed in the undergraduate press. This was the war which had corrupted all human values, the war in which your girl friend turned prostitute while you were at the front.

It was precisely in the realm of private morals that the sophisticated young broke most openly with traditional values. Conventional sexual ethics were very much in dispute, with D. H. Lawrence's *Pornography and Obscenity* serving as a text for undergraduate discussion, as did Aldous Huxley's *Brave New World* (although this was in fact a critique of brave new attitudes). In a dig at the old solemn values, Gavin Ewart composed a poem beginning, 'Imagine all the dons in the attitude of buggers'. No one remembers Kim having a girl friend at Cambridge, nor boy friends, in the technical sense. But in anti-war sympathy at least, he was part of the current. One of the first glimpses of him at Trinity shows him acquainted with a pacifist Hungarian artist, Szigeti Szucs, who published a book of angry drawings from the front, called *My War,* in the style of George Grosz, if a little less savage. He was a quiet little man who, a contemporary recalls, often found his way to Kim's room.

'In the outer world issues have to be faced and decisions taken. Here they are rarely faced and rarely taken,' lamented an undergraduate newspaper, the *Cambridge Gownsman,* with a touch of wistfulness in April 1930. It was true that on the surface Cambridge seemed as uncaring as ever but, as this comment showed, consciences were beginning to stir. The demolition work on bourgeois society wrought by the war and the sceptical twenties had been very effective. Minds had been cleared and made receptive for new ideas. Into the vacuum charged left-wing politics.

Kim's introduction to these ideas took place in a direct and personal fashion. He was not weaned from Beethoven and the Russian classics by reading socialist theory or by first-hand experience of social injustice. Instead he learned the first principles of socialism from men whose own harsh schooling had turned them left. The remarkable fact is that his first real friends were coal-miners. There were at the university at that time half-a-dozen former workers, among them two ex-colliers who had fought their way up from the coal-face to the pinnacle of British élitist education by means of scholarships from the Miners' Welfare Fund. A genuine proletarian at Cambridge was a rare, even an outlandish phenomenon: to many in the regiment of privileged youth, they were like dogs walking on their hind legs. A contemporary commentator, John Steegman, considered they would be better off elsewhere: 'Discouraging though it may be for social reformers, the man from the elementary school is unquestionably excluded from everything that makes Cambridge worth while.'[1] Older than the other undergraduates, matured and coarsened by work, with uncouth accents and empty pockets, the miners found adjustment painful.

The more prominent of the ex-miners was Harry Dawes who coped with Cambridge by his gritty refusal to take on protective colouring. He insisted on being himself. So obstinately did he cling to his working-man's cloth cap that he was taken, on occasion, for a member of the Pitt Club. His dedication to the cause of the workers had been forged by ten years on the coal-face and the harsh ordeal of the General Strike of 1926. In spite of his patchy education he was a lively and effective speaker, causing the debating hall of the Union to resound with his proletarian evangelism. Reports of his speeches in the undergraduate press referred to his fierce working-class sincerity, which sometimes embarrassed his well-bred audience. As early as November 1930 he was recommending the wholesale nationalization of British agriculture and the abolition of the landlord, 'pure parasite in many cases, incompetent ninny in others'. Dawes, an exact contemporary of Kim, read Economics and did well, staying on at Trinity after taking his degree for a fourth year of research. It may well have been under his influence that Kim switched to Economics in his third year (after taking a third in the summer of 1931 in Part I of the History Tripos). With the spreading world depression, economics was, of course, the subject to study, particularly if

1. Steegman, op. cit., p. 95.

one's mind was beginning to open to politics. Nor could Kim have been indifferent to the intellectual glamour of John Maynard Keynes, or of Dennis Robertson, who became Kim's economics tutor, then engaged with Keynes in a public debate on the causes of the slump and its remedies.

Dawes was the first person at Cambridge really to take Kim up, to jostle him out of his self-sufficient isolation and introduce him to that other world outside, then becoming an object of curiosity to undergraduates in the privileged sanctuary of their colleges. Dawes was a most spontaneous and likeable person who readily gave his friendship. He was very popular with many people who had never known an ex-miner before. This was certainly Kim's situation, and in fact Dawes was probably the first working man he ever got to know.

As a friend of Harry Dawes Kim met another ex-collier, Jim Lees, who came straight from the coal-face to Cambridge in 1930 and who was, if anything, still more to the left: a member of the Independent Labour Party, that leftist ginger group of British socialism, and drifting towards Communism. His pit had been closed for thirty weeks after the General Strike and that year Lees had drawn only two days' pay before Christmas. This victim of capitalism had for his younger, more privileged friends something of the aura of a sage. He gave them a taste of the cutting edge of workers' militancy, but his appeal was not only political: at a time when Bernard Shaw was an undergraduate idol, Lees was preaching the excitements of James Joyce's *Ulysses*. Kim and Lees became very fond of each other.

In the first months of their acquaintance Lees found Kim a sombre figure. 'He didn't go round much with anyone, and I thought him rather humourless but also very generous in an unostentatious way. Austere and high-principled, he hardly ever drank.'[1] To Lees, who a year earlier had been in the pits dragging a tub of coal chained to his middle, Kim seemed a privileged chap, with a distinguished father and lots of money. But he noticed that Kim did not behave like a person of privilege. He did not seem aware of his advantages, and had

1. Jim Lees, a personal communication to the authors.

Philby

no sense of upper-class values. Nor was he concerned about the
fate of the proletariat: he was just indifferent to it, treating
every man on his merits.

The truth is that Kim too was in his way an outsider. In spite
of Westminster, the whole focus of his upbringing was abroad,
in India and Arabia. It was that overseas, imperial aspect of
Britain which he knew about, rather than the realities of
Britain's social structure. With his father turned Muslim and
selling motorcars in the East, he may have found it hard to
place himself with conviction in a British hierarchy. His very
ignorance of England protected him from snobbery.

What sort of socialism did Kim learn from the miners? In
a nutshell they were campaigning for a militant alternative to
the feeble, gradualist, irredeemably constitutionalist policies of
their own leaders. Their bitter analysis sprang from the
General Strike of 1926 and its disastrous consequences. In this
trial of strength with capitalism, the working class had been
ignominiously defeated. Its will had been broken. Union membership had slumped. The Labour movement seemed on its
knees. Such men as Dawes and Lees despised the leadership of
the movement as defeatists who had never really believed in
the success of the strike, who had flinched from recognizing
the class character of the workers' demands, who had shied
away from challenging their enemies with an assertion of
working-class strength outside Parliament on the streets.

British socialism was still paralysingly demure when Ramsay
MacDonald brought Labour back to power in 1929, and it was
this government's deplorable record that the colliers were
attacking when Kim got to know them. Far from wielding a
socialist sword against the deepening economic crisis, Mac-
Donald sought a truce with his Tory opponents in Parliament,
wondering how far it was possible 'to consider ourselves more
as a Council of State and less as arrayed regiments facing each
other in battle'.[1] Anything that was militant or that smacked
of class conflict was jumped on, no less by the Trades Union

1. From MacDonald's first speech as Prime Minister. See *Hansard*,
Vol. 229, for 2 July 1929.

Congress than by the parliamentary party. So unradical was its programme that G. D. H. Cole described it as one in which 'socialism found neither place nor mention'. Independent Labour Party (ILP) proposals for a minimum living wage were dismissed as 'flashy futilities', while Oswald Mosley's recommendations of cheaper money, higher pensions, and greater public control of industry and banking were given equally short shrift. Inexperienced, irresolute, inhibited by its own nature from embarking on revolutionary transformations, Labour under Ramsay MacDonald failed hopelessly in tackling the biggest problem confronting it – that of one and a half million unemployed.

Panic-stricken in the face of events it could not control, the Labour government simply broke up. On 24 August 1931 MacDonald, in the conviction that his first duty was to the country, abandoned the Labour Party and joined the Conservatives and Liberals in forming a National Government in a bid to beat the crisis. But immediately the new team was battered by a series of fresh emergencies: a naval mutiny at Invergordon, the Japanese invasion of Manchuria, a flight of funds from London forcing Britain off the gold standard. Deciding that his National Government needed a fresh mandate from the nation, MacDonald called a general election for 27 October.

From one term to the next Cambridge was hurtled into politics. From July to October 1931 the walls of the ivory tower crumbled before the magnitude of the crisis outside, and personal indulgence in playing, learning and growing up was seen to be glaringly inappropriate. With Britain lashed by the tidal wave of the world slump and Labour drowning, with the defector MacDonald trying to keep his premiership afloat in the floodwater, politics were the only thing that mattered. In an atmosphere of unprecedented political ferment, Cambridge tackled the great issues: Was the slump an uncontrollable world phenomenon, or was it due to the greed and incompetence of the British ruling class? Could the ills of the British economy be cured by piecemeal tinkering, or was a radically new approach necessary? Could Parliament ever solve the country's problems, or did revolution provide the only hope? Was social democracy finished? Was MacDonald a traitor or a national saviour?

Nowhere were the arguments more passionate and agonized than in the thin and divided ranks of the Cambridge socialists. Driven out of business by the failures of the Labour Government, the university Labour Club had collapsed in the spring of 1931. For a month or two the socialists were without a forum, until Harry Dawes with some kindred spirits leapt into the breach to found the Cambridge University Socialist Society. This was a decisive moment in the evolution of Cambridge in the 1930s. From then on the CUSS was the home of the new Left, the platform for the debate which was to shape a whole undergraduate generation. Working men at Cambridge on scholarships had laid a foundation for leftist thinking; but with notable exceptions like Harry Dawes, these proletarian scholars were extremely cautious, sharing the profoundly non-revolutionary philosophy of the trades unions in which they had been brought up. Now, however, with the formation of the CUSS, the leftward movement really began to gather pace as public schoolboys, from an altogether different social and moral background, took up the cause. Unlike their less privileged precursors, they felt they had a right to lead and to express themselves, with the result that when Britain developed a radical intelligentsia – comparable to the much longer established tradition on the Continent – it was an essentially middle-class phenomenon.

Kim, not yet twenty, was thrown in at the deep end of these exciting developments. Drawn into the CUSS by his mentor, Harry Dawes, its secretary and prime mover, in October 1931, Kim gained his political education in the society and over the next two years moved with the prevailing current from political innocence to militant social democracy, and finally to Communism.

His journey began with the election campaign of October 1931 in which Kim, in what was probably his first experience of active politics, canvassed in the Labour interest. All that was left of parliamentary socialism had regrouped under Arthur

Henderson to fight the turncoat MacDonald and his national coalition at the polls. This Labour rump was no more radical or clear-thinking than the ill-fated Labour government that had gone down before the crisis. Parliamentary gradualism – the view that capitalism would smoothly make way for socialism by constitutional means – remained its credo. But what else was there for a budding socialist to support?

From the start of the election campaign, described by the *Manchester Guardian* as 'the most fraudulent of modern times', MacDonald took up the challenge offered by his old colleagues and turned his guns on them. Asking voters for a wide ranging 'doctors' mandate' to rescue Britain from the deathbed, he denounced Labour's programme as 'Bolshevism run mad'. In Cambridge, as in the country at large, Labour was thrown on the defensive. All Harry Dawes's eloquence could not prevent the Cambridge Union from defeating by 146 votes to 62 the motion that 'This House would welcome a triumphant Labour victory at the polls.' Outside the Union Dawes and his social democrats also had a hard time. Phalanxes of Tory hearties came in force to break up the first CUSS meeting of the term in Matthew's Café that October, shouting, heckling and singing patriotic songs. 'Within a few minutes the disturbance had become so great that the manageress was forced to intervene and close the meeting,' reported the undergraduate press. 'This announcement was greeted with cheers, and then, like a battle-cry came the thunderous roar: "Loyalty first, socialism afterwards!" At this point, Mr H. Dawes, of Trinity, the Secretary, sent for the Proctors and the Police. Later the loyalists used stink bombs.'[1]

In Cambridge where Kim and his CUSS friends were canvassing for Labour the candidate was Geoffrey Garratt, an ex-Indian civil servant who had turned to gentleman farming and writing. Somewhat left of centre, he was a bit of a misfit in the Labour movement, being neither a trade unionist nor an intellectual theorist. He admired the Russian revolution, criticized the Labour leadership for its deep-rooted suspicion of the Soviet experiment, and believed that Britain could at least have

1. *Varsity*, 17 October 1931.

a shot at a bloodless, socialist revolution.[1] In mid-October 1931 Kim and four other keen young socialists, Blackburn, a young science don and his wife, John Midgley, and D. W. Ewer (son of 'Trilby' Ewer of the *Daily Herald* and later Professor of Zoology at the University of Ghana), canvassed the agricultural constituency in an open tourer. Their task was to travel ahead of the candidate to keep his meetings warm in widely scattered, draughty village halls.

It was a holocaust. At the general election on 27 October Labour was annihilated, securing only fifty-two seats against the National Government's 554 (Garratt, too, was buried in the landslide, although to his credit he held the Labour vote at its 1929 figure, polling 11,013 votes against 23,742 for the Unionist candidate, Captain R. G. Briscoe). The catastrophic defeat was to be of supreme importance for the development of Kim's own thought, and indeed for the progress of the left in Britain. The Labour Party appeared to have committed suicide. Henderson and his successor, the septuagenarian George Lansbury, still clung to their feeble, submissive reformism and appeared to have learned nothing from the disaster, recommending no stronger medicine at their post-mortem conference than a programme of long-term education for the electorate: action here and now, outside Parliament if necessary, was not even considered. Such arguments for doing nothing cut little ice in Cambridge. With no experience of politics but the crisis, with no Fabian inhibitions, with no understanding of the traditional caution and moderation of the British working class, the young socialists of the university plumped as one man for radicalism. For them the illusions of social democracy were exposed as hollow; the whole philosophy of gradualism, central to Labour Party doctrine, was utterly discredited. As Shaw had said, you might as well try to fry eggs with a sewing machine as get socialism through Parliament. All went left, driven by furious convictions which John Strachey was soon to express: 'It was necessary for me to see

1. See *The Mugwumps and the Labour Party* (London, 1932), in which he expressed disillusion with the ineffectual role of Labour intellectuals – Mugwumps – in British politics.

with my own eyes and at close range the mingled impotence and treachery of social democracy in action; to put my fingers upon the stigmata of the poltroonery of Henderson, Lansbury, and Greenwood; and my hand into the gaping spear wound of the turpitude of MacDonald, Thomas and Snowden, in order to know that this corpse would never rise again.'[1]

It was the world of tomorrow beginning to happen.

1. 'The Education of a Communist', in *Left Review*, No. 3, December 1934, p. 65.

3 The Student Soviet

> HungeR and WaR
> On the door,
> Inside 10
> 'Big' men.
> Outside 44,000,000
> Men women (and ch,ooo,ooo).
>
> 'Revolutionary Poem', by Charles Madge,
> published *Cambridge Left*, Winter 1933–4

In late June 1931, as Labour stumbled towards collapse, a handful of Marxists met discreetly in Cambridge to form the first Communist cell in the university. From this cell was to grow a movement which gave the new explosive radicalism born of crisis a dogma and a structure. Almost immediately the Communists identified left-wing social democrats such as Harry Dawes and his CUSS stronghold as their chief rivals for undergraduate minds. It was this conflict between the forces of the left, won by the Communists in 1933, which thrust Kim into his lifelong commitment – an early victim of the intellectual revolution of the 1930s.

The Communist Party of Great Britain was eleven years old when it decided that students were ripe for recruitment. Founded in 1920 it had faced an uphill task in attempting to forge a revolutionary party in unrevolutionary England. It had failed pretty abjectly to penetrate the working class still overwhelmingly loyal to Labour, and it (and its newspapers) survived only on Soviet subsidy. In 1931, however, the deepening recession, Labour's disgrace and the awakening political consciousness in British universities encouraged the CPGB to believe that its hour had come. Within a few months of each other embryo Communist organizations were set up in London, Oxford and Cambridge. At University College, London, the Gower Socialist Society, founded in the autumn of 1931, met in a pub for over a year because the university authorities refused to recognize it. A Marxist Society saw the light of day at the London School of Economics at the same time, while Oxford's October Club was established in January 1932.

But Communist headquarters at King Street, London, made its earliest and biggest effort at Cambridge. Judging the moment propitious in June 1931, it sent one of its leading luminaries, Clemens Palme Dutt, an expert on student work, to nudge the intellectuals into action. Although little was left to local initiative, the formation of the cell that June afternoon seemed spontaneous. About half-a-dozen sympathizers – young dons, research students and one or two undergraduates – had been informally invited to meet Dutt to discuss the new mood in Cambridge. Someone, it may not even have been Dutt, suggested it would be a good idea to form a Party cell in the university. Before the meeting broke up that afternoon, the cell existed, and its membership, strategy and immediate targets had been decided upon.

Incontestably the man who had done most to prepare the ground for this decisive step was a young Trinity economics tutor, Maurice Dobb, who was then just about the only known Communist in the university. Even further afield he had a reputation as a pro-Soviet propagandist and pamphleteer forever denouncing, in books and in his articles in the *Sunday Worker*, the 'marionette show' of bourgeois democracy, and extolling the virtues of Russia's new race of man, 'disciplined by the machine and by labour'.[1] He combined steadfast party allegiance with mastery of Marxist economics, an amiably donnish manner, and the diction and indeed much of the appearance of a Cambridge aesthete. He had started his work of quiet proselytizing as early as 1925, and given it more formal shape in the winter of 1927–8 by founding a small discussion circle called the League Against Imperialism (a name borrowed from a national left-wing pressure group run by an eccentric diplomatist turned 'comrade', Reginald Orlando Bridgeman).

Dobb's League in Cambridge was never more than a handful of young people meeting round his fireside to discuss econo-

1. Cf. Maurice Dobb, *Russia Today and Tomorrow* (1930); *In Soviet Russia, Autumn 1930* (1930); and *Soviet Russia and the World* (1932).

mic theory and socialist practice. But for those who attended it was an exhilarating intellectual experience: Dobb's Marxist analysis was in such marked contrast to the economics they learned at lectures, as well as to the timid economic thinking of the Labour Party. The League met in his tall, narrow house in Chesterton Lane which, once his doctrines began to spread, became a second home for left-wing undergraduates, and earned the nickname 'the Red Household'. Without Dobb, Trinity could not have become in the early thirties the undisputed centre of Cambridge Communism. The formation of the cell in June 1931 marked the beginning of the decade of his greatest influence: numerous generations of undergraduates are in his debt and among many economists whose views he helped form was his contemporary, Joan Robinson, then an assistant lecturer and who later held the chair of economics there. Long consigned by his modesty or his politics to the margins of academic life, Dobb's gifts eventually won him recognition: a Trinity Fellowship in 1948, a university readership in 1959, Fellowship of the British Academy in 1971. He died in 1976.

No doubt it was Dobb who handpicked the little band of the faithful to meet Clemens Palme Dutt that afternoon. Who were they? One was John Desmond Bernal, a thirty-year-old physicist and crystallographer later to gain great eminence, a Marxist convert of the twenties. He gave his blessing to the cell but, preferring not to be actively associated with student Communism, did not become a member. Two other men largely responsible for the intellectual stiffening of the cell were Roy Pascal, a young Fellow of Pembroke College who shared Dobb's house, and D. H. Stott, a psychologist (whom his friends used to tease by calling him 'Daily Herald' Stott, which, in view of the *Herald*'s conformist Labour politics was an insult to an active Communist). These men did not shine as party organizers but their intellectual distinction helped make Communism not only respectable but also attractive to the best undergraduate brains.

The 'proletarian' founder members of the cell were Kim's collier friend, Jim Lees, and Bugsy Wolfe, a young Jewish East

Ender then studying biochemistry under J. B. S. Haldane, whom he recruited for the party. Lees had arrived at Cambridge a left-wing social democrat but, disgusted by Labour's record in power, had by the spring of 1931 crossed the line into the Communist camp. In fact he stayed there no more than twelve months, returning early in 1932 to the less exposed Labour movement. It was still thought dangerous to be a Communist, as undergraduates had been sent down from Oxford for political agitation. The early thirties were also a time of high graduate unemployment. Lees's wife was expecting a baby and he was worried about job prospects, a caution characteristic of those early working-class Communists who were just breaking into bourgeois life. On going down in 1933 Lees was relieved to be offered a teaching post worth £200 a year at Nottingham University – where he remained until his retirement in 1969. As for Bugsy Wolfe, he lent the cell a cutting edge of real class bitterness. He had arrived at Cambridge in 1929, straight from political rough-houses in Stepney and consumed with a violent loathing of the Labour Party, which he saw as the chief obstacle to revolution in Britain. Later in the thirties he too opted out of politics to settle into academic life in Glasgow.

Maurice Dobb's Cambridge cell might, however, have remained an obscure, inbred sect, with little impact on the university at large, had it not been for one remarkable young man: David Haden Guest. He was the towering figure of that first generation of Cambridge Communists, from the formation of the cell in June 1931 to the arrival in October 1933 of John Cornford, the revolutionary tornado who swept the movement to its triumphant climax in the middle thirties. Cornford inherited an established student party: its first promoter was Guest.

A mixture of great brilliance and naïveté, he had already demonstrated his precociousness at Oundle in a flood of essays and poems. He came up to Cambridge the same term as Kim to read philosophy and mathematical logic at the feet of Ludwig Wittgenstein. But the philosopher, who preferred disciples to interrogators, found his incessant and turbulent questioning

53

a thorn in his flesh. However, philosophy for Guest was soon thrust into second place by politics.

After only two terms at Cambridge he went to the University of Göttingen in the summer of 1930, attracted by the advanced philosophical thinking in Germany. Before he returned to Trinity a year later he had seen enough at first hand of the beginnings of Nazi violence to convince him that Communism alone could save the world from this barbarism. To appreciate the impact of this experience it should be recalled that the Germany then threatened by the Nazis had a very special place in the imagination of most English intellectuals. It seemed to them the most radical, the most promising part of the bourgeois world where the defeat of 1918 had swept away the shackles of class and philistine convention, releasing a powerful current of daring left-wing thought. This was among the attractions of Germany in the late twenties for such men as W. H. Auden, Stephen Spender and Christopher Isherwood before the explosion of Nazi hate. British intellectual life in contrast seemed stifling and constipated.

Guest came to Germany a socialist and a pacifist, but these temperate views did not long survive. The turning point was his arrest at a Communist youth demonstration on Easter Sunday 1931. Held in solitary confinement for a fortnight he was released only after going on a hunger strike. 'I shall never get myself into danger again so long as I live,' he wrote, 'or at least only on *very urgent matters of principle*.'[1] (In fact he was to die on a Spanish battlefield six years later.)

He went back to England soon after this ordeal, bursting upon Cambridge like a revolutionary prophet, invested with the glamour of having served in the front line of the ideological war on the Continent. The fact that the holder of a British passport had been jailed without trial on trumped-up charges no doubt also helped to bring home to many minds the wickedness of the Nazis. There at the birth of the first Communist cell, Guest soon took over the leadership to become an unstoppable force in Cambridge politics. This was a triumph for

1. 'Göttingen 1930–1', by Max Black, in *David Guest*, ed. Carmel Haden Guest (London, 1939), pp. 58 ff.

Maurice Dobb: the movement was off the ground on under-graduate wings.

The first decision the cell faced was the choice of its main target. Should it direct its attack against the still largely apathetic student body, living much as it had done before 1914, a citadel of unquestioned privilege? Or against proletarian Cambridge, the drab lines of workers' cottages beyond the railway bridge in Romsey Town? 'In Cambridge there was "town" and there was "gown",' Nicholas Monsarrat wrote in his autobiography, 'and there could be no damned nonsense about mixing the two up. We were "gown" and we were pleased as Punch about it ... A good deal of impenetrable snobbery was involved, and we clasped it to us firmly.' It was due partly to Bugsy Wolfe that the cell chose to concentrate on the 'town', rather than the 'gown'. Like other working-class students he had a touch of caution and defensiveness in his attitude to gilded, confident, undergraduate Cambridge. To evangelize the colleges seemed quite hopeless. This may have fed his belief that the main target of the cell should be the town.

How did they go about it? In those early months there was a good deal of brave tub-thumping at empty street corners, distributing leaflets, selling the *Daily Worker*, protesting against high council house rents and inadequate school buildings. All this activity left the town unmoved and very largely unchanged: a few converts were made, a town branch was eventually organized, but the real impact was on the proselytizing students themselves. It taught the first generation of middle-class undergraduate converts that Communism was action as well as discussion. It brought them into actual contact with the workers. It allowed them to see their student movement as part of the workers' struggle to defend their standards at a time of massive unemployment in the country at large.

Back in Trinity after such sorties to Romsey Town, they mugged up Marxist theory. One of Guest's first acts on taking over the cell was to found a Marxist study group, which in effect took over the functions of Maurice Dobb's League against Imperialism. It discussed *Das Kapital* and other socialist classics, chapter by chapter, long into the night. After these sessions, held in Guest's scruffy, spartan room at Trinity – bare except for a large bookcase, a piano, and a picture of Lenin – he led the comrades in revolutionary songs. There was nothing temperate about his Communism. He seemed constantly at white heat, working at menial tasks from morning till night, preaching, arguing, heckling. His contemporaries remember him marching into hall at Trinity with the hammer and sickle prominently displayed on his lapel. But more often than not he simply forgot to eat, or even shave or change his clothes. He was a faintly dotty, intellectually brilliant Communist saint who could not look after himself.

There was something more than a shade priggish and self-righteous about these first-generation Communists. They were immensely certain that in Marxism they, and they alone, had the key to the scientific understanding of society. The confidence that they were right allowed them to patronize others. The workers may have been their theoretical ideal, but they were also viewed as a rather dim-witted lot, capable of grasping only one point at a time, and then only if it were dinned in. Maurice Dobb's early pamphlets, for example, spelled out the issues with the greatest crudity. But inside the privacy of the cell, the bright young converts went in for orgies of logic-chopping. They could and did, argue endlessly as to whether 'Merchant Capital' was the same as 'Merchant Capitalism', a phase postulated by the Bolshevik heretic, Pokrovsky, as occurring between 'feudalism' and 'industrial capitalism'.

The Cambridge cell's first year was a period of intense self-absorption, a time of girding up ideological loins in conditions of semi-clandestinity. It forged its own identity by cutting itself off from, and vowing total hostility to, every other force on the left – not only the Labour Party but left-wing social democrats and even the I L P. Seen through its ultra-sectarian spectacles, all who were not Communists were 'social fascist reptiles', rotten brethren to be struck down.

Chief among these were, of course, the social democratic leadership of the Cambridge University Socialist Society, the undergraduate institution above all others which the Communists had to penetrate and take over if their power was to be recognized. Still in its infancy in late 1931, the Communist cell faced a strong SD phalanx in the CUSS, which as well as the society's secretary, Harry Dawes, included another trade unionist, Bill Ingham, from Nelson, Lancashire, who as a wartime conscientious objector enjoyed much prestige in undergraduate socialist circles. The CUSS chairman was A. L. Symonds, of Jesus College, who fourteen years later won Cambridge for Labour in 1945. Two other middle-class stalwarts were R. W. B. ('Otto') Clarke, an able and ambitious young economist, later Sir Richard Clarke, a senior Whitehall administrator, and Anthony Blake of Magdalene College, later a City insurance broker. Blake was to follow Dawes as CUSS secretary in 1933, when *Granta* reported that he was the most hard-working left-wing politician in the university. 'He is that not uncommon phenomenon – a socialist with an aristocratic vice. He fences.'

These commanders were supported by a small army of foot soldiers – of whom one was Kim Philby. Otto Clarke recalls that in those early months of the CUSS, when its target was more the moribund Labour Party than the Communists, only just beginning to show their teeth on the left, this earnest young man was a 'sensible, reliable member of the SD caucus. But he was no great intellectual and you would not have picked him out for distinction. He seemed then a useful bureaucrat, the sort who would have made a good career in Unilever.'

It would be wrong to suppose that a hard-and-fast frontier separated these social democrats occupying the centre of the ground from men to the right and left of them. The debaters in the CUSS were ranged in a disorderly continuum from the mildest critics of MacDonald's National Government to the most violent advocates of revolution. The Society was ideologically in a state of constant flux, but with the current running leftwards. In this moving stream, it was not always clear who was to the left of whom. The Communists had begun to organize themselves in Cambridge, but they were not yet in a position to emerge from their study circle and make a real bid for power in the Society. In 1931 Communist Party membership was not yet fashionable, and could mean that one was cut by former friends. In any event, such was the blurring of boundaries that the Communists were not alone in clamouring for drastic revolutionary remedies to cure the sickness of capitalism. So grave was the world crisis that few members of the CUSS, if any, disputed the general Marxist analysis that capitalism was near extinction. The question was not whether socialism was necessary, but how to bring it about. It was a debate not of ends but of means. Left-wing social democrats such as Harry Dawes and Otto Clarke argued fiercely that 'a revolution of some kind' was necessary to strip the privileged class of its powers. In the Cambridge Union in October 1932, Dawes attacked the central doctrine of Fabian reformism by proposing the motion 'that the inevitability of gradualness is an exploded and impracticable creed'.

In fact while Dawes was still tilting at Fabian moderation on his right, the Marxist challenge to his views had already emerged on his left. His social democrats still provided the main officers of the CUSS, but the intellectual centre of gravity was moving into the Communist camp. The frenetic activity of the first Cambridge Communist cell was beginning to bear fruit. The original hard core of David Guest, Bugsy Wolfe, Roy Pascal and D. H. Stott had brought in a second generation of recruits, so that some twelve months after its formation the cell numbered about twenty members, largely centred on Trinity and still looking to Maurice Dobb for doctrinal guidance, although increasingly organized by the undergraduates themselves. By mid-1932 the Communists had split the CUSS into two wings, locked in theoretical debate – but also in a less high-minded struggle for power.

Perhaps the most important of the new recruits was Maurice Cornforth, like Guest a Trinity philosopher (now a director of the Communist publishing house, Lawrence and Wishart), who had come up to Cambridge to work for a PhD, after taking a degree in London. He fell immediately under Guest's influence. He had seen Guest at a meeting 'bubbling over with excitement' about Lenin's *Materialism and Empirio-Criticism*. 'I went straight home and read the book, and thereupon decided to join the Communist Party.'[1] Cornforth's importance was as an administrator of this crucial phase of Cambridge Communism. He and Guest made an impressive team, with Guest supplying the fire and Cornforth the organizational structure. As their activities grew, Cornforth became secretary of a town branch of the CP, with a proletarian membership, while Guest was secretary for the University.

Two other promising newcomers to the cell were James Klugmann and Donald Maclean, who had both come up to Cambridge to read modern languages in October 1931 from Gresham's, a school whose radical tradition in the twenties attracted the sons of left-wing politicians. At Cambridge they became close friends, eventually rising to the first rank of the Communist hierarchy. By 1933–4, Maclean had made his name as a speaker, reviewer and propagandist, while Klugmann was lieutenant to John Cornford, the outstanding student leader of the mid-1930s. Today, Maclean is in Moscow, while Klugmann is a senior functionary and the historian of the British Communist Party.[2] Klugmann's lively sister Kitty married Maurice Cornforth shortly after he arrived at Cambridge and they set up house above a pawnbroker's in King Street. This became the organizing centre of the Cambridge cell. There was a good deal of Klugmann money, and the Cornforths, although not approving of bourgeois wealth, were not averse to spending it to promote the cause. They found it spiritually and psychologically more enriching to dedicate their lives to the movement than to embark on a conventional career. So absorbed did Cornforth become in Party work that he left the university without completing his PhD.

Ever more numerous and more confident, the Party organized innumerable, almost daily, rallies, conferences and discussions. It redoubled its canvassing in the 'town' which was a good training ground for speakers; while back in the colleges young Communists met in study groups, trying to relate Marxism to history, to science, to religion. They strove to get

1. Maurice Cornforth, 'The Growth of the Student Movement', in Carmel Haden Guest, op. cit., pp. 95 ff.
2. James Klugmann died September 1977.

Philby

Marxism accepted as a philosophy in the curriculum. They held luncheon parties and talked endlessly. But private conversations and personal relationships were, above all, the sure basis on which success was built. Elaborate lists were kept of sympathizers, near-sympathizers, and in general of everyone Communist students knew. Systematic collecting and converting and recruiting were the main occupations.[1] They set themselves to become the best workers in their own factory – the university. They argued that Marxism led to good degrees, and one of their slogans was 'Every Communist is a good student'. They saw themselves as members of a secret commando force, bound together by an iron Marxist discipline, marching to the assault of sleepy, unsuspecting Cambridge. With the obvious exception of David Guest, whose casualness and eccentricity of dress were notorious, most of the members of the movement were not bohemians but dressed well and behaved respectably. Indeed, if one's clothes were shabby and one's hair long, one risked being approached for recruitment on the grounds that slovenly habits were a sign of rebellion, listlessness and lack of purpose. Communism offered a remedy.

Confronted by all this evidence of swelling Communist strength, the social democrats were thrown on the defensive. Inside the CUSS, the Communists were still a minority of the 200-odd members, but they mustered greater arguing power. They gained of course from the way in which events in Britain and the world crowded in to support their diagnosis that Western capitalism was doomed, but perhaps their greatest asset was their utter conviction. Springing from a pragmatic tradition, the social democrats could not be so sure of the answers. At political meetings, David Guest would get up and scream and gesticulate at social democratic speakers with passionate disregard for conventional civility. His bulldozing certainty undoubtedly influenced even those who laughed at him.

Kim spent his last year and a half in Cambridge right at the centre of this political excitement. Quiet and unassuming as he was, not in any sense a political prima donna, yet he was en-

1. 'Cambridge Socialism', by A Group of Contemporaries, in *John Cornford: A Memoir*, ed. Pat Sloan (London, 1938).

60

gulfed in the debate and followed its every twist. After many months of service in the ranks of the CUSS, helping his friends Harry Dawes and Otto Clarke to fight off the growing Communist challenge, he rose in October 1932 to be treasurer of the Society and was thus well placed to watch the power balance shift in the Communists' favour. It was a contest which divided his friends as it divided his own mind. He was caught in an intensely exhilarating tug-of-war.

Sunday was the most political day of the week. In the morning there was a meeting of the Breakfast Club, an exclusive left-socialist group of five or six members which had been meeting informally from late 1931 and into which Kim was co-opted. It included Otto Clarke, R. H. ('Freddie') Cook (later a distinguished classical archaeologist), and a few others, mostly from Clare College. Kim's friend, Anthony McLean, was a member until he crossed the line and joined the CP in January 1932 when his Sunday mornings were taken up selling the *Daily Worker*. Thus he missed a breakfast meeting to which Kim brought his father to meet the group on one of St John's visits home from Arabia. Jim Lees met Kim's parents at that time and remembers St John as a very bearded figure, and Dora as distinctly handsome. They made a considerable impression, and there was no suggestion that money was not in plentiful supply. To his friends Kim seemed intensely proud of his father. He frequently recounted to Lees stories of his father's virility, shared his father's bitter disappointment when Bertram Thomas was first across the Empty Quarter, and spent whole days on the very eve of his final exams correcting the proofs and compiling the index of St John's account of his own desert crossing.

On Sunday afternoons the young socialists would often attend the Film Society to see a classic of the early cinema, perhaps *Earth*, or *Storm Over Asia*, or some other Russian masterpiece brought to Cambridge by 'Comrade' R. L. Dreschfield's Society for the Promotion of Cultural Relations with Soviet Russia. An ardent Soviet propagandist, Dreschfield was, like Donald Maclean, at Trinity Hall. In the cinema Kim's own preference was for René Clair, and Anthony McLean remembers him and Otto Clarke doing a mime based on *Le Million* up the stairs to Kim's rooms at Trinity. It was fashionable if you were left-wing in those pre-Hitler days to be pro-German, but Otto used to say that René Clair almost made him feel pro-French. From the film show, Kim and the others used to go on to a CUSS tea, held about six times a term in a café near Christ's, and usually addressed by a speaker from London.

But although pretty firmly at this time in the social democratic camp, Kim did go about with members of the Communist faction. Two of his closest friends, Jim Lees and Anthony McLean, were Communists and no doubt they influenced him (although Lees left the Party in the spring of 1932 and McLean went down that summer, a year ahead of Kim). Through these contacts he also came to know David Guest, the presiding prophet of Trinity Communism, but he did not attend Guest's Marxist study group. However, from early 1932 he regularly saw copies of the *Daily Worker* (passed on to him by Harry Dawes who in turn got them from Anthony McLean). McLean remembers that Kim praised the *Worker* with unexpected warmth: 'The only paper without trivia, mendacious advertisements, and social chit-chat,' or words to that effect. In May 1932 Kim and McLean attended a Union debate in which Maurice Dobb and another young Trinity don, George Kitson Clark, spoke on opposite sides of the motion 'that this house sees more hope in Moscow than Detroit'. As was to be expected Dobb was passionate in defence of Russia, attacking capitalist individualism which, he claimed, spelled ruin, and more particularly America 'where the big trusts operate like gangsters'. In rebuttal Kitson Clark ended, according to *Varsity Weekly*, 'with the old magnificent cry of human individualism, the state may have my body; to me is my soul and mind'.[1] Part of Dobb's argument was that, unlike America, the Soviet Union produced nothing so nasty as a pornographic film. 'What about *The Village Of Sin*?' a White Russian heckled from the floor. 'It's only called that abroad,' Dobb retorted. Kim was not convinced. As they left the debat-

1. 21 May 1932, Vol. V, No. 37, p. 3.

ing hall he told McLean he felt Dobb had doctored the evidence. He was already closer to Moscow than Detroit, but not yet there.

At a loose end during the Christmas 1932 vacation – his parents were as usual abroad and Camberley offered little excitement for a young man eager for new experience – Kim decided on a lonely exploration of the unemployment-stricken provinces. Jim Lees arranged for him to rent (at £3 a week) the Nottingham flat of W. J. H. Sprott, a former Cambridge man who had taken up a lectureship at Nottingham University. In the early thirties Nottingham was known as 'the Queen of the Midlands' and was supposed to have a whore on every street corner, but Kim's tenancy was respectable and even austere. Later in the same vacation, Lees found Kim lodgings with a real coalminer, Bob Wright, who had a house at Huthwaite where Lees's wife came from. This may have been Kim's first contact with the drab discomforts of working-class life, but his hosts found neither guilt nor embarrassment in their earnest and politely inquiring lodger. If Kim had a social conscience he did not make a song and dance about it. He noted the facts of social injustice, and no doubt they played their part in his political evolution, but he was not an hysterical socialist like so many of his contemporaries.

That was one pole of Kim's life at the time. Another was Guy Burgess who had come up from Eton to Trinity in 1930 and had since set Cambridge buzzing with his wit, intellectual agility and general outrageousness. Guy was known to everyone who mattered, and shone as much among the scholars as the snobs. He was a Pitt Club man, at ease in the car-racing, poker-playing, beagling set. But he had also been elected an Apostle, a member of that Cambridge club which was so exclusive and certain of its excellence that it could afford to call itself simply 'the Society'. Election to the Apostles was thought to be a mark of outstanding and all-round distinction, and Guy, whose conversation was a fireworks display of epigram and erudition, was an obvious candidate. Another of Guy's accomplishments which at that time by no means excluded him from the Apostles' company was his daring and promiscuous homosexuality. For that matter homosexuality was accepted in Cambridge as a whole. The dons tended to be either married or homosexual, although not all of the homosexuals were sexually active and many suffered from feelings of guilt. The Cambridge economist, Sir Dennis Robertson, in whose rooms Kim and Burgess first met, went to see Freud in Vienna seeking a cure, while Goldie Lowes Dickinson, an eminent but ageing Apostle, used to lament that he could no longer have policemen. Heterosexual activities were viewed with less tolerance, and in any event there was remarkably little mixing of the sexes in the university. Girls from Newnham and Girton sat in the front row at lectures and normally no one talked to them: their colleges provided a seemingly inexhaustible store of adolescent jokes. In the Michaelmas term of 1932 the President of the Union clashed with the Senior Proctor over a proposed motion for debate: 'that the sexual morality of Christian civilization is unscientific and harmful'. The Proctor took objection 'to the word "sexual", which, he alleged had an unpleasant ring about it'. The debate was cancelled.[1]

When politics became fashionable Guy became political. From one night to the next he appeared to have read all the books and to be fluent in the higher reaches of socialist dialectic. But he was not beguiled by practical socialism or by the presence of ex-miners at Cambridge, even if some fun could be derived from them. Burgess had met Jim Lees in the room of the history don, George Kitson Clark – the very rooms where a year earlier Kim had made the acquaintance of Anthony McLean. From the twenties to the present day, Kitson Clark has seemed for generations of undergraduates as permanent a feature of Trinity as the Great Court.[2] Burgess

1. Letter from S.D., Middle Temple, in *The New Statesman and Nation*, 23 December 1933.
2. Mr Kitson Clark
   Tries to keep it dark
   That he has of late
   Been putting on weight.
   Trinity Magazine, Lent 1931.

took Lees up, earning a mild reproach from an elderly American don, Gaillard Lapsley, whose snobbery had earned him the title of 'the Unknown Etonian'. 'Guy, dear boy,' he said to Burgess one day, 'I see you about with the common fellow Lees. Do you think it wise? Surely it will damage your social standing?' 'But Gaillard, you're so old-fashioned,' Guy retorted. 'Fraternizing with the working classes can do my social reputation nothing but good.' Jim Lees had no wish to indulge Guy's interest in him as a bizarre specimen, and so only reluctantly accepted his invitation to lunch with Victor Rothschild, a socialite Harrovian who was also a Trinity contemporary (now Lord Rothschild, the scientist and administrator).[1] After lunch cigars were passed round. 'Take one, Jim,' Guy urged in a deliberately audible whisper, 'they're worth three-and-sixpence apiece!'

Kim was too fond of Lees, too involved in genuine issues and too kind a person anyway to enjoy such malicious baiting, but there is no doubt that he found Burgess immensely companionable and may well have envied his entrée to brilliant and well-connected Cambridge. As the logic of the future was to dictate, it was the friendship with Burgess which endured, not that with Lees, and which in fact dogged Kim's whole life, possibly shaping it more than any other human contact.

Such then was the range of Kim's acquaintance at Cam-

1. 'I spent an entertaining afternoon at the Speed Trials on Saturday. The general standard of driving was good ...

'Victor Rothschild provided a genuine thrill when his lovely Mercedes came into view. The manner in which he pulled up to avoid Denis Conan Doyle's Austro-Daimler, which was lying broadside across his path, was masterly.

'He was travelling at over 100 mph when he crossed the finishing line. Fortunately he was slowing down just before the mishap otherwise I do not think we should have seen the Mercedes in Cambridge again.

'This would have been a tragedy for there are so few cars of this quality belonging to undergrads. these days.

'He seemed little perturbed by his accident, and was entertaining guests at an amusing cocktail party in Jesus Lane, later in the evening.

'Victor Rothschild is an ardent dance music enthusiast and plays the piano with considerable technique.' (An Undergraduate's Diary, in *Varsity Weekly*, Vol. IV, Number 31, 27 February 1932.)

bridge, from proletarian activists at one end to men of such contrasting magnetism as David Guest and Guy Burgess at the other. Kim was of their company but not really intimate with any of them except perhaps Lees. He was almost an unsociable undergraduate, not addicted to parties where so many young men's friendships are cemented. Impressed by his seriousness, his friends believed that he did not really approve of socializing. Like a figure on the edge of a group photograph, he was simply there, judiciously noting, decently maturing, but not shining, not standing out. In Moscow years later Burgess was to describe the Kim he knew at Cambridge as 'always solitary but always popular'.

Just outside Kim's circle of political contacts was Donald Maclean, a forceful recruit to Communism who by 1933 had so distinguished himself among undergraduates that Kim could not avoid noticing him, although they were barely acquainted. Where Kim was still feeling his way in politics, Donald, exceptionally mature at twenty, already knew what was wrong with contemporary Britain: 'The economic situation, the unemployment, vulgarity in the cinema, rubbish on the bookstalls, the public school, snobbery in the suburbs, more battleships, lower wages ...'[1] Here were the supremely confident tones of fashionable middle-class Marxism, but there was more to Maclean than that. His contemporaries were already aware of the ambiguous, multi-layered personality that was to see him through his espionage career. In November 1933 *Granta* interviewed him:

Q Mr Donald Maclean, I presume?
DM How do you do?
Q It is my job to examine the undergrad's personality. Would it embarrass you if I took a glance at yours?
DM Not a bit. But which one? I have three dear little fellows. Here comes Cecil. Perhaps you would like to begin with him.

1. *Cambridge Left*, Winter 1933–4, a review by Donald Maclean of R. D. Charques, *Contemporary Literature and Social Revolution*, pp. ii, iii.

CECIL Oh my dear, you *did* startle me. I was just slipping into my velvet trousers when I heard you call. What *is* the fuss? Has anyone shaved off our hair, or destroyed the Picasso?

DM No, nothing like that, Cecil. I want to introduce you to *The Granta* representative.

CECIL Oh how sweet! You must come to my next party. I am going to have *real* passion flowers, and everybody is going to dress up as a poem ... *Do* come.

Q Delighted. But what are your favourite pursuits?

CECIL Oh, I usually spend the morning being a figure on a Greek vase – so Attic and delightful. Of course I'm very keen on being critically aware: after all, as Mr Leavis says, it is the *only* thing.

DM Now run along Cecil and get on with your tapestry-work.

CECIL (sulkily) Very well, goodbye. I hear that dreadful creature Jack coming – I must fly.

DM Jack, this is *The Granta* representative.

JACK Hullo, chaps. I was just having a steak at the George. Awfully good fellows there – and dam' fine waitresses too. (He winks.) ...

Q ... May I ask how you spend your day?

JACK Oh, I just crack around, you know. Buy a few club-ties here, and smash up a flick there. Bloody marvellous.

Q Have you no ambitions, Jack?

JACK Rather. My heart's set on getting into the Hawks. They are such wizard blokes. Besides, the blazer is topping – it looks grand with a Crusader's tie and Sixty-Club trousers.

DM That's enough, Jack – you'd better go and oil your rugger boots.

JACK OK, Cheerio.

DM I hope I'm not boring you, but you haven't met Fred yet. He's very busy just now, trying to find out whether Middleton Murry is material or merely dialectic. Shall I get him?

Q Yes do, Mr Maclean. I'm anxious to see all your personalities.

FRED What do you want? I'm working. Who is this?

DM Be civil, Fred. This is *The Granta* representative. He wants to find out what you do and what you think.

FRED (a large smirk of pleasure spreading across his face). Oh I see. Good morning. Have a cigarette?

Q (suspecting a bribe) No thanks.

FRED Well. The point is this. Everybody ought to work. That's what I'm here for. I want to get on. Take Shakespeare or Henry Ford – they knew what was what. I belong to eleven societies and three lunch clubs. I once read a paper on Lessing's *Laokoon* (in German, of course.) I hope to get a first. It's all due to *hard work*. Any questions? None – well that's all right. I am afraid I must go and see a man about a thesis. Goodbye.

DM Well, that's that.

Q It was very interesting Mr Maclean – but, tell me, which is your favourite personality of the three?

DM I like them all equally. I see no standard against which to set them, no hierarchy in which to put them – they are all of the same value to me.

Q One more question. Why do you have these personalities at all?

DM Because society demands it. Cambridge expects one to be either Cecil, or Jack, or Fred. If one isn't, Cambridge is annoyed. It is a pleasant game – and I enjoy playing it.[1]

Kim never achieved the eminence of a *Granta* interview: not recognizably a Cecil, a Fred or a Jack, Cambridge left him to his own sober devices, and these, in steady, well-considered steps, led him to Communism by the summer of 1933. Beatrice Webb once observed that the serious study of economics created socialists, even when their teachers were orthodox economists. This, it may be assumed, was Kim's experience. He had switched to economics in October 1931 at the very moment when unemployment in Britain was at its peak of 22 per cent, and the Economic faculty at Cambridge in an agony of self-doubt. The debate about the relevance of academic economics to the crisis raged as fiercely inside Trinity as anywhere else, in study groups organized by the Communists, or for bigger confrontations, in the Junior Combination Room. On one occasion, when Dennis Robertson and Maurice Dobb debated the Depression, all the left turned up, adjourning after the meeting for drinks with Anthony Blunt, a friend of Guy Burgess (now Sir Anthony Blunt, Professor of Art History, London University, and Director of the Courtauld Institute). Guy was there, firing questions and discussing volubly.

1. *Granta*, 8 November 1933, Vol. XLIII, No. 968, p. 90.

In this discussion with the Marxist Dobb, Robertson did not represent the orthodox Cambridge economics school. From the mid-twenties he and of course Maynard Keynes had challenged the classical view that full employment was the natural order of things, and unemployment a self-correcting aberration. To justify this rosy view, orthodox economists invoked Say's Law, a primitive exhibit from the museum of political science which stated that supply created its own demand, that is to say that the process of producing an article resulted in just enough purchasing power to buy it. According to this gloriously optimistic capitalist theory of equilibrium, over-production was hence impossible. What in the Britain of the 1930s was preventing the normal working of the theory? The orthodox answer was that prices and interest rates, and above all wages, were too high and that the only way to climb back to full employment was to cut them. The workers must therefore agree to earn less, and the state itself must set an example by cutting government expenditure. Keynes and Robertson attacked this view, calling for more government expenditure, not less, as a simple way of mopping up unemployment. Not until 1936, however, when Keynes published his revolutionary *General Theory*, did his views triumph, but by then Kim's generation had already found its own solutions.

By 1932–3 classical economics seemed to young Cambridge socialists unbearably irrelevant to the distress around them. The National Government's cuts in unemployment benefits, and particularly the Means Test introduced in November 1931, aroused their violent indignation. They made heroes of the workers' leaders who were sent to jail for protesting, and were moved to even deeper commitment by the ragged hunger marchers. The north-east contingent of the 1932 hunger march came through Cambridge, and this sight, bringing home the bleak reality of the Depression, was a landmark in the growth of student Communism, for many the moment of political awakening. David Guest led a body of students out to meet them, and returned into the town with them, proudly carrying their knapsacks. Undergraduates scurried around organizing meals for the unemployed and negotiating a loan of the Corn

Exchange for them to sleep in. The marchers were impressive types, tough, hand-picked trade unionists, capable of exercising self-discipline. This demonstration of proletarian solidarity in the face of a ruthless economic system brought a surge of new recruits into the Communist movement.

To students of economics like Kim, the discovery of Marx came as a blinding revelation. They found that seventy years earlier he had predicted the crisis, diagnosed its causes, and even prophesied the outcome. Standing the classical concept of equilibrium on its head, he had suggested that unemployment could be endemic and that capitalist society could produce more than it consumed. But the Cambridge school ignored him.

The thrill of discovery gave way to the white heat of indignation. We felt ourselves surrounded by a wall of intellectual dishonesty, ivory-tower escapism, and apologetic accommodation. We felt in duty bound to smash that wall, both for ourselves and for our fellow students. Sweeping aside the inhibitions engendered in us by the half-truths and intellectual evasions of our training, we became inspired missionaries for a new integration of thought and action, a new science of life ...[1]

If thinking about economics led inevitably to radicalism, so too did the shock and horror at what was taking place on the Continent. The rise of fascism was a mobilizer of young minds as effective as the impact of the Depression. For anyone with lingering hopes that socialism might be achieved by constitutional means, fascism was the final blow, or in J. D. Bernal's words, 'the culminating disillusion of the bourgeois intellectual'.[2] Hitler's excesses – his murderous persecution of Jews and liberals, his destruction of democratic liberties, his nonsensical race theories – were for humane young idealists so many nails in the coffin of their moderation. To the CUSS, the fascists were deadly serious symptoms of the disease which they feared was spreading from the Continent to Britain. Sir Oswald Mosley himself presided over a luncheon in Cambridge

1. M. W. Lang's introduction to 'The Growth of the Student Movement', in Carmel Haden Guest, op. cit.

2. J. D. Bernal, 'The End of a Political Delusion', in *Cambridge Left*, Vol. 1, No. 1, pp. 10–15.

in October 1932 to launch an undergraduate branch of his British Union of Fascists. His leading acolyte at the university at that time was Frederick Lawton, of Corpus Christi, whom *Granta* described as a revolutionary hearty, prowling round Cambridge 'with an eager, hungry look in his eyes, ever ready to pounce upon an idea, and never finding one'. Many influential people in England openly expressed sympathy for Mussolini and Hitler, while the police seemed tenderer to fascists than to anti-fascists. The left saw British democracy collapsing into what Stafford Cripps called 'country gentleman's fascism'.

Like David Guest before him, Kim went to Germany, Hungary and Austria to see what was happening for himself. Accompanied by his Westminster friend, Tim Milne, then at Oxford, he wandered about Continental Europe in the long vacations, taking with him a great stick which he kept in his rooms at Trinity. Jim Lees remembers him struggling to learn some Hungarian before the summer vacation of 1932, while Professor Hugh Trevor-Roper, who then lived on the same staircase as Tim Milne at Christ Church, Oxford, recalls Milne talking of his 'Communist' travelling companion, Kim Philby. John Midgley met him in Berlin in March 1933, within days of the Reichstag fire, the incident which triggered off Hitler's purge of the German Communist Party. Calling on Midgley at the Hegelhof, a student hostel where a bed was to be had for a mark a night, Kim betrayed a touch of characteristic puritanism. Glancing through Midgley's wardrobe, he exclaimed, 'Two dressing-gowns! What on earth do you need two dressing gowns for?' Together the two young Englishmen witnessed uniformed Nazis blocking the entrances to Jewish shops and painting *Jude* on the doors. In halting German Kim started to explain to bystanders that such anti-Jewish demonstrations were unknown in England, and was told rudely to clear off. From such experiences was conviction born.

Disgusted by social democracy and frightened by fascism, the young left turned to Soviet Russia, which, from 1932 onwards, captured their imaginations as never before. While the capitalist West seemed, in Hugh Dalton's phrase, 'one great blot of tragedy', Russia, then embarked on its herculean first Five-Year Plan, was the country of full employment, of the rational use of resources. The Soviet economy seemed to be rising triumphantly in a world in decay. But its appeal to Western intellectuals was as much cultural as economic: Russia treasured its scientists while in the West they were out of work; writers, not film stars and gangsters, were headlined in Russian newspapers; Maxim Gorki was cheered when he appeared in public and his works sold in millions, Russian films became a cult. But above all the attraction of Russia was that it did not seem a nation like any other: to Communists of the thirties, for whom nationalism had been discredited by the First World War, Russia was the bridgehead to a new global society. 'The only possible future for Britain,' John Strachey proclaimed in *The Coming Struggle For Power*, 'is as a free Republic of an at first European, and later world-wide, Union of Soviet Republics.'[1] The clinching argument for Marxists was their conviction that the thugs of capitalism – arms merchants, banks, oil companies and so forth – were conspiring to wage war on their beloved Russia. This was the threat which powered the great Anti-War Movement into which the Communists channelled the deep-rooted pacifism of that generation. With flags flying David Guest travelled as a student delegate to the Anti-War Congress at Amsterdam in 1932. *Student Vanguard*, the organ of British University Marxism founded in November of that year, advertised (in conjunction with Intourist) a three-week tour of the beleaguered land of socialism at a specially reduced rate of £18 inclusive.

The greatest moment of fulfilment for the Cambridge Communists was their seizure of control of the CUSS and the rout of their old enemies, the social democrats. The Communist caucus always met separately before committee elections to decide how their votes should be concentrated, and with these tactics a mere thirteen Party members took over the leadership of the Society in mid-1933, just before Kim went down. Thus instead of being a debating society, the CUSS became a channel for Communist propaganda. In the same expansionist

1. London, 1932, p. 395.

spirit, Marxists captured (but also killed) the Heretics, an anti-clerical society founded in the twenties by C. K. Ogden, I. A. Richards, and Sargent Florence, to offer an alternative to compulsory chapel. Maurice Dobb recalls attending a meeting at which the all-Communist platform – chairman, secretary, and treasurer – outnumbered the floor. A still more prestigious prize was the Apostles, already weakened by homosexual exclusiveness and then nearly extinguished by the Communist takeover. The extension of Communist influence was reflected in the undergraduate press. In February 1932 John Midgley launched *The Outpost* as an independent radical journal, but by June he had been ousted by Maurice Cornforth, and *The Outpost* could make no pretence of impartiality. *Cambridge Left* which appeared the following summer was Marxist from the word go, and printed such verse as Charles Madge's 'May Day':

> One morning you will wake and find
> Suddenly into the sky has climbed
> The wonderful unheard-of day,
> The never-ending First of May.

By 1933, two years after the founding of the first Cambridge cell, the Communists had stormed the august fortresses of the colleges. As the *Spectator* regretted, 'The days when a question could be asked in Parliament because a Trinity lecturer advised his class to read the *Communist Manifesto* are sadly passed.' Of course not all the anxious young men flocked to the Party. Some went left, some went right, some went religious, in what C. E. M. Joad called 'the flight to the herd'. As well as the Communist Party, bodies such as the Christian Union and the Student Christian Movement flourished. The Buchmanites launched a 'drive' in 1933, drawing into their net, as *Student Vanguard* put it, 'public school men of the more refined and emotional type' who fell victim to the 'element of irrational surrender' in the movement. Indeed, surrender to faith was demanded by all these cults, Communism included, and all in the then current atmosphere of drift and disillusion provided spiritual satisfaction. True, Kim and his contemporaries had argued their way step by step to Communism, weighing the evidence which the world offered. To that extent their Marxism was, in Kingsley Martin's words, 'a deduction from the facts'. But perhaps George Orwell is closer to the truth when he suggests in *Inside The Whale* that after the wholesale debunking of the values of their grandfathers, Kim's generation needed something to believe in. The Party 'was simply something to believe in'.

Here was a Fatherland and – at any rate since 1935 or thereabouts – a Fuehrer. All the loyalties and superstitions that intellect had seemingly banished could come rushing back under the thinnest of disguises. Patriotism, religion, empire, military glory – all in one word, Russia. Father, king, leader, hero, saviour – all in one word, Stalin. God – Stalin. The devil – Hitler. Heaven – Moscow. Hell – Berlin. All the gaps were filled up. So, after all, the 'Communism' of the English intellectual is something explicable enough. It is the patriotism of the deracinated.[1]

In these years of radical effervescence it was not easy to discriminate between the finer shades of the left. The true distinction between Communist and left Socialist was that the first carried a Party card and the second did not, a distinction which seemingly left Kim among the not yet committed. But his political associates inside the CUSS were in no doubt as to the distance he had travelled. Otto Clarke remembers questioning him, just back from Berlin, about the fate of the great German Communist Party which had so quickly crumpled under Hitler's attack. This fatal blow to Communist power in Western Europe had triggered off a passionate and anguished debate in left-wing circles in Cambridge – and indeed everywhere. What was the correct left-wing interpretation of the German disaster? Had the Communists been fatally mistaken in directing their fury against the luckless social democrats, rather than against the Nazis? Could Stalin have betrayed the CP to Hitler? Was he really on the left?

'What Stalin does *is* left!' Kim retorted with finality. By definition and beyond argument, the word from Moscow was

1. In *The Collected Essays, Journalism and Letters of George Orwell*, Vol. 1, Penguin Edition, London, 1970, p. 565.

the genuine left-wing line. Kim's answer convinced Clarke that he had at last crossed the frontier into the Communist camp. Thus in his last term at Cambridge, Kim was converted to Communism. Winning a college prize worth £14 that summer, he celebrated his conversion by spending it entirely on Marx. He did not join the Cambridge cell and never carried a Party card, but this was an accident, due simply to the fact that his decision occurred too late in his university career for it to seem worth-while to join the local organization. This accident was to serve him in good stead.

On the eve of their final examinations in June 1933, Kim and Lees dined together in hall at Trinity. 'It's the bloody Tripos tomorrow,' Lees said. 'Let's have a gin and ginger, then,' Kim replied, and, to Lees's slight amazement at this display of wealth, he ordered two doubles.[1]

1. Jim Lees, a personal communication to the authors.

4 Red Vienna

> I found him at last, with a Viennese wife – a
> dark, untidy comrade – neither of them looking
> very domesticated. He strikes me as too gentle
> to be a good politician.
>
> NAOMI MITCHISON'S *Vienna Diary*, 1934

St John Philby was home from Arabia that summer of 1933
when Kim came down from Cambridge with a good second-
class degree in economics and his head full of socialist politics.
Father and son were well pleased with each other. In spite of
living so far apart and meeting rarely, they had developed considerable mutual esteem which was to survive their very
separate careers to the end. There was in this relationship a
touch of characteristic self-congratulation, a sense of their own
worth, a consciousness that we Philbys knew our own minds
and obeyed our own judgements. Until that moment Kim had
been a dutiful son, fulfilling at Westminster and Trinity St
John's expectations; and now, equally dutifully, he launched
himself into adult independence, with the self-reliance and
earnestness which his father required of him. How he disposed
of his life from then on was to be his own decision. But St
John's influence lived on in him. By surrendering to Islam and
the desert, St John had surely provided his son with a model
for his act of faith in Communism. For both there was the
appeal of a cause larger than themselves, a cause demanding
self-abnegation, if not masochism; and both embarked on their
journeys with a quiet confidence of being right.

In reward for his work on the index and proofs of *The
Empty Quarter*, the book published by Constable in 1934
which established St John's reputation as an explorer, Kim
was given £50 by his father and the freedom to spend it as he
liked. He chose to go to Vienna, and to get himself and his
knapsack there he bought a motorcycle. Ostensibly his purpose was to improve his German, in preparation for a bid to

enter the Foreign Service, but in fact he wanted to watch the murderous contest between fascism and the left then engulfing Europe. Vienna was the place to be.

Kim was typical of his generation in feeling the need to stop theorizing and do something. Both Communists and Fascists in the thirties shared a cult for action that seemed to provide an escape from the drift and disillusion about them. 'Go out and get your head broken at Olympia. Stand for hours in the rain selling the *Daily Worker*. The command "Go" is a force releasing and recreating energy,' Storm Jameson wrote in *Left Review* in November 1934. This hunger for physical action, for translating words into deeds that might change society, drove some of the early Cambridge comrades to 'good works' in England. For example, David Haden Guest went to work with the Young Communist League in the slums of Battersea – where this once unwashed but high-minded ideologue was born anew, spruce, clean and happy. Maurice Cornforth, the Cambridge cell's chief-of-staff, threw up philosophy to become an agricultural organizer in East Anglia. A year or two later John Cornford broke with his bourgeois background to serve the Party among the Birmingham working class, while Donald Maclean, in spite of his first-class degree in modern languages, dreamed only of teaching English to workers in the Soviet Union, until his Russian friends persuaded him that he would be of more use in the Foreign Office. Kim's path to self-fulfilment lay in Central Europe.

Especially for a young man like him, more interested in foreign than domestic affairs, the rise of the Nazis and their destruction of the German labour movement were the major political facts of the time. First the social democrats had been defeated, now the Communists were in turn being decimated – the most powerful Communist Party outside Russia. The whole of the European left was profoundly shocked by the disaster, and the outcome which Kim and his friends had so endlessly debated in Cambridge was still unclear. Could the tragedy have been averted? Who was to blame? What was the right anti-fascist strategy now? The whole future of civilized Europe seemed at stake as, in one of the greatest manhunts modern Europe had known, the Nazis hounded down German Communists by the thousand after the Reichstag Fire. The Nazi onslaught shattered not only the German Communist Party, but also the Comintern whose Berlin headquarters was abandoned. Refugees poured out of Germany, mainly into Austria on those Berlin–Vienna trains featured in Christopher Isherwood's novels. On his visit to Berlin at Easter Kim had seen the beginning of the persecution, and now, avid for news, he trundled back across Europe on his motorbike, this time towards little Austria, wedged dangerously between Hitler's Germany and Mussolini's Italy. It is one thing to read Marx and John Strachey and the Comintern's International Press Correspondence arriving at theoretical conclusions in the ordered world of an ancient university. It is quite another to see these conclusions come true in the smoke and blood of battle. Over the next few months Kim saw the destruction of 'Red Vienna', the stronghold of the Austrian labour movement. It was an experience powerful enough to determine the course of a whole life.

Kim was twenty-one when he arrived in Vienna in the late summer of 1933 and found himself modest lodgings. If England had seemed crisis-ridden, the situation in Austria, reduced by defeat in the First World War to a poor, insignificant little country, was near catastrophic. Out of a total population of six and a half million, four hundred thousand adults were unemployed. The splendid baroque façades of the city hid real hardship and a profound sense of insecurity. Apart from the world depression and the dangerous upheavals in Germany next door, the chief anxiety for the working people of Vienna was the threat to their own power. The Social Democrats had ruled the city since 1918, first under Victor Adler and then under Otto Bauer, a moderate Marxist whose sense of compromise had held the Austrian labour movement together, reconciling moderate with extremist at a time when everywhere else the workers' parties were splitting into socialists and Communists. Bauer's 'Austro-Marxism', studied as a hopeful phenomenon in Maurice Dobb's discussion group in Cambridge, represented just that blend of Marxist theory and

humane reformist practice which a compassionate British convert to Communism might be expected to find attractive. In
fifteen years of achievement, Vienna's socialist administration
had made a social theory real, translating into bricks and mor-
tar pioneering blueprints for education, child welfare and
medical care. The party organized sports and travel societies,
choirs and drama groups, holiday camps. But above all it had
rehoused nearly 200,000 slum-dwellers in giant blocks erected
in the outer suburbs. These *gemeinde Häuser*, with their cliffs
of frontage, kindergartens, playgrounds and communal baths,
seemed to admiring visitors airy and generous, each a model
town or Greek city-state. The Karl-Marxhof, for example,
built between 1927 and 1930, housed no fewer than 15,000
people. Gas, electricity and water were provided at cost. Each
May Day a quarter of a million people turned out to march
eight abreast under the party banners to the Town Hall across
the Ring. Karl Seitz, the social democratic mayor, was the most
popular man in the city.

Now all this achievement was at risk. Working-class Vienna
had always been bitterly opposed not only by big business, but
also by its rural hinterland, dominated by aristocratic land-
lords, disgruntled army officers and clerical politicians of the
Christian Social Party – the Clerico-Fascists, as the socialists
called them. These two camps, the progressive and the reactionary, lived side by side but virtually without contact, like
two distinct civilizations. Fearing each other, both looked outside the borders of little Austria for support: the Social Democrats to their brothers in Germany, the Christian Socialists to
Italy and the Vatican. But when Hitler destroyed the left in
Germany, this balance was upset: the Austrian socialists found
themselves exposed and, increasingly harassed by their local
enemies, were tormented with the prospect of defeat. The
powerful German Socialist Party had collapsed without a
fight. Was the same terrible fate in store for them?

Already there had been much evidence to feed their anxiety.
As early as 1927 police savagery in breaking a general strike at
a cost of scores of dead strikers had demonstrated the weakness of the workers when it came to a showdown. Then, in

April 1932 all the enemies of the Austrian social democrats united to put Engelbert Dollfuss in power as Chancellor, although with a parliamentary majority of only one. More ominously Dollfuss's anti-socialist coalition included the Heimwehr, a sort of swaggering voluntary nationalist army, raised in the provinces in defence of rural Catholic Austria. Dollfuss found himself in the unenviable position of having to use these rustic bully-boys to protect his fragile régime against what he saw as its two major threats: Hitler's Nazi followers in Austria, already subversively working for Anschluss, and of course the workers' phalanxes on the left. The survival of Austria as an independent state in a Central Europe in turmoil depended on the tolerant coexistence of socialist Vienna and its anti-socialist hinterland. But, terrified by Hitler and frightened of being overthrown by the socialists, Dollfuss turned to Mussolini for help. It was given on one condition – the destruction of Red Vienna. So when his majority of one in the Chamber was overthrown by the absence of a single supporter in March 1933, the Chancellor seized the opportunity to dissolve parliament and rule by decree. Swiftly he followed up this dictatorial move by muzzling the socialist press, taxing the urban working class for the benefit of the peasantry and, most important of all, outlawing the workers' own militia, the Schutzbund, which though poorly armed and ill led was Vienna's principal source of reassurance.

With his sympathies firmly on the side of the persecuted socialists, Kim was soon familiar with the ins and outs of this complex and potentially explosive situation. From the beginning his search to understand and his earnest concern would have driven him into contact with young socialist intellectuals and trade unionists. Like every British visitor to Vienna, he must have visited the *gemeinde Häuser* and marvelled at the triumphs of Otto Bauer's social policies. He must certainly have sought out Communist refugees from Hitler's purges in Germany who filled the cafés with their anguished discussions. The Cambridge debates about the future of the European left here took on tormented flesh and blood. Perhaps he even met men he had seen on his visit to Berlin the previous Easter. Inevitably he gravitated to the office of Eric Gedye, Central European correspondent of the *Daily Telegraph* and the best-informed Briton in Vienna at that time.

Gedye was a champion of democracy, a great campaigning journalist such as the 1930s produced who felt responsible not only for informing the British public, but for shaking it from its lethargy. A passionate liberal democrat rather than anything further left, he saw, earlier than most, that the barbarism transforming Germany and threatening her neighbours would very soon put at risk all civilized societies – including Britain. Against complacency and appeasement at home he directed his knowledgeable but high-coloured journalism and later his book, *Fallen Bastions*, a horror story of Central Europe's collapse before fascism. His articles in the *Daily Telegraph* brought him a stream of visitors eager to learn, and also eager to feed him the titbits of information they had gleaned themselves. This was Kim's position. Gedye, attracted by his concern for the plight of anti-fascists and respecting his inside knowledge, used him as a tip-off man for the activities of the Heimwehr. They became friends.

Through the Austrian Relief Fund for the Victims of German Fascism, Kim had found a room at a price he could afford[1] in the flat of a girl two years older than himself who was active on the far left of Austrian politics. Alice Friedman was a Communist, a rare enough political animal in a socialist Vienna that had so far contrived to keep radicals and moderates under the same roof. 'As long as we have a Bauer at the top, we do not need any Communists,' his followers used to boast.[2] Litzi, as Alice was known, took her young English friend home to stay with her family in the ninth district of the city. Her father, Israel Kohlman, was a minor government official of Hungarian Jewish origin. Litzi had left home at eighteen to marry Karl Friedman, a left-wing Zionist, but on the break-up of her marriage had returned to live with her parents. She was a small, dynamic person, with fuzzy black

1. Elizabeth Monroe, *Philby of Arabia*, London, 1973.

2. Joseph Buttinger, *In the Twilight of Socialism: A History of the Revolutionary Socialists of Austria* (New York, 1953), p. 182.

hair, dark lively eyes and a warm, friendly, even passionate character. A friend of the family remembers her at this time as 'very young, very enthusiastic, and very Red'. What did she see in Kim? First of all they shared the same intense commitment to the left, the same tools of analysis, the same presuppositions. But all this, common enough in her circle, was lit up by the glamour of his Englishness, a prestigious and powerful attribute in Central Europe: an English passport could still open many doors. Moreover, this Englishman appealed to her by his good manners, his honesty, his calm judicious judgements, his courage. There is no doubt that Kim was a very decent young man. After a while Kim and Litzi moved out of the Kohlman household and set up house together in a small flat in a working-class district.

The overwhelming question for young militants of their sort was what the left should do in the face of Dollfuss's ever more violent persecution. Every day brought new evidence. In October, for example, 60,000 workers turned out to celebrate a choral society's anniversary, and the authorities forthwith shut down the club. By Christmas 1933 the socialist municipality of Vienna was paralysed.

The social democratic leader, Otto Bauer, had built his whole career, as well as the achievements of Red Vienna, on the principles of moderation, compromise and non-violence. Now, with everything at risk, he had no new tactics to offer. His confidence had been shaken by the destruction of his old allies the German socialists. In addition, he was reluctant to use force or even industrial action against his domestic enemies, Dollfuss and the Heimwehr, seeing them as the best buffer available against an invasion by either Hitler or Mussolini. And so he continued to urge restraint and patience on his restive and increasingly terrified supporters. The young in particular challenged his leadership, arguing that unless the social democrats fought back their movement would be damaged beyond repair. Convinced that Bauer's party was doomed, some young rebels were already making preparations to go underground by founding a clandestine organization called Spark (after Lenin's *Iskra*). Its leaders, Ilsa and

Leopold Kulcsar, began recruiting underground workers and made contact with the *Neue Beginnen*, the new socialist underground then starting to take shape in Hitler's Germany.[1]

Less important, because of its tiny membership, but even more bitterly critical of Bauer was the Austrian Communist Party, to which Litzi belonged. It set about distributing anti-régime tracts, holding secret meetings, exchanging passwords, and generally building an underground network to rival that of the Spark. Perhaps its most useful role was to provide shelter for Communist refugees from Germany. Strictly speaking such activities were punishable by imprisonment, but they were still too trivial to attract the serious attention of the authorities. So it was in an exhilarating but not very dangerous game of hide-and-seek that Kim and Litzi found themselves caught up. They themselves were in deadly earnest, however, and it was these circumstances which drove Kim across the uncharted frontier between Austro-Marxism and Communism *tout court*. In October 1933 Jim Lees, then in his first term as an assistant lecturer at Nottingham University, received a letter from his old friend in Vienna. Kim was scathing about the Austrian social democrats who, he wrote, had capitulated to Dollfuss. He was finished with them.

In the New Year the enemies of Austrian socialism closed in for the kill, and ironically it was Hitler's supporters who provided the occasion. In January 1934 Austria was swept by a wave of Nazi terrorism, and amid rumours of an imminent Nazi *coup* the Heimwehr mobilized for action. However, it soon became obvious that it was socialist Vienna, not the Nazis, they were gunning for. Sadly, the socialists themselves

1. As a Communist Ilsa Kulcsar had in 1925 accepted a secret assignment from the Russians to find a Romanian opposition leader and channel funds to him. She carried out her mission from a base in Budapest, but was uncovered by the Hungarian secret police and spent four months in jail. The Russians made no move to help her, or to reimburse her legal expenses. On her release from prison, she left the Party but returned to active work on the left wing of Otto Bauer's social democrats. (Ilsa Barea, formerly Kulcsar, a personal communication to the authors.)

sparked off the holocaust. Richard Bernasek, the young
Schutzbund leader for Upper Austria, increasingly critical of
Otto Bauer's passivity, warned Vienna of his determination to
launch a preventive attack on the Heimwehr. Bauer urged him
to hold back. But the police intercepted the messages and at
dawn on 12 February raided Bernasek's party offices at Linz.
Government and Heimwehr forces then moved in across the
country to crush the ill-prepared social democrats.

Driven at last to action, Otto Bauer ordered a stoppage of
the Vienna trams – the pre-arranged signal for a general strike
– and called on the Schutzbund to mobilize but to hold its fire
unless attacked. Dollfuss was more ruthless. He proclaimed
martial law and dissolved the party by decree. Mayor Karl
Seitz was arrested in his own town hall, a cordon of barbed
wire was thrown round the Inner City where the main municipal buildings were located, and the police moved in to
occupy party headquarters, labour centres, factories – and the
great housing estates which the Clerico-Fascists had always
denounced as proletarian fortresses. Everywhere party, administrative and Schutzbund leaders were rounded up.

Decapitated, the social democrats collapsed in utter disarray. No one seemed to know whether the general strike was
on or off. Bands of distraught workers searched for the hidden
arms caches, but in many cases the one man who knew where
the weapons were concealed was already under arrest. At the
Engelhof women tore up the gardens with their nails looking
for guns. Thousands of bewildered Schutzbundlers ran from
place to place on the afternoon of the 12th and the night that
followed, asking what they could do, where they could fight.
But there was no one to give them orders. On the fringes of
the fighting zone, massed workers stood by, stunned and em-
bittered by the Schutzbund's failure to defend them. Socialist
Vienna was like a country whose professional army had been
routed.

Small groups of armed workers, cut off from one another,
fell back to the shelter of the tenement blocks, but artillery
was brought up to blast them out. The spectacle of densely
inhabited municipal housing shelled by government Howitzers

shocked the world, and left those who witnessed it sick with anger: it was as if the finest thing the broken thirties had produced was being crushed. The young poet Stephen Spender was there to lament:

There were some suffered from the destruction of houses
More than from the death of men: they weep for their houses
That endured enormous wounds ...[1]

Kim's friend, Eric Gedye, exploded with rage: 'These fair dream-cities, with their promise for the whole world, which had grown up out of the jungle of slumdom, dirt and dependence, were being trampled back into the jungle again by beasts who would not tolerate their existence.'[2]

The immediate aftermath of the rising was if anything more terrible than the brief outburst of fighting. More people were wounded by Heimwehr and police beatings than by shells and rifle fire. Heimwehr swarmed into the shattered tenements, then flying the white flag, and slashing bedding and upholstery with their bayonets in the search for weapons. Schutzbundlers fleeing for their lives took refuge in the sewers and air passages under the tenements. Some escaped through manholes, but others were driven out to the cry of '*Kellerratten* [sewer-rats] need hanging!' A few badly wounded men were kept in the sewers for weeks, tended by doctors, mostly Jewish, at the risk of their careers. Nine socialist leaders were summarily tried and hanged. Altogether the February fighting claimed a toll of over 300 dead and 800 wounded.

By edict and ordinance the social democrats were driven out of public life. The party's entire property was seized – workers' rest homes, printing presses, playgrounds, holiday camps, down to typewriters, flags and footballs. The trade unions were broken up, the party was smashed, hundreds of socialists lost their jobs. Morale collapsed in an atmosphere of terror. The remaining leadership fled abroad, Otto Bauer and the Schutzbund commander, Julius Deutsch, to Czechoslovakia, many

1. 'The Death of Heroes', the third part of his long poem, *Vienna* (*1934*), (London, 1936).
2. G. E. R. Gedye, *Fallen Bastions*, London, 1939, p. 113.

others to the Soviet Union where they were briefly treated as heroes before perishing by the score in Stalin's purges from 1935 onwards.

Faced with the possibility of injury, even death, Kim could have remained on the sidelines; after all, Otto Bauer's quarrel with Dollfuss was not his. Instead he flung himself headlong into the battle, giving shelter and bringing relief where he could. He burst in upon Eric Gedye at the height of the crisis to beg for cast-off clothes for a group of Schutzbundlers trapped in the sewers so that they could attempt to escape. Recalling the incident Gedye recounted that he allowed Kim to ransack his wardrobe and make off with three suits which were not really so old. 'I have always cherished part-worn suits – but it was hard to refuse a man his chance of avoiding the vengeance of the Clerico-Fascists.'[1]

Kim was not the only Englishman to be stirred by the plight of the Vienna working class. Numbers of English socialists and sympathizers hurried to Austria, bringing with them not only funds but also their British passports under whose protection many a wanted man was escorted to safety across the frontier. They came to swell a small resident community of British and American left-wingers of whom perhaps the most prominent were Hugh Gaitskell, then studying economics with Professor Hayek on a Rockefeller grant, his future wife Dora Frost, and Mrs Muriel Gardner, a rich and enterprising American woman who helped finance the Spark group's illegal activities. She had a flat in town, a car – an unimaginable luxury in Austrian left-wing circles in those days – and a timbered cottage especially built for her in the Wienerwald. After the February catastrophe Gaitskell rushed to London to collect more funds and helpers for the cause. A young Welsh lawyer, Elwyn Jones (later Harold Wilson's Attorney-General), came to Vienna, as did Stephen Spender (to stay in Muriel Gardner's woodland cottage) and the writer Naomi Mitchison who, in English tweeds and woollen stockings, toured the shattered *gemeinde Häuser* distributing relief, and whose *Vienna Diary* helped bring the ugly facts to the attention of the British public.

1. The late Eric Gedye, a personal communication to the authors.

All these people and their local friends were in and out of each other's lives. Immediately after the rising, when Leopold Kulcsar was jailed, his wife Ilsa took refuge in Hugh Gaitskell's one-room flat. When conditions became a little more normal Ilsa returned the compliment. She rented a large apartment in the Herrengasse, conveniently situated in a big block with several entrances, where Gaitskell came to live as a lodger for several months, including a spell with Dora. As Dora (now Baroness Gaitskell) recalls: 'We were a very small group of foreigners, who knew each other well, all felt the same politically, and shared a great feeling of solidarity with the ordinary people living in the municipal flats. We had a real feeling that European war was near, and that we had in fact heard the first shots fired. This was an extremely important year in Hugh's life – his first live contact with European Fascism. The political experience of witnessing the destruction of the socialists by Dollfuss made a deep impression on him.'[1]

It did too on Kim, but he and Litzi were too far to the left to be really part of the Gaitskell group, although they were known to them. In Ilsa Kulcsar's words, 'Philby was there of course, but only as one might glimpse a person out of the corner of one's eye.' The Gaitskells and their friends were socialists not Communists. Indeed they were deeply concerned to do what they could to prevent the defeated Austrian workers from turning in desperation either to Communism or to Fascism. And as socialists they were rather suspicious of, and irritated by, the activities of the underground Communist networks such as the one to which the Philbys belonged.

For by this time Kim and Litzi were man and wife. On 24 February, just a week after the rising had been put down, they were married in the Vienna Town Hall, Kim describing himself on the certificate as a 'student, without religious faith'. Announcing this unexpected development to his parents and no doubt hoping to soften the blow, he wrote that his marriage, the object of which was to give Litzi a British passport, could be dissolved once the emergency was over. But St John's and

1. Baroness Gaitskell, widow of the Labour Party leader Hugh Gaitskell, a personal communication to the authors.

Dora's dismay could not be appeased either by his chivalry or by the hint that all might yet be well: they never forgave Litzi her 'capture' of their twenty-two-year-old son.[1] In Vienna it was recognized among the foreign visitors that Kim and Litzi were in love and that their relationship was not merely expedient, but when news of Kim's marriage reached Gaitskell, he exclaimed to Ilsa Kulcsar, 'That silly young man has gone and done it!' The hard-working foreign helpers viewed such marriages between high-minded English youngsters and Austrian Communist girls as romantic nonsense. For one thing the girls were not in any particular danger: only the socialist party leadership and former Schutzbundlers and their families were being actively hunted down, and, moreover, holders of British passports were needed to ferry such fugitives across the frontier. A wedding usually meant the loss of a valuable escort. But from the viewpoint of the Communist underground, the danger to Litzi might have looked graver.

What among other things distinguished the Communists from the socialists was that they cared as much about their German comrades persecuted by Hitler as about the Schutzbundlers persecuted by Dollfuss. It was in the German cause that Kim tracked Naomi Mitchison to her hotel on 1 March, a week after his wedding, in the hope that this influential visitor could help. As Miss Mitchison recorded in her *Vienna Diary* (p. 78): 'I came back to the hotel, to find several telephone messages, and an urgent note from an unknown man. After lunch the unknown turned up, a nice young Cambridge Communist, all "het-up" about some of the Reichstag prisoners, and wanting to know if I or anyone I knew could fly at once to Berlin and see about it.' Kim was still with her when they were joined by the brother of one of the prisoners on whose behalf he was seeking her help – 'dark and white-faced and little, hunted looking'. Although full of sympathy Naomi Mitchison first took the precaution of checking up on Kim to see if he was 'all right', as the Austrian CP was known to be stiff with government spies. But the next day she ferreted out some information for Kim and rang him up to ask him to come

1. Monroe, op. cit., pp. 207, 209.

round. 'He couldn't, so reluctantly I decided I must go round to him – after all, the information I had might conceivably be a slight means of saving someone's life. But I was too tired for anything but taxis – and he lived at an address no taxi seemed to know. I found him at last, with a Viennese wife – a dark, untidy comrade – neither of them looking very domesticated. He strikes me as too gentle to be a good politician. Probably the best politicians of all are really tough women' (p. 79).

The February uprising and the rout of the social democrats totally discredited Otto Bauer's policies of caution and compromise – not only for the already converted like Kim and Litzi, but for a great mass of young socialist militants. Bauer's earlier critics were now vindicated and, in the angry bitter mood which followed the massacre, the trend everywhere was sharply leftwards. Why did the party show so little fight at the moment of testing? Was not this faint-heartedness in the very nature of social democracy? Spontaneously, underground groups sprang up calling for resistance on a 'real revolutionary basis'. Before the rising the Austrian CP could boast of only a handful of party workers; now it mushroomed overnight. In the university, as Joseph Buttinger, the chief chronicler of Austrian socialism, reported, 'there had been a hundred Social Democrats for every Communist; now ... three-quarters of the Social Democratic students had gone Communist'.[1] In an agony of breast-beating and self analysis young recruits joined the many squabbling underground groups, whether Communist or left-socialist such as the Spark, swelling their membership to about a thousand by March 1934. Bauer in exile was challenged by new leaders inside the country calling themselves 'Revolutionary Socialists' under the slogan 'We are beaten but not defeated.' But this did not check the drift still further left. Perhaps the biggest success scored by the Communists at this time was to penetrate and take over the defeated Schutzbund, bringing it back to life under their own leadership and renaming it the Autonomous Schutzbund.

It was Kim who first alerted Eric Gedye to this shift of power in the underground. Never having probed his tip-off man on his

1. Buttinger, op. cit., p. 79.

politics, Gedye had always presumed him to have socialist rather than Communist contacts, but this incident made him wonder. Without much explanation Kim introduced Gedye to an Austrian girl who, he said, could put him in the way of an exclusive story. Gedye recounted the sequel:

This girl arranged to meet me one Sunday morning at a tram stop, and in real undercover style, drilled me in how I was to recognize a series of guides whom I was to follow discreetly – until the last of them led me to my destination.

This proved to be a small clearing in the heart of the Vienna forest. Here, in ones and twos, some forty young people slowly gathered, while what appeared to be loving couples kept a lookout from the bushes. From their rucksacks four young men produced large pieces of red cloth which they clipped together to make a banner and attached to a sapling as a flagpole. The young people lined up as on parade, their leader delivered a brief, anti-Fascist address, the Red Flag was waved, the Internationale quickly sung, and a photograph taken of the parade – but from behind, only the backs 'facing' the camera.

From the fact that the banner was inscribed 'Kirov Cadre' I began to suspect that this was an illegal meeting of the Autonomous Schutzbund which was then taking shape under Communist control.

Only later did I put two and two together and realize that these were Kim's friends.[1]

In the late spring of 1934, less than two months after the dramatic events of the workers' rising, Kim took his Austrian wife to London. They travelled by train via Paris. As a young militant couple committed to the anti-fascist cause, they could have stayed on in Austria to fight with their comrades, but they chose not to. Perhaps the enemy seemed overwhelmingly strong: at any rate events were to prove them so. And for Litzi, both Communist and Jewish, there were already enough premonitions to make her want to leave the country. In July the Nazis assassinated Engelbert Dollfuss, but failed to seize power. Kurt von Schuschnigg became Chancellor. By 1936 Italy had dropped her championship of Austrian independence and Austria was marked out for a Nazi takeover. When the

1. The late Eric Gedye, a personal communication to the authors.

German army marched in, in March 1938, it met with no resistance. Many of the workers defected to the Nazi cause. Even the Vienna working class, reared on social democracy, had no heart to defend the native dictatorship which had destroyed Red Vienna.

And so the Philbys headed for home. Men who returned to England from Central Europe at that time felt they had grasped a blinding truth: the world was going fascist, it was being overwhelmed by the Nazi dark age, and only Communism could save it. Social democracy had utterly failed. It had collapsed in Britain in 1931, in Germany in 1933, and in Vienna in 1934. Those who lived through these crises and understood their import felt themselves separated by a great chasm of experience from those who had not. Wholly convinced that their analysis was correct, and burning with a sense of urgency, they had compelling motives for political action. Indifference was impossible. But what political action? It was to be a full twelve months before Kim embarked on his career as an agent of Soviet intelligence. He was recruited in England although he may have been noticed in Vienna.[1] The evidence suggests, however, that on leaving Austria he was no more than an overt militant, free from espionage entanglements. But after all he had seen and felt and struggled against, he was looking for a vocation to match his fervour and his resourcefulness. He was soon to find it.

1. At least one young Englishman was approached by a Communist agent in Vienna at that time. John Lehmann was then in Austria acting as the 'secret correspondent' of the fellow-travelling Amsterdam-Pleyel Anti-War International, run from Paris by Henri Barbusse and Romain Rolland. John Strachey directed its British section. (See Lehmann's *The Whispering Gallery*, London, 1955.) The Communist agent who called on Lehmann on three occasions urged him to provide regular political information: in the struggle against fascism everyone should do his bit. But under this pressure Lehmann panicked. On his next visit to London he blurted out the whole story to John Strachey, who told him not to worry about it any more, and from then on he was left alone. He assumed that in some devious way Strachey had warned the comrades off. (John Lehmann, a personal communication to the authors.)

5 Mild-mannered Desperado

> Practically every man I have knows he will
> have to earn his living when he goes down ...
>
> A CAMBRIDGE DON, 1932

'I'm quite prepared to marry one of these girls, so long as I don't have to go to bed with her.' This was Guy Burgess's reaction to Litzi on her arrival in London with Kim in the early summer of 1934. Couples of their sort were not uncommon at a time when chivalrous young Englishmen were snatching maidens from the fascist dragon on the Continent. There was quite a fashionable traffic in refugees. Most of these marriages were fictitious, contracted solely to get across a difficult frontier on a British passport, and the partners usually drifted apart shortly afterwards.

It was at first presumed that Kim's and Litzi's relationship was of this nature. At a party given for them soon after they turned up in London, the journalist Clare Hollingworth remembers friends advising Kim, 'Don't *marry* the Jewish refugee; help her, of course, but don't be silly enough to marry her!' Jim Lees found her 'not very pretty, but quite bedable'. Others tended to exaggerate the age difference between this 'rather bossy woman' – so much the standard continental female party member and her earnest, pipe-smoking, mildly-stuttering young husband. To most, Litzi seemed by far the stronger personality of the two. She was still the 'dark untidy comrade' of her Vienna days, and her English was uncertain – the language of the household was German, as Otto Clarke recalls from a visit to them in 1934. He presumed Litzi was a left-wing social democrat, because everyone knew that the socialists had led the left in Vienna and the Communists were hardly thought of. In any event, it would have been difficult for an Englishman at the time to distinguish between left SDs and CPers. But among the people the young Philbys saw regularly were many Communists, refugees for the most part from the

Continent. These central European friends assumed without question that Kim, like his wife, was a Communist: 'It never even entered my head that he could have been anything else,' one of them remarked. 'It would have been most unusual for a girl of her type to live with a non-Communist.'

To save the rent, Kim and Litzi set up house with Dora Philby in the family home in Acol Road, West Hampstead. Dora's gloom about her daughter-in-law was confirmed on meeting her. She found Litzi hard, pert and managing, and held her responsible for Kim's radical views. 'You wait till you see her,' Dora wrote ominously to St John in Jidda. 'I do hope he gets a job to get him off this bloody Communism. He's not quite extreme yet but may become so if he's got nothing to occupy his mind.' It was precisely because of his politics that Kim was at a loose end: he had sacrificed his Foreign Service prospects to his convictions. Returning from Vienna, he made out an application for the Civil Service Examination, then sent the form to Cambridge for his three referees to insert their judgements of him. Two of these, his economics tutor, Dennis Robertson, and his father's old friend Donald Robertson, Regius Professor of Greek, scrupled to recommend him and told Kim so by letter: his sense of political injustice might well unfit him for administrative work, Dennis Robertson wrote, bringing Kim hot-foot to Cambridge to discuss the matter and eventually persuading him that his best course was to withdraw the application. Robertson's caution suggests more political grasp than was usual at the time: a year later Donald Maclean's tutor noted in his report to the Civil Service Commission that Maclean had been politically very active, but without specifying in what sense, a question no one at the Commission troubled to take up.

Frankness itself, Kim readily acknowledged to his Cambridge elders that in a conflict of loyalties politics might prove stronger than respect for the interests of the Foreign Service, and that was that. St John, disappointed and pugnacious, offered to help him fight the Civil Service Commissioners if he were turned down for views honestly held. In reply Kim reasonably urged that the Commissioners could not be expected to select candidates who could not be trusted in a crisis: 'The ideal would be for people of extreme views to keep them dark from everyone, their own families included. But it is very difficult to hide views when they are in the process of formation, and indeed unless they start extreme there is no incentive to do so.'[1] Clearly, just back from the battlefield, Kim hardly gave his career first priority.

On that visit to Cambridge or another he addressed the now Communist-dominated Socialist Society to raise funds for the struggling Autonomous Schutzbund that was emerging in Vienna from the rubble of defeat. Diffident by nature and hampered by his stutter, he had neither the manner nor the skill for effective public performance, but to the untried students he must have cut a romantic figure. (Another young Vienna veteran turned up at a CUSS Sunday tea at about this time with a revolver in the belief that firearms were carried to political meetings as a matter of course.)

Cambridge Communism had long since ceased to be sectarian and was well on the way to being modish. It was the era of the Popular Front, of co-operation between Socialists and Communists. The CUSS membership was soaring: a year earlier, when Kim was an undergraduate, it had been perhaps 200; now it was double that figure and was to go on climbing. By 1938, the Society had a membership of almost 1,000 in a university of fewer than 5,000 undergraduates. When Kim came to talk about Vienna, the dominant figure in student Communism was the charismatic John Cornford.[2] From the moment of his arrival in October 1933, the term after Kim had gone down, he had given the Communist organization in Cambridge a new confidence. Semi-clandestinity was replaced by brazen publicity-seeking, high-minded theorizing gave way to political aggressiveness. Cornford believed in the slogan of propaganda by deed, to which the vigour of his personality and his extremely emphatic way of speaking lent substance. He switched the attack from the 'town' – to which the first genera-

1. Monroe, op. cit., pp. 208–9.
2. For a detailed account of John Cornford's life, see Peter Stansky and William Abrahams, *Journey to the Frontier* (London, 1966).

tion of Cambridge Communists had devoted themselves – to the colleges. Asked on one occasion what single thing in the universe gave him most satisfaction, Cornford replied after thinking for a minute, 'The existence of the Communist International.'[1]

One of his most remarked-upon converts was Guy Burgess, then doing a fourth year at Trinity, on a research scholarship which his dazzled tutors had offered him even before his degree examinations. Only a year earlier politics had been an intellectual game and the weary canvassers in Romsey Town a subject for mockery. Now, under the influence of John Cornford, whom the febrile Guy admired more than anyone in the world, he was eloquently and passionately committed. Jim Lees recalls lunching with Maurice Dobb, patron saint of the Trinity Communists, earlier that year. 'Pity Kim never joined the Party,' Dobb said. To console him, Lees pointed out that he had gained a new and prestigious recruit in Guy Burgess. Dobb was gratified: 'He's a very brilliant and talented boy.'[2] It was to this new recruit that Kim entrusted the task of raising money in the University for the Austrian Communists, the first step in their life-long clandestine association.

Back in London with Litzi, Kim could no longer avoid the problem of making enough money to keep them. He had no private income, no job, and his father was thousands of miles away, still in the early years of a chancy business career and with younger children to educate. As Kim's ambition to enter the Foreign Service had been stifled at birth, he had to look for a substitute; he settled on journalism, a natural choice for a young man so interested in international affairs. But neither in journalism nor anywhere else were jobs easy to find when Kim first went on the labour market in the summer of 1934. Out of a total 'black-coat' force of about two million, including clerks as well as professional men, between 300,000 and 400,000 were unemployed. As the Depression whittled away the remaining job opportunities, the menace of graduate unemployment was

1. Victor Kiernan, 'Recollections' in *John Cornford: A Memoir*, ed. Pat Sloan (London, 1938).
2. Jim Lees, a personal communication to the authors.

repeatedly evoked in the university press. Not only was industry in decline, but also the professions, notably teaching
which contracted with the reduction in the flow of public
money to schools and universities. For intellectuals there was
hardly anywhere to turn: literary magazines did not pay and
the BBC was not then the vast dispenser of patronage it has
since become. Poets turned to clerking. As A. J. Liebling put it,
'the principal preoccupation of almost everybody in the 1930s
was getting by'.[1]

The nondescript niche Kim eventually found himself, at £4 a
week, as sub-editor and hack contributor to the *Review of Reviews* was typical of the times. He got the job in the late
autumn of 1934 after a few penny-pinching months, and kept
it for two years during which the *Review* merged with *World*
to become the *World Review of Reviews*, under Vernon
Bartlett. Kim rated a desk, a secretary, and a room in Bream's
Buildings, Holborn, hardly large enough to accommodate all
three of them together. In 1936, towards the end of his interlude in this backwater, his secretary was a girl just out of
school called Joyce Clayton (now Mrs Joyce Leather) who remembers him as being 'kind, reticent, shy and pleasant to work
with' but also daringly unconventional: at a time when professional men wore dark suits on weekdays, he sported an oat-
meal tweed suit, Viyella check shirts and handwoven woollen
ties. Sitting across the table from him, she would overhear his
telephone conversations with Litzi: *'Hast du denn zuviel
getrunken?'* The *Review* was a dull, middle-of-the-road
monthly, largely made up of articles reprinted from British and
American journals. It published a great many cartoons, but the
most constant non-political feature was a motoring page. Kim
told his old friend, Jim Lees, that he wrote 'most of the letters
and a good many of the other contributions'. To fill up the
magazines, Kim resorted to pseudonyms, signing himself for
example Adrian Russell, his two middle names. He was obviously a useful stand-by to the editor, Wilfrid Hope Hindle. In
the March 1935 issue, Kim's name appears with the exalted

1. A. J. Liebling, *The Most of A. J. Liebling* (New York, 1963), Fore-
word.

title of Acting Editor, and he may thus have been responsible for printing this limerick, commenting on the pro-German results of the Saar referendum the previous January:

> There once was a man of the Saar
> Who said 'We are Germans nicht wahr?
> And under dem Fuhrer
> We feel much securer
> But Gott really knows if we are.'

Another contributor, Sir Roger Chance, remembers meeting Kim in Bream's Buildings: 'He seemed an extremely nice, intelligent young man, with a bad stutter; very left-wing, of course, as all young men have to be.'[1] Chance visited Germany after the rise of Hitler – writing from there for the *Review* – and felt a certain sympathy for National Socialism in its early stages when he contrasted it with the anarchy of France under Léon Blum. Kim's views on Germany, he noticed, were 'wholly opposed to those of Neville Chamberlain'.

Kim's contributions were plain and almost ponderously sober for a young man of twenty-three, but they yield occasional fleeting glimpses of his thinking. He was anti-clerical, a sentiment presumably strengthened by his first-hand experience of the Viennese Clerico-Fascists. He was scornful of the record of Christianity in the face of the new Nazi 'blood and soil' faith. On Middle East affairs he spoke with authority – no doubt because of his father's links with Arabia. His obituary note on T. E. Lawrence in the *Review* in 1935 was sensible and hard-headed, in remarkable contrast to the uncritical adulation poured out by the rest of the press. Lawrence, he wrote, had misjudged both the balance of power in the Arabian Peninsula and world interest in the Middle East: 'He was sent to Arabia to perform a concrete task, and performed it to perfection. But the surprising success of his operation and the brilliance of his personality lent a false glow to the material he had at hand. He was himself certainly deceived as to the permanence of his achievement ... The dominant figure in contemporary Arabia is not Lawrence, still less Faisal, but Ibn Saud ...' Here the

1. Sir Roger Chance, a personal communication to the authors.

voice of St John Philby speaks clearly through his son. On occasion the *Review* seems almost a family affair, with St John contributing a long travelogue, entitled 'Mecca to Maida Vale', describing a journey from Jidda to Britain in a Ford V8 seven-seater sedan in 1935. Illustrating the article is a picture of Kim's mother in a yashmak, standing by the great car in the middle of the desert. The caption reads: 'King Ibn Saud accorded permission for my wife to accompany me provided she conformed outwardly to the Arab code of female etiquette.' The same issue of the *Review* carried a dull piece by Adrian Russell.

Apart from this work for the *Review*, Kim had another contact with the anxious, ill-paid world of part-time journalism. One of Litzi's left-wing friends from Vienna was Peter Smolka, a young Austrian from a well-to-do industrialist background, who had come to the London School of Economics to do post-graduate work. In late 1934 he set up a small news agency, London Continental News Ltd, to collect and distribute information from Central and Eastern Europe. Kim, who shared Smolka's interest in alerting the British public to what was happening in those troubled countries, joined him on the board of this youthful venture. They sold the news they collected to the Exchange Telegraph company, which Smolka eventually joined in 1938 when EXTEL – particularly its monitoring service for listening in to foreign broadcasts – was a haven for left-wing refugees from fascism. In the Index to the Foreign Office Archives for 1934 there is a reference to the two young men setting up London Continental News Ltd, but the original report is not available. According to the Foreign Office it has been 'destroyed in the normal process of weeding out documents of no administrative or historical importance'.

With one thing and another, Kim was contriving to get by, but he had clearly not yet found the vocation he dreamed of.

He might feel he was serving the cause by fund-raising in Cambridge and feeding Eastern European news to the British press, but the dull weekly stint at the *Review* could hardly have satisfied his burning sense of urgency. After Vienna life was frankly flat. And then, at some point in that winter of

1934–5, word reached him that he had been noticed, that if he came up to expectations there was a job for him to do, a job which would rescue him from the irrelevance of hack journalism and put him in the front-line again. He was approached by the Russians.

The leftist boom in Britain's ancient universities was then arousing considerable excitement in Moscow – and nowhere more, no doubt, than in the intelligence organizations. For the first time since the October Revolution the British Establishment seemed to be breeding scores of Soviet sympathizers to breach its own walls. At the 1934 Congress of Soviet Writers, Karl Radek drew attention to the phenomenon: 'In the heart of bourgeois England, in Oxford, where the sons of the bourgeoisie receive their final polish, we observe the crystallization of a group which sees salvation only together with the proletariat.'[1] In Cambridge John Cornford perhaps did more than any undergraduate to arouse the Russians' interest and it is likely that he established close links in London as much with the Russian Embassy as with British Communist Party headquarters in King Street. It may even be that the stir he created and the swelling movement he directed caused the Russians to give belated attention to Kim's first generation of student Marxists whose potential may earlier have passed unnoticed. When the leftward trend became so general as to be inescapable, the early converts doubtless came under closer scrutiny.

Who exactly put the Russians on to Kim must remain conjecture. He may not have known himself. It could have been a Cambridge Communist, or someone in the British Party whose task it was to keep an eye on the student Marxists. It could have been an alert officer in the Soviet Embassy in Vienna, or indeed in the Soviet Embassy in London, tipped off by one of the East European Communists the Philbys were friendly with. Another possible channel was Andrew Rothstein, son of the Soviet diplomatist Theodore Rothstein, an important member of the Communist hierarchy in London whose role then was to steer British intellectuals towards King Street and defend

1. The Comintern's *International Press Correspondence*, 14 September 1934.

Soviet policies in the British press. He was a sort of lay brother to Ambassador Maisky at the Embassy. Perhaps the most plausible explanation is that Kim's introduction to the Russians was made by his own wife Litzi who, some intelligence sources suggest, was herself in Soviet employ. There remains a nagging question. Could three young men so different in temperament and gifts as Philby, Burgess and Maclean have been recruited from a single Cambridge generation without there being in Cambridge a tip-off man working in the Russian interest? Such a man would have needed close and regular contact with the students, a sympathetic understanding of their feelings as they evolved in those crucial years; he would have had to know them and the milieu in which they lived well enough to judge their characters accurately and to spot their potential. Was there such a fourth man?

Whoever made the link, it is certain that the British Communist Party knew little or nothing of Kim's fate thereafter. From the mid-twenties onwards the Russians had been at pains to maintain at least an outward and formal separation of Soviet intelligence from the local Communist parties – a policy adopted to protect the parties from the scandal which followed the uncovering of spy rings. In Britain the affair of the Zinoviev Letter and the police raids on the Soviet trade mission in May 1927 had led the Baldwin government to break off relations with the Soviet Union. So it was decreed by Stalin that contacts between the Party and the intelligence apparat should be kept to the minimum.

In each party this minimal link was the responsibility of a high-ranking official – usually a member of the politburo – who was assigned to 'special duties'. These were co-operating with Soviet intelligence and talent-spotting for it, without necessarily informing the rest of the party leadership of such activities. It was evident to British party members in the thirties, but never explicitly stated, that certain party functionaries had 'international connections'. They were in touch with the Soviet Embassy, the Comintern, or with one or other of the various Communist front organizations – and therefore with Moscow. For example the trade unionist Douglas Spring-hall was the Red Army's intelligence talent spotter in the British Communist Party, and in this capacity recruited Alexander Foote who went on to become a Soviet wartime agent in Switzerland.[1]

Kim was a natural choice for Russian intelligence. Not only was he a whole-hearted convert to Communism but, as he had proved in Vienna, he was a convert eager to do what he could for the cause, even at the cost of his personal convenience and safety. Although young, he was better informed than many in England about the realities of the power struggle on the Continent: he knew that the war against fascism had already begun. Perhaps the clinching argument for his Russian recruiters was that he spoke German, for at that moment their interest was less in subverting the British establishment than in charting the development of its relations with Hitler. They must have noted with approval that their young recruit was not only brave but sensible, reliable, judicious. He had a trained mind and could write a good report. Since Kim was earmarked for clandestine work, his unobtrusiveness was itself an advantage. He had never hit the headlines at Cambridge nor flaunted his Communist views since. Most important of all, he held no Party card and was therefore, for official purposes, 'clean'. He was the epitome of the 'mild-mannered desperado', Beatrice Webb's phrase for British intellectuals who took up Communism.

Did Kim suffer any qualms at the thought of becoming a Russian agent? Did the knowledge that this was treachery make him hesitate? The evidence suggests that, on the contrary, he leaped at the chance. As he himself has written from Moscow with a touch of obtuse complacency, 'One does not look twice at an offer of enrolment in an élite force.'[2] His subsequent career was to demonstrate that Kim took warmly to organizations, finding satisfaction in the teamwork, the sense of hierarchy, the insider's knowledge and power. Already at

1. Alexander Foote, *Handbook for Spies* (London, 1949), pp. 16, 17.
2. Kim Philby, *My Silent War* (London, 1968), p. xix.

Cambridge his contemporaries had noted that his patience and method fitted him for a bureaucratic future. At the moment of decision, however, the attraction of the Russian service was its promise to fill the vacuum in his life. Under his father's influence, Kim had grown up to need a moral purpose; he could not happily drift along, without a target, without a schedule of work, without a job to match his view of his abilities. He desperately wanted to do something positive in the struggle against fascism, and the Russians gave him the opportunity. But Kim lacked the toughness of character which allowed his father to freewheel all his life, making his own rules as he went along. Kim's application of St John's ideas led him to dissent but with the paradoxical result of harnessing him for life to a whip-cracking Communist discipline.

Joining an intelligence service is not like getting an ordinary job, where one day you do not have it and the next you as definitely do. Before acceptance a candidate usually undergoes a long period of probing and investigation. The presumption is that in Kim's case this process of exploration began as early as the autumn of 1934 and led some months later to his being recruited – but still only on probation. His first steps in espionage were directed by an intelligence officer on the staff of the Soviet Embassy: 'Week by week, we met in one or other of the remoter open spaces in London; week after week I would reach the rendezvous empty-handed and leave with a load of painstaking advice, admonition and encouragement. I was often despondent at my failure to achieve anything worth while, but the lessons went on and sank deep.'[1]

These activities led in the summer of 1935 to changes in the pattern of his private life, which provide the first, small clues to the momentous decision he had taken. With the discretion and restraint which were his nature, he started to bury his left-wing past, to break with his left-wing friends, to seal off old channels of communication, and to adopt a wholly new persona as a right-of-centre sympathizer with the Continental enemies of communism. He did not cry his new attitudes from the rooftops but waited for his friends to find them out. His

1. Kim Philby, op. cit., p. xv.

old Cambridge contemporary, Anthony McLean (the same McLean who had lent Kim Tolstoy's *Resurrection* and never got it back), thought to look him up in London that September, and telephoned. 'I'm very busy,' Kim objected. McLean said he would be back in town in a month or two, and wondered whether Kim would be too busy then. 'Yes,' Kim said, 'I shall be too busy to see you.' It was a very cold brush-off.

That same autumn, Maurice Dobb, who had seen Kim in Cambridge on his return from Vienna, wrote to invite him to contribute a chapter to a volume of essays he was editing under the title *Britain Without Capitalists*. It was to be a study of various British industries, criticizing the way they were then being run and suggesting how socialism could improve them. But Dobb got no answer. 'A little while later, it must have been late 1935 or early 1936, I decided to call a meeting of all the possible contributors to put the project into final form. I phoned Philby to ask if he were coming. He was distinctly negative. "I don't want anything to do with it," he said. It was as if he had given up all his left-wing associations. I thought it a little shabby.'[1] The volume eventually appeared, published by Lawrence and Wishart in 1936.

To Lees, who knew him really well, Kim felt the need to be a little more explanatory: when they met that autumn on one of Lees's frequent visits to London, Kim told him he thought that Communism was finished and that any sensible man, in the present state of the world, would go fascist. 'But I can't bring myself to do it,' he added ingenuously, 'after all, I have some responsibility for Litzi.'

But to new acquaintances, Kim already seemed a fellow-traveller of the fascists. The really telling evidence was his frequent visits to the German Embassy in London and his membership of the Anglo-German Fellowship, a body bristling with well-connected names which the Nazis made use of to improve their image in Britain. The Fellowship's President was Lord Mount-Temple, and the honorary secretary Mr E. W. D. Tennant, a city businessman whom a foreign diplomat de-

1. The late Maurice Dobb, a personal communication to the authors.

scribed in a memorandum to the Foreign Office as 'a sincere fanatic, who has an almost mystical admiration for Hitler and the Nazi régime'. The memorandum continues:

The propaganda department of the Anglo-German Fellowship is in constant contact with the German Ministry of Propaganda and Enlightenment in Berlin ... The Ministry in Berlin sends the Fellowship in London a lot of literature – printed in England – for distribution in this country. Some of the stuff is in pamphlet form. It includes also a sort of journal giving press opinions. The aim of the last-named is to suggest to the British public that it is being misled by the British press about both German and British government policies ...

A Foreign Office official minuted: 'The Germans are spending more money and energy in this country than the Soviets.'[1] Some of the German money went on entertaining top people – and others. Kim's name appears on the guest list of formal dinners given by the Fellowship of 14 July 1936 for the Duke and Duchess of Brunswick, and on 15 December for Ribbentrop the German Foreign Minister.

So successful was Kim in carrying out his Russian task to penetrate the Fellowship that early in 1936 it employed him to start a German-financed trade journal. Prudently he kept on his dull job with the *Review* for a while, but now enlivened routine by flying repeatedly to Berlin for talks with the Propaganda Ministry, and even with Herr Ribbentrop himself with whom he had struck up an acquaintance when the latter was Ambassador in London. Coming in to land at Berlin, knowing the terrible fate of the German comrades, Kim must have felt he had broken into the enemy's lair. But Kim's trade magazine never saw the light of day. The Fellowship's backing was transferred to a rival publication, the *Anglo-German Review*, which appeared in November 1936, under the editorship of C. E. Carroll, and which as time went on became more overtly and hysterically pro-Nazi. Indeed, the Fellowship itself was soon overshadowed by a still more aggressively pro-German organization called The Link, founded in July 1937 by a retired naval officer and political innocent, Admiral Sir

1. *FO Archives*, 1936, C 3917/3917/8.

Barry Domvile. Domvile was friendly with C. E. Carroll, but was unimpressed by the Fellowship's effectiveness. It seemed to do little except hold dinners and 'catered mainly for the well-to-do ... It was also well patronized by Judmas, and its off-shoots in British social and business circles.'[1] He therefore conceived The Link with the more practical purpose of bringing together German and British organizations, professional bodies and towns.

Behind all this activity was a personal motive: 'In 1934 I was told privately by the secretary to the Admiralty that if I wanted further commands I would have to become a Freemason. I declined, as I had always been opposed to naval officers joining secret societies. As a result I was placed on the Retired List in 1936. I found myself a free man, and I decided to find out for myself what Masons, Jews and other secret forces at work in our Society, were up to.'[2]

These were the sentiments which brought him to sympathy with Hitler. He never met the Fuehrer, although he once watched him drive past in an open car. Sir Barry's diary records that Hitler looked 'absolutely terrific; absolutely A1'. He met Himmler and found him 'a very charming young man'. The Link survived until the outbreak of war and in 1940 Domvile was jailed in Brixton under Section 18b of the Defence of the Realm Regulations.

Like Kim but with less reticence, Guy Burgess broke publicly with Communism and in 1936 was also to be found in pro-German circles. He too was a frequent visitor to Germany. He served briefly as secretary and travelling companion to 'Jack' Macnamara, Conservative MP for Chelmsford and a prominent member of the Anglo-German Fellowship. Margot Heinemann, a powerful Newnham College socialist and John Cornford's girl friend, loudly denounced Guy's change of heart, while Maurice Dobb, who heard of it belatedly, wrongly attributed it to the shock of Cornford's death

1. Sir Barry Domvile, *From Admiral to Cabin Boy* (London, 1947), p. 64.
2. The late Sir Barry Domvile, a personal communication to the authors.

in Spain in December 1936. ('Guy wrote to me saying that from then on he would be "primarily a democrat, possibly also a socialist".') But if Kim is to be believed, the truth was that Burgess had been recruited on Kim's own recommendation to the Soviet intelligence service.[1]

At Cambridge Burgess had far outshone Kim, but since then Kim's greater practical experience of politics on the Continent had put them on more equal terms. Since Kim's brief visit to Trinity after his return from Vienna in 1934 they had seen a good deal of each other in London, and Kim, in the first flush of enthusiasm for espionage, must have estimated that Guy, so clever and so well connected, would be a great catch. The Russians concurred, and soon, within a very few months of each other, the two young men were exploring the ins and outs of Anglo-German relations. Although no one can have foreseen it at the time, their contributions to the Soviet cause were to be very different. Steady of character and morally committed to his work, Kim was to prove the more effective spy; for Burgess, espionage was an element in his social revolt, one more outrageous gesture of self-assertion. He might well have got a secret kick out of his flirtation with fascism: some types of mind like acting a role and fooling everyone. To link this maverick to his own careful career was an early mistake from which Kim never fully recovered. Donald Maclean, the third Soviet spy of that vintage, was recruited independently, shortly before his entry into the Foreign Service in 1935.

In July 1936 Guy Burgess invited Jim Lees to London from Nottingham for a weekend. To kill two birds with one stone Lees wrote to Kim in the hope of seeing him too. Kim replied that he would be in Berlin that week and had planned to stay on for the weekend, but would make a point of returning to lunch on the Saturday. It was the weekend the Spanish Civil War broke out.

1. Is it fanciful to suppose that the conversation between Burgess and his Soviet contact went something like this?

'Be brave, Comrade Norris. Think of Lenin.'

'I'm afraid, ha, ha, I find more inspiration in the Marquis de Sade.'

(Christopher Isherwood, *Mr Norris Changes Trains* (London, 1935), p. 91.)

As Jim Lees recalls,

It was the most awful lunch – roast beef, almost raw: Litzi couldn't cook an English dinner; but the booze made up for it. I remember Kim saying that Franco's rebels were romantics who could not possibly threaten the Spanish Republic. Of course no one could have foreseen German and Italian support for the rising. But then Kim and I quarrelled violently about what was happening in Central Europe, with him defending the Germans and maintaining that the left was finished. That was why he had taken his job with the Fellowship, he said, and (in an aside to me) that was why he would have to get rid of Litzi.[1]

Lees marvelled at Kim's facility for picking up ideas, doctrines and people, and then dropping them when the wind changed. But he was convinced that Kim's conversion to fascism was genuine. Disgusted he stalked out of the house and had no word from his friend for nine years – not until the last year of the war, when the crusade against Hitler had long since put an end to the debate of the 1930s.

Was the recruitment of Philby, Burgess and Maclean just a lucky throw for the Russians, or was it the fruit of a carefully thought out long-term plan? Alexander Orlov, in his *Handbook of Intelligence and Guerrilla Warfare* (1963), argues that Soviet intelligence deliberately switched in the early 1930s from attempting to recruit already well-placed government officials – an effort that had brought small results – to signing up promising young men on the threshold of their careers.

The political climate of that period was very favourable for such an undertaking, and the young generation was receptive to libertarian theories and to the sublime ideas of making the world safe from the menace of fascism and of abolishing the exploitation of man by man. This was the main theme on which the NKVD 'residenturas' based their appeal to young men who were tired of a tedious life in the stifling atmosphere of their privileged class. And when the young men reached the stage when their thinking made them ripe for joining the Communist Party, they were told that they could be much more useful to the movement if they stayed away from the

1. Jim Lees, a personal communication to the authors.

Party, concealed their political views, and entered the 'revolutionary underground' (pp. 108, 109).

Orlov's evidence suggests that Russian thinking on agent recruitment was different from that of Britain and other European powers whose standard procedure was to 'recruit into access', to pick men already capable of meeting intelligence requirements. Spymasters looked for the weak point in the target to be penetrated rather than for the apprentice with potential. It was thought wasteful in time and effort to recruit and train agents in the pious hope that they would one day have access to secret material. Moreover in the ups and down of politics the enjoyment of access could be transitory: the secretary to a prime minister, for example, could overnight become secretary to an out-of-work politician.

An alternative to the uncertainties of these methods of recruitment was the creation of 'illegals', a technique in which the Russians were to prove skilful. This is the placing in the target country of highly trained men under deep cover, charged with the task of creating their own access. Colonel Abel in the United States and Gordon Lonsdale in England are post-war examples of this Soviet method. It may be assumed that most services today operate a tandem recruitment system: on the one hand their cadre officers seek to recruit agents into access by all the usual means of inducement, coercion and the exploitation of ideological sympathy; on the other, they train and place their own 'illegals'. Throughout the 1930s, the period which Orlov was writing about, the Russians were no doubt still working towards that degree of operational sophistication which so startled the Western world when it was brought to light in the spy trials after the war.

In the brief period 1935 to 1937 England provided a large pool of potential spies for Russia. Hundreds of British intellectuals, distrusting and despising their own government, transferred their loyalties to the internationalist, anti-fascist ideal of the Soviet state. They would have been ready to provide Russia with secret information had they been asked to do so.

We know of three privileged young men signed up by the Russians. Perhaps there were more. But as the 1930s wore on the pool dried up; some Communist sympathizers were absorbed back into a revitalized Labour Party under Clement Attlee and Stafford Cripps, fully alert to the dangers of Communist penetration, many disenchanted by the Moscow trials, the Soviet attack on Finland, and the Nazi-Soviet pact. Finally, Russia's chances of recruitment in Britain were much diminished by the outbreak of war and the thinly veiled defeatism of the Communists' 'imperialist war' line. At last it was possible for Englishmen to take up arms against Hitler without commitment to Communism.

Yet for converts of Kim's vintage, belief in the Russian promise was not a volatile emotion to be quenched by the disappointments of history. Those who took the ultimate step of becoming spies did so in a spirit of great disinterestedness. Young men embarking on a career usually want to know what the prospects are, but this was a job which could offer none, demanding in contrast only sacrifices. The Russians may not always have appreciated what feats of loyalty they asked for – and secured. Trojan horse tactics such as Kim and Burgess were engaged in – penetrating the enemy camp the better to subvert it – meant abandoning the left just when it had become fashionable. To leave this winning side in 1935–6, to drop one's friends, to put oneself outside the fold, to join the right and mouth its despicable arguments – all these demanded devotion and self-discipline. The history of Soviet relations with Western Communist Parties is rich in examples of the Russians' failure to grasp the high-minded selflessness of their European sympathizers; equally the latter were sometimes repelled by the insensitivity and red-tape mentality of their Soviet 'handlers'. For example Kim's Cambridge contemporary, the physicist Alan Nunn May, who passed atomic secrets to the Russians in 1945 for ideological motives, was paid off with two bottles of whisky and some 700 dollars concealed in an empty bottle. Nunn May found the transaction repugnant: 'The whole affair was extremely painful to me, and I only embarked on it because I felt this was a contribution I could make to the safety of mankind. *I certainly did not do it for gain.*'[1]

Perhaps the major sacrifice demanded of Kim was his separation from Litzi. His Jewish and Communist wife was too incongruous in the new right-of-centre persona he was building up, and she had to go. Did she agree to be dropped in the interests of his new intelligence career? It must be presumed that she was an accomplice. 'The Party comes first! Mountains of wrecked lives are buried beneath that epitaph! When a man belonged to the Party, he really *belonged* to it. Body and spirit without reserve. Despite the cynicism which grows in the hearts of men who have devoted their lives to the cause – we loved our Party, and we were proud of its power, proud of our own serfdom, because we had given it all our youth, all our hopes, all the enthusiasm and selflessness which we had once possessed.'[2]

Without Kim, Litzi's life followed the chequered path of a left-wing European refugee. She settled in Paris in 1937, and travelled to Austria in 1938 to bring her parents to safety in London. There she spent the war years with another refugee Georg Honigmann, a German Communist who had found a niche in EXTEL's radio monitoring service. Neither he nor Litzi made a secret of their politics. When the war ended the British military authorities posted Honigmann to Hamburg to help set up a proposed German news agency, and he was given permission to travel by way of Berlin. But he never arrived in Hamburg, and was thought lost in the great confusion of the immediate post-war months in Germany. In due course he surfaced in East Berlin where he worked on a newspaper and where Litzi eventually joined him. A visitor to East Berlin in the late 1960s found him separated from Litzi and directing a satirical cabaret, while Litzi was working as a sound dubber for the East German film corporation, DEFA. She was then a small, good-looking, sophisticated woman in her fifties, living

1. Dr Alan Nunn May's written statement, made before his arrest in February 1946, quoted in the *Report of the Royal Commission* on the Igor Gouzenko case, 17 June 1946.
2. Jan Valtin, *Out of the Night* (1941).

in a quiet street of large detached villas in an elderly eastern suburb of Berlin. Her spacious book-lined room, with low settees in primary colours, suggested the setting of a well-paid woman at the BBC. The effect was emancipated, rather British – but Litzi had not been back to London: 'It would obviously be difficult for many reasons.'[1]

The puzzle remains why Kim did not divorce her until after the Second World War, almost ten years after they had parted, when he was already the father of several children by another woman. Was it that he feared divorce proceedings might draw unwelcome attention to himself and to his metamorphosis? Was it that in the mood of wartime London divorce just did not enter their heads, and that it only became a problem when Litzi joined Honigmann in East Berlin and wished to marry him? Or was it because they hoped that their separation, dictated by their Russian masters, would not be final? In later life when Kim mentioned his first marriage, he dismissed it as a schoolboy prank, a Scarlet Pimpernel episode.

When the Spanish Civil War took on the dimensions of a major conflict, with implications far beyond the country's borders, the Russians judged it was time to give Kim something more testing to do than charting the antics of the Anglo-German Fellowship. On the Republican side they were not short of reliable informants, but they had little means of access to Franco's camp. Who better for the job than an upper-middle-class Englishman of impeccable education and mild right-wing views? All he lacked was a pretext. The most obvious cover for him to travel under was that of a newspaper correspondent – but the trouble was he had no newspaper to represent. He may have used his association with Peter Smolka's London Continental News to secure the necessary journalistic credentials, but if so Smolka, one of the left-wing friends whom Kim was keen on dropping at that time, knew nothing about it. What is certain is that the lack of proper newspaper accreditation for this first trip to Spain, at the time no more than a trivial flaw in a convincing front, was to show

1. Frau Lisa Honigmann to Neil Ascherson, a correspondent of the *Observer*.

up glaringly when, many years later, his past came under investigation.

Whom did Kim suppose he was working for, as he prepared to leave London in the autumn of 1936? It is highly unlikely that the Russians would give such a raw recruit any glimpse of the organizational structure of their offensive or security organizations. Eager newcomers would be told they were joining the 'revolutionary underground', or becoming agents of the Comintern – as Guy Burgess, in a moment of indiscretion, described himself to Goronwy Rees.[1] In any event, from 1933 onwards the Comintern's espionage functions had become increasingly important, and by 1936 it was totally interlocked with the Russian intelligence service. This was the result of a long process of subjugation extending back to the 1920s. Over the years non-Russians in the Comintern's Moscow offices were ousted and replaced by Soviet citizens, so that when, in 1928, Stalin consolidated his hold over the Soviet state machine, he was able to turn the Comintern first into an instrument for disciplining foreign Communist Parties and then into an organ of espionage.

By 1929 Berlin, the stronghold of German Communism, had become the principal foreign base for Soviet intelligence operations and the field headquarters, or Western Secretariat, of the Comintern. Berlin was chosen because Moscow was too remote from Western Europe and North America, and so the threads of Russia's clandestine operations in these areas ended in Berlin, linked to Moscow by a single line of communication. This elaborate organization was shattered by the Nazis when they came to power in 1933: Berlin was abandoned as an operating centre and the functions that had been performed there dispersed throughout Europe. A vast reorganization was set on foot. Soviet military intelligence moved to Amsterdam and Paris, the passport *apparat* went to the Saar, while the Western Secretariat of the Comintern was set up in a large modern office block in the heart of Copenhagen under the cover of a firm of architects and engineers. The journey Moscow–Leningrad–Helsinki–Copenhagen led through re-

1. Goronwy Rees, *A Chapter of Accidents* (1972).

latively safe countries and couriers could make it in forty-eight hours by train and boat.

This defensive dispersal served Russia's purposes in the immediate aftermath of the great setback to the Communist cause in Germany; but as Hitler grew in power and menace Soviet intelligence regrouped yet again, the better to penetrate the Third Reich, now its chief target. Switzerland, and more importantly France, became from 1937 the new bases for operations, and it was to Paris that Kim, a small cog in a large machine, was summoned for training before his Spanish mission. Here he was fitted out with codes and contact addresses, given his targets and briefed on Soviet requirements. He spent some weeks in the French capital before moving south to surface in Spain early in 1937. His period of probation for the Russian service was almost over.

6 Graduation in Spain

> He's not only reporting for the Franco side,
> but he seems to think they're right.
>
> ST JOHN PHILBY on his son

Spain buried many of Kim's friends, but it was the making of him. He emerged from the three bloody years of civil conflict an experienced journalist, a seasoned agent of Soviet intelligence, and a more or less mature man. As he grew up, an element of gritty ruthlessness came to the surface of his character, hardening the youth who had married Litzi and thrown himself so earnestly into the anti-fascist struggle. His father's life was rooted in Arabia and his own loyalties in Russia, but Kim's real debt was to Spain: from his first visit there as an observant child of twelve, this corner of Europe was a recurring motif in his life, and from 1936 to 1944 it was right at the centre of his preoccupations. It was because of Spain that he was eventually recruited by British intelligence, and because of his work on Spain that he was thereafter singled out for promotion. But success and achievement were only hopes in early 1937 when, on Russian instructions, he headed for Franco's Spain. His Soviet intelligence brief was to worm his way as close to the centre of Nationalist operations as possible, to bed down there on a long-term basis, and to report to Moscow first-hand information on all aspects of the fascist war effort.

But his intelligence career almost ended before it properly began. Under the flimsy cover of a freelance journalist and, with no avowable source of funds since the Russians were paying the bill, Kim was anyway dangerously exposed; and, within a few weeks of his arrival, this disguise was almost blown when he was hauled in for interrogation by the Guardia Civil in Cordoba, escaping detection as a Soviet agent only by swallowing his coding instructions.

The real threat to him came however not from his fascist

enemies, nor from anything he did or failed to do himself, but from inside the Russian service he had so recently joined. General Walter Krivitsky, the head of Soviet military intelligence in Western Europe, defected in 1937 and told a British MI5 interrogator, Jane Archer, that the Russians had sent a young British journalist as a spy to Spain. But Krivitsky did not know his name, which paper he was working for, or which side of the civil war he was covering. This was not surprising: as a military intelligence officer Krivitsky would know little about agents working for Russia's civilian service. During the active life of a spy many different individuals, typists and archivists as well as case officers will inevitably learn a good deal about him, but the protection of his identity will always be the organization's most closely guarded secret. Even high-level defectors cannot necessarily name the agents working for their own service. As head of military intelligence Krivitsky would no doubt have been receiving the 'product' of Soviet civilian espionage in Spain, and as a guarantee of their credibility such reports would probably be accompanied by some general indication of their source. Over a period of time regular readers of the 'product' could perhaps deduce the source's name, but Krivitsky did not stay with the puzzle long enough. If his scrap of information was followed up by the British, which is doubtful, it did not lead to Kim – perhaps paradoxically because he was at the start hardly a journalist and without newspaper accreditation. Even when Kim's whole career was combed for clues by MI5 in 1951, Krivitsky's evidence was somehow overlooked. Four years after his defection, Krivitsky was found dead in February 1941 in a Washington hotel. Betrayal from inside his own service – the nightmare of all spies – was three times in his life to put a bomb under Kim's dangerous house of cards. This time he escaped unscathed.

Blissfully unaware of Krivitsky's revelations, but only too conscious that he needed a good reason for being in Spain and for talking to the Nationalists, Kim set about wooing *The Times*. From the moment of his arrival in February 1937 he sent it a stream of unsolicited articles, and one or two of the better ones were printed. He could count on one fortunate circumstance: Robin Barrington-Ward, the assistant editor of *The Times*, had also been to school at Westminster and continued to be greatly attached to it, serving as chairman of its appeal fund. It was natural that he should be only too pleased to give another old boy a lift up in the world. St John Philby clinched the matter by inviting Barrington-Ward to lunch.

Events collaborated. On 26 April 1937 Franco's German-equipped air force plastered the centre of the Basque town of Guernica with incendiary bombs – an act of war against undefended civilians less usual then than now. A cry of outrage went up all over Europe. Two days later Guernica fell to Franco's forces which immediately put about the story that most of the damage was done by the Basques themselves in a cynical bid to inspire resistance and win over world opinion to their side. *The Times*'s coverage of this highly controversial event was widely noted: its dispatch from the stricken town a week after the bombing leaned over backwards to give Franco the benefit of the doubt. Kim had seen his opportunity and seized it. He reported that a commission of civil engineers had been appointed to investigate the causes of the fire that swept the town:

It is feared that the conflagration destroyed much of the evidence of its origin, but it is felt here that enough remains to support the Nationalist contention that incendiaries on the Basque side had more to do with the razing of Guernica than General Franco's aircraft ...

It has been asserted that Guernica was subject to bombing of exceptional intensity, but the distinctive marks of an aerial bombardment are not numerous ... Few fragments of bombs have been recovered, the façades of buildings still standing are unmarked, and the few craters I inspected were larger than anything hitherto made by a bomb in Spain. From their positions it is a fair inference that these craters were caused by exploding mines which were unscientifically laid to cut roads ...

In view of these circumstances it is difficult to believe that Guernica was the target of bombardment of exceptional intensity by the Nationalists for an experiment with incendiary bombs, as is alleged by the Basques. In the investigators' opinion, it will be difficult to establish exactly how the fires started.[1]

This pharisaical piece of writing was Kim's passport into the confidence both of the Spanish nationalists and of Geoffrey Dawson, the editor of *The Times*. Pro-Franco commentators noted approvingly that *The Times* 'became a very different paper after the exposure of the Guernica swindle'.[2] Kim was summoned to London to be interviewed on 20 May by Barrington-Ward who noted in his diary, 'He looks good,' and there and then appointed Kim special correspondent with Franco's army as from 24 May 1937, with an expense allowance of £50 a month. Grub Street days were over but, more to the point, he had got himself the most imposing cover Fleet Street could offer.

Philby was a master at taking the pulse of an office, a skill which was to stand him in good stead on many occasions, but it called for no great cunning to write the sort of dispatch Dawson and Barrington-Ward wanted to read. Although neither man was a specialist in foreign affairs, they sat in sole authority on the subject. They did not choose to draw on the considerable talents and judgement of the paper's correspondents, but preferred their own personal sources, such as Dawson's ministerial friends, Baldwin, Chamberlain and Halifax. From 1935 onwards they were at pains to print nothing that they considered might upset their policy of establishing good relations with Germany. 'I do my utmost, night after night, to keep out of the paper anything that might hurt their susceptibilities,' Geoffrey Dawson wrote to his Geneva correspondent, H. G. Daniels, in May 1937.[3]

Kim covered Franco's Spain for *The Times* for over two years, from May 1937 until August 1939, five months after the fall of Madrid and Franco's final triumph. It was a messy, sprawling war, already ten months old when Kim took over his

1. *The Times*, 5 May 1937.

2. William Foss and Cecil Gerahty, *The Spanish Arena* (1938).

3. Quoted in Sir Basil Liddell Hart, *Memoirs*, Vol. II (London, 1965), p. 149.

duties. He had not been there to report the first terrible battles when the Nationalists were flung back from Madrid in the autumn and winter of 1936-7; but he arrived in time to witness the relentless Nationalist destruction of Republican resistance in the north-west.

Whatever was really going on in his mind and heart at the time, it was in Kim's character to apply himself conscientiously to his work. As a journalist, he had the sober virtues of an honest craftsman, gifts which perfectly accorded with what *The Times* demanded of him. He was a straight reporter in the leisured, literate, sometimes literary, tradition of the time. Still only twenty-five, and with no previous experience as a foreign correspondent, he did a more than competent job, producing clear, well-organized, confident reports. But hardly a word he wrote is worth remembering. The 1930s were the great age of the foreign correspondents, of men who wrote with passion and commitment and whose testimony counted in forming international opinion. The slow death of the Spanish Republic was recorded by a dazzling company of writers and pamphleteers whose prose still reverberates today. Kim cannot be classed with them. At bottom he was too careful and bureaucratic a writer ever to set hearts thudding, but in any event he was on the wrong side and perforce had to muzzle his real ideas and feelings. What can be said is that he rose to the challenge of the job and, as the tide of war moved Franco's way, he upgraded a rather minor niche in *The Times*'s Spanish coverage into one of at least equal importance with the rival dispatches from the Republican side.

Salamanca, the old capital of Leon, west of Madrid, was Kim's base in 1937, but that summer and autumn his reporting of the war took him on long forays to the north and west. He was among the first to enter Santander, taken by Franco's forces on 25 August:

Throughout the morning a number of cars, full of released prisoners, careered through the untidy streets to shouts of Tu arriba Espana! Viva Franco! from the multitudes on the pavements. Many houses were already showing the red and gold nationalist colours. Our progress was considerably hampered by the fact that your Correspondent's escort was wearing the first Nationalist uniform seen in Santander, by virtue of which he was regarded for a short space as the paramount authority in the city. Beneath the plaudits was the sullen sound of retreating militiamen from the front walking silently down the main avenue, known for the last 13 months as the Gran Avenida de Rusia ...[1]

He was there, too, when the Nationalists overran the last Republican stronghold in the North-west – the port of Gijon. He sent *The Times* an elegiac piece on its fall on 21 October: 'Defeat broods over Gijon. At night the stars are dimmed by the glare from the fire at the Campsa petroleum depot started by an aerial bomb. In the daytime great clouds of black smoke roll over the city. Sheets and towels are hung from windows as tokens of surrender. The shops are empty and the population is silent.'[2]

By the end of 1937, Kim could congratulate himself on considerable success. He had wormed himself into a position of trust with the Nationalists, securing two interviews from Franco himself. He was filing long reports to London almost daily, his cover was immaculate, and both his sets of employers must have been well satisfied. He was even an object of envy: this quiet young Englishman had hooked perhaps the most desirable foreign lady then living in Spain. Lady Lindsay-Hogg was thirty-five. She had divorced her minor baronet husband, Sir Anthony, in 1933, but continued to use the title although her own name, Frances Doble, had glowed quite brightly in London café society in the late twenties and early thirties.

Daughter of a Canadian banker, Frances – or Bunny, as her friends called her – had become a star of light romances and melodramas, living much the sort of life glorified in the plays in which she appeared: she was constantly seen at champagne parties, after-theatre dinners and country-house weekends. She was a woman of great attractiveness and spirit, but marked beyond the possibility of change by the values of those tinsel years. She played the lead opposite Ivor Novello in *Sirocco*, a

1. *The Times*, 27 August 1937.
2. *The Times*, 26 October 1937.

bad play by Noel Coward, in which a 'most urgent Italian chased her round a table and rolled her on the floor in the urgency of his passion'.[1] The play was booed off the stage. She appeared in *The Constant Nymph* and *The Chinese Bungalow* and even in a sentimental 'talkie', *Dark Red Roses*, in which the character of an open-hearted baronet was played by none other than her future husband. Magazines like *Picture Show* and their glamour-hungry readers drooled over her. 'There is a vast amount of what is known as sex attraction in Frances Doble. There is a great depth of quality in her beautiful speaking voice; her silky hair has the sheen of dark satin, her brown eyes are like dark pansies, her smile enchanting and her figure exquisite ... She is a great artiste, highly cultured and extremely well bred.' The peak of her career was *Ballerina*, a tear-jerking story of love sacrificed to art, in which Frances danced a (brief) *pas de deux* with Anton Dolin. 'At the end, a little man named Haskell, leading authority on the ballet, approached her with tears in his eyes: "I thought you were Pavlova ...".'[2]

To put it mildly, Frances's political views were conservative. She doted on titles, connections, country houses, the names that made the gossip columns. In 1934, a Canadian journalist in London, interviewing 'the lovely Canadian girl' for the folks back home, remarked *en passant* that among much chit-chat about the theatre, 'we talked of the ineffable glory that was Hitler'. Her politics were ecstatic rather than reasoned. When Kim met her in Spain in 1937, she was a passionate Royalist, but largely because in London she had struck up a friendship with King Alfonso of Spain who had gone into voluntary exile in 1931. She had met him in 1932 at an after-theatre party:

'Senora! May I join you?'
He was carrying a bottle of champagne and two glasses. I curtsied and then we sat side by side by the fire.
'I hear that you love my country and I should like to talk to you about it,' he said.
A friendship grew up between us and our friends made a point of

1. *The Times*, 25 November 1927.
2. *The Toronto Star*, 16 January 1934.

inviting us to the same parties. Sometimes he called on me at my flat. It was always a ceaseless chatter about Spain. What did I think of the bulls, of Spanish music, of painting? He was a tall man with a good figure, and a heavy-featured, rather brutish face. I adored him.[1]

King Alfonso died in Rome in 1941, and is buried in the Escorial.

Kim's liaison with Frances Doble was a blue-chip alliance between *The Times* and a glamorous symbol of what the Spaniards took to be British high society. Kim affected a cool impartiality, but Frances was all for Franco. 'I'm *passionately* for this side!' she used to say, 'with all my heart and soul! Heavens, don't tell me you have no interest in who wins!' She would try to jolt him out of his neutrality, but Kim did not like arguing. And when, as the Nationalist armies swept onwards, she exclaimed: '*We've* won another battle,' he would just smile wryly. Frances kept a civil war diary in a big office ledger, which she liked reading aloud to her friends. When Kim was working, she would correct his articles. 'You taught me to write,' he told her gallantly.

Frances remembered Kim as

deeply sentimental but not very demonstrative. He was sober and serious with a taste for classical music. He didn't joke a great deal. I wouldn't say he was wildly attractive to women, but there was something very appealing about him. He didn't care how he dressed, but was always very neat and clean. He drank, of course, though not to excess, and was popular with the other journalists. We often talked about his father's exploits in Arabia, or about Vienna and the Austrian girl he married there, but he never breathed a word about socialism, communism, or anything like that.[2]

Nurse-maided by Franco's press officers, the foreign journalists criss-crossed Spain in a hearty, rambunctious body; negotiating their dispatches past the censors each evening was their chief hurdle. Not much on the Nationalist side was left to the correspondents' initiative: there was no striking out by oneself

1. The late Lady Lindsay-Hogg, a personal communication to the authors.
2. ibid.

in search of a scoop, no hazardous individual reconnoitring. 'The journalist who moves a single kilometre alone in Franco's territory is jailed at once or expelled.'[1]

When the fronts were quiet, life for the press corps centred on the Grand Hotel in Salamanca – Franco's military headquarters – where the big table in the dining room was reserved for German military observers, an earnest party presided over by a general.

At a smaller table nearby sat the newspaper correspondents, among them Randolph Churchill, Pembroke Stevens, Reynolds Packard and his wife, and Philby of *The Times*; Churchill's clear, vigorous voice could be heard deploring with well-turned phrase and varied vocabulary the inefficiency of the service, the quality of the food, and, above all, the proximity of the Germans, at whom he would direct venomous glances throughout the meal. 'Surely,' he exclaimed loudly one night at dinner, 'there must be one Jew in Germany with enough guts to shoot that bastard Hitler!'[2]

A frequent stop on the press circuit was Saragossa, in Aragon, where the hotels were shabby and overcrowded, but the company always interesting. The correspondents, sleeping two or three to a room, would hear the German and Italian airmen leaving at four or five in the morning to fly over Barcelona or the Teruel trenches. But the pilots were taciturn; printed notices under the glass covers of the table in the lounge warned: 'Do not drink too much or you will raise the hopes of those who wish to make you a victim of espionage!'[3]

Decorously, rather separate from the other correspondents, Kim and his titled lady travelled about Spain together in a car. The Spaniards were much impressed and no journalist got bigger smiles than Kim from the escorting officers. He was an object of admiration even to the Germans who had come to Franco's aid. In his book *My Silent War* he recounts how he was wined and dined for a year or so by Major Von der Osten, alias Don Julio, an officer of the German Secret Service, whose

1. A Journalist, *Foreign Journalists under Franco's Terror* (London, 1938), p. 260.
2. Peter Kemp, *Mine were of Trouble* (1957), p. 106.
3. Karl Robson, 'With Franco in Spain', in Wilfrid Hindle, ed., *Foreign Correspondent* (London, 1939), p. 265.

'real interest in me was to get an introduction to a lady of my acquaintance. When I obliged him, he propositioned her forthwith, both espionage-wise and otherwise. She turned him down indignantly on both counts, and his manner to me became distant.'

When not on tour, Kim and Frances used to settle down for a few days at a time in one or other of the active centres of Franco's Spain: Salamanca, headquarters of the army, or Burgos, seat of the civil administration. Salamanca, where Frances had a room in an old palace, was an altogether livelier place, bursting at the seams with troops, foreign advisers in exotic uniforms, and observers from half Europe. At Burgos, the deeply conservative capital of Castile, Frances kept a suite of rooms, but, for form's sake, Kim always stayed at an hotel.

For two precious months, from mid-October to mid-December 1937, there was a lull in the war. Both sides took breath and bound their wounds. Then, on 15 December, in bitter weather, the Republic struck out at the bleak walled town of Teruel, in the lonely wastes of Aragon – famous as the coldest spot in Spain. This atrocious battle, fought in blizzards so cold that men on both sides went down with frostbite and limbs had to be amputated, was the bloody summit of Kim's war. The Nationalist garrison held out until 8 January 1938, then it was the Republicans' turn to defend the city against a Nationalist counterattack which, slowed by heavy snow, did not retake Teruel until 20 February.

Kim witnessed these murderous reverses of fortune, taking his share of the hazards of war. Most of Teruel's 13,000 inhabitants fled. Those who remained squatted in muddy shelters beneath their houses, while the shells hissed back and forth above their roofs. Just after Christmas, when the fighting was at its fiercest, Franco allowed a few carloads of pressmen to visit the front. In cruelly cold weather, 18 degrees below zero, Philby and a group of other journalists drove up towards the fighting on 31 December, through mean villages crowded with soldiers and refugees. In the party were Karl Robson of the *Daily Telegraph*, Richard Sheepshanks of Reuter's, Edward Neil of the Associated Press, and Bradish Johnson, a *News-*

week photographer. Apart from Kim, Robson, whose eye-witness account follows, was the only one to survive the experience:

Round about noon we turned off the main road and drove into the village of Caude (eight miles north-west of Teruel) ... We stopped near a barn, and got out to ask passing soldiers for news of the battle ... A heavy battery in action a hundred yards away annihilated consecutive conversation. Ears, feet and hands ached with cold ...

A startling sound split the air – the unmistakable *swish* of an approaching shell in the last second of its career. A stupefying crash, and a blast that seemed to lift the car. I crouched low while a shower of debris clattered on the roof and cracked the rear window. Silence. Then urgent shouts in the street, and running footsteps, stilled as each of three more shells thudded heavily into the village.

One felt absurdly defenceless sitting in that car. Three mules lay dead, by the side of a pond, a fourth standing agitatedly beside them. Their leader had disappeared. Seeing a group of soldiers taking cover beside the barn, I ran over and joined them. As we gratefully rose in unison after every burst I looked around for the others.

For a while I could see no sign of them. Then Philby came running across the road. Blood trickled brightly from his forehead down his face on to his clothes. 'They're in there!' he yelled, pointing to the second car. Sickeningly I saw three figures, with grotesquely blackened faces, lolling motionless in their seats. A shell had exploded within a foot or two of the left front wheel of the car immediately behind the one in which I had been sitting. The bonnet and door were riddled with black-ringed holes. A press officer got there first. When the door was opened Johnson tumbled out dead. Somebody threw a rug over him. Sheepshanks, who had been sitting next to Johnson, was breathing in quick, deep snores, his temple torn open, and consciousness gone for ever. Neil was sprawling at the back of the car, dazedly recovering from the first shock of the explosion. His left leg had been torn and broken by scores of splinters; he could not move, and he could scarcely speak.

A Republican artillery observation officer, it seems, had watched the cars turn off the main road and drive into Caude. Staff officers, of course; and word was given to shell the village. In the meantime Sheepshanks, Neil and Philby had got into the car to talk and smoke. Neil and Philby sat in the back, Sheepshanks in front.

Shortly afterwards they had been joined by Johnson, who took the driver's seat.

Sheepshanks was laid on a stretcher and carried off to a dressing station up the street. Then we began to extricate Neil from the back of the car. He was heavily built, the car was a two-door saloon, and we had to crouch now and then as a shell landed near. Neil smiled his infectious smile. 'Good work, boys. Sorry I'm so damned heavy. Keep an eye on my typewriter, will you?' Then, catching a glimpse of the covered body, 'Who's that dead, Robson?'

They were roughly patched up and slid into an ambulance to be taken to a casualty station at Santa Eulalia. Philby had been incredibly lucky. His head wounds were not serious . . .[1]

Sheepshanks died in hospital that night without regaining consciousness. Neil had a slow and painful journey back to Saragossa. The Associated Press commissioned a surgeon to fly to his bedside, but gangrene set in swiftly, and he died before the doctor arrived.

On the night of the accident, Kim joined Frances at Saragossa. She remembered him walking into the restaurant with a soiled bandage round his head and wearing a woman's moth-eaten fur coat: he had lost his own coat in the explosion. His hands trembled from shock. The next day, 1 January, was his twenty-sixth birthday.

As the miraculous survivor of the Republican shell, Kim became a prize exhibit of the Nationalist press officers. On 2 March he was received by General Franco, who conferred on him the Red Cross of Military Merit. If he needed a seal on the perfection of his cover, this was it. It was a moment rich in irony when the only Communist member of the British parliament drew indignant attention in the House to this Fascist award.

On behalf of Mr Gallacher (Fife W, Comm), Mr Kirkwood (Dumbarton, Lab) asked the Prime Minister whether he was aware that Mr H. A. R. Philpot had been offered the decoration of the Military Merit Cross by General Franco: and whether Mr Philpot had been authorised to accept this decoration.

1. Karl Robson, 'With Franco in Spain', in Wilfrid Hindle (ed.), *Foreign Correspondent* (1939), pp. 254 ff.

Mr Butler: I assume that the Hon Member is referring to Mr H. A. R. Philby, a newspaper correspondent serving with General Franco's forces. I have seen in the press a report of the award of a medal by the Spanish nationalist authorities to this gentleman. Mr Philby has not sought and has not been given any official authority to accept the distinction in question.[1]

Someone in Moscow must have enjoyed the joke.

'The battle for Teruel is over,' wrote the newly decorated Kim, when the city had once more fallen to the Nationalists, 'and with it another stage in the civil war. It is unlikely the Nationalists will again give their opponents time to rest and recuperate, and a new chapter must begin soon ...'[2] His prediction was borne out as the Nationalists began their lightning progress through Aragon in March, the Republicans crumbling before them. But by mid-April the pace was slowing and the jubilant mood of Franco's armies gave way to war-weariness when their campaign was brought to a halt by the Republicans' desperate stand on the Ebro in late July 1938. It was here on 1 August that David Haden Guest, the Communist hero of Kim's Cambridge days, was killed, fighting in the XVth International Brigade.

The long engagement on the Ebro, fought from July to November 1938, for many weeks in stifling heat, was the last point at which hope for a Republican victory could still be entertained. Kim brought up the rear of the advancing Nationalists, filing workmanlike dispatches, always sympathetic to Franco and sometimes lapsing into Hollywood prose: 'Blood still flows on Valencian olive-groves; still girdles the domed white city of Madrid; still mingles with the streams that water the sun-smitten vale of La Serena, serene in nothing but name.'[3] As the war turned north into Catalonia, he defended the Nationalist bombing of Barcelona and other ports on the grounds that war material from Russia and France was reaching the Republicans through them. Killing civilians by aerial bombardment – thirteen thousand died in Barcelona after two

1. *The Times*'s parliamentary report, 6 April 1938.
2. *The Times*, 23 February 1938.
3. *The Times*, 10 August 1938.

days of Nationalist bombing in March – was still enough of a novelty to need defence. From January 1939, after the fall of Barcelona which Kim witnessed, the Nationalist advance was more of a victory parade than an offensive. Republican refugees streamed into France. He stayed in Barcelona, a city engulfed in cheering, clapping mobs, hysterical with relief that their war at least was over. In his dispatches, he dwelt on the barbarity of the Republicans; the discipline of the Nationalists and the work of reconstruction they now undertook. He also had space to record a tiny off-beat incident: 'A lieutenant entered your Correspondent's bedroom and explained briefly that he was the owner of the flat, put a chair on the bed and extracted from the recesses of a lamp hanging from the ceiling a small piece of screwed-up tissue paper. Having examined its contents, he pocketed it, apologised for the intrusion and disappeared as quickly as he came with the recovered treasure ...'[1]

As late as February 1939, the Republic still held a third of Spain, including the capital, but its authority had disintegrated. Britain and France recognized Franco's régime on 27 February, and Madrid fell without a fight a month later.

Over the years of the Spanish war, some of Kim's journalistic colleagues thought they detected a whiff of the intelligence agent about him. No one, of course, connected him with Russia. Rather, there was a strong suspicion that he was in British pay, as it was known, or at least believed, that the British secret service sometimes employed correspondents of *The Times*. His strategic grasp of the campaigns on the different fronts, his sheer level of information, seemed to give substance to this view. For some of the pressmen, this supposed secret role made Kim's mild pro-Franco sympathies more palatable, although journalists reporting from the Republican side of the war regarded his cool, unmoved dispatches as a betrayal of the democratic cause.

Kim's disguise as a fascist sympathizer was always skilful, never insistent: he adopted an air of neutrality towards the conflict, as behoved the representative of the mighty *El Times*,

1. *The Times*, 30 January 1939.

but let it appear, without actually saying so, that his personal attitudes were conservative and gentlemanly. Other journalists stormed at the censorship; some, such as Noel Monks of the *Express*, were even expelled for what they wrote. But Kim was always on the most friendly terms with Nationalist officials, and in particular with Pablo Merry del Val, the man in charge of Franco's press and propaganda services. Avoiding blatant partiality, he always managed to give a flattering gloss to Nationalist Spain, making a point of mentioning the normality of life, the maintenance of law and order, the high standing of Franco's credit abroad, his concern with the people's well-being. 'He's not only reporting for the Franco side,' a puzzled St John Philby told his old friend Sir Reader Bullard of the Foreign Office, 'but he seems to think they're right.'[1] But Kim could not be accused of overplaying his pro-Franco role: Sir Robert Hodgson, the senior British diplomat in touch with Franco in 1937, is at pains in his book *Spain Resurgent* to defend himself against a report made by 'Philby of *The Times*' that he had given a Falange salute during the playing of the Spanish national anthem.[2] With such unemphatic touches of evidence Kim contrived to appear objective.

There were spies by the dozen on both sides in the Spanish Civil War, and the French border was the clearing house for much of their information. For news of the Royalist camp, the press corps would go to San Sebastian on the Basque coast to drink, dance and rub shoulders with well-born exiles from the rigours of Madrid who had taken refuge in the smarter hotels of this seaside resort. Kim, having no sense of rhythm, kept off the dance floor, but Frances cut a dashing figure foxtrotting and tangoing with condes, marqueses – and the other journalists. At Hendaye, the little town astride the frontier, the place of rendezvous was the Grand Hotel Imatz, where the air was heavy with conspiracies of every colour: some spied because they were paid to; some spied because it was the thing to

1. Sir Reader Bullard, a personal communication to the authors.
2. Sir Robert Hodgson, *Spain Resurgent* (London, 1953), pp. 81, 82.

do – almost the only thing to do.[1] In the early months of the war, Hendaye was also the seat of the British Embassy to Spain. At that time the British government had no official relations with the Nationalists, but diplomats often crossed into Franco's territory to deal with the problems of British subjects living under his jurisdiction. Later a British Agency to treat with the Franco government was established in the Golf Hotel in St Jean de Luz. The head of this Agency, Sir Geoffrey Thompson, made a point of grilling the British pressmen when they dropped in on this neutral staging-post on the edge of the conflict. 'There was little that Philby did not know about the extent of the German and Italian military participation on the Franco side.'[2] Such, no doubt, was the nature of the information which Kim was supplying to the Russians. His orders were to transmit his information by hand to Soviet contacts in France or, in the case of urgent communications, to send coded messages to cover addresses outside Spain. This fitted in very well with the pattern of his movements as a journalist, and it was on one of his regular excursions to the Basque coast that he again met Guy Burgess who, Kim later revealed in his book, brought him fresh funds.

Even more than Hendaye, St Jean was a remarkable place for intrigue. Alan Moorehead, then covering the war for the *Express*, noted that every traveller – black-marketeer, diplomat, secret agent, or journalist – paused there for a while on his journeys in and out of Spain. You could buy anything there from a forged passport to a million-peseta small-arms contract.

The centre of all this agitation was a cheerful little restaurant called the Bar Basque that still exists in the main street, and sooner or later everyone of any consequence made their way there in order to read the newspapers and pick up the latest gossip. There was no item of news about the fighting, whether it was the shipment of tanks from Russia or Moors from Morocco, the destruction of Guernica

1. Alan Dick, *Inside Story* (London, 1943), p. 101.
2. Sir Geoffrey Thompson, *Front-line Diplomat* (London, 1959), p. 138.

or the rising of the Fifth Column in Madrid, that was not either invented in the Bar Basque or dicussed there with embellishments early in its course round the town.[1]

Many British residents of Spain had fled to St Jean from the shellings, air raids and imprisonments of the Civil War, and to make themselves feel more at home had founded the Baloney Club amid the rustic walnut and red plush of the Bar Basque. Several of the war correspondents were roped in as associate members – Alan Moorehead, Walter Duranty, the red-haired, knickerbockered Virginia Cowles, and of course Kim.

Behind the careful make-believe, what must Kim really have felt? His life was a lie. It must sometimes have been a painful one. John Cornford was killed in Spain a couple of months before Kim got there, and David Haden Guest before he left. He saw the Republic die and the detested fascists triumph. Even his guarded neutrality must have been a terribly irksome pose to maintain. By reporting the Franco side of the war with rather less than total objectivity, he had set himself publicly apart, once and for all, from a stream of left-wing thought and feeling which the war had powerfully inspired. Sympathy for the Republic was a sentiment shared by most intelligent, humane, liberal-minded men of his generation. Kim was doomed not to keep their company. The disgust and condemnation of men he admired must have been the hardest thing to bear.

But the conflict itself gave him qualities which helped him to endure these miseries. Like developing fluid working on a negative, the war brought out in him traits already in his character: a sense of discipline, a touch of stoicism and austerity, an ability to devote himself to the job in hand without constantly putting in question the abstract ideal – an ideal which must in any case have been eroded by what he had seen of cynical Soviet policies in Spain and by what he must have heard of the great Stalinist purges of 1936–8. In his relationship with Frances, Kim learned the subtle arts of emotional deception. From then on, he was able to keep his women in a

1. Alan Moorehead, 'To the Edgware Road', in *Cornhill Magazine*, Autumn 1970.

watertight compartment, giving them sincere affection, even devotion, but keeping them separate from what was most important to him.

He was still not all steel, however, and on one occasion could not resist defending himself against the contempt of a man he respected. Eric Gedye, the veteran Central European correspondent of the *Daily Telegraph*, remembered Kim in his Vienna days as a fervent young socialist, and was therefore astounded and perturbed to find him in 1937 reporting the Franco side of the Spanish war for Geoffrey Dawson's rightwing *Times*. He wanted an explanation and an opportunity presented itself. Gedye chanced at this time to meet again the Austrian girl Communist whom Kim had sent him three years earlier to lead him to the secret Schutzbund parade in the Vienna woods. This young woman was about to set off for Spain on a journalistic assignment: 'Mostly in joke, I told her that if she should run across our mutual friend, Kim Philby, to tell him I was sorry to find him in such bad company. Months later, when I'd forgotten the incident, she telephoned me out of the blue with a message from Kim. It was simply this: "Tell Eric not to be misled by appearances. I'm exactly what I've always been." '[1]

For one brief moment, Kim's *amour-propre* caused him to let slip his guard.

Kim left Spain in August 1939 on a three-week holiday, but he never returned, although Frances waited for him in St Jean de Luz where her Canadian banker father owned a villa. They met briefly in Paris later that year when Kim was on weekend leave from another war – the Phoney War which the press covered from the Arras headquarters of the British Expeditionary Force. In Paris, too, at this time, Kim found his wife Litzi. They must have had a lot to say to each other.

1. The late Eric Gedye, a personal communication to the authors.

7 Miss Marks & Spencer

Nothing Recorded Against.

MI5 ON KIM PHILBY, 1940

The first British soldier killed by the Germans in the Second World War died in France on 13 December 1939, three and a half months after Britain's declaration of war. It was an isolated clash, north of the Maginot Line, and the Phoney War still had another five months to run before the German thrust across the Low Countries and into France in May 1940 sent the British Expeditionary Force reeling back towards Dunkirk, and knocked France out of the war.

For these eight months before the sudden catastrophe, the only reality was boredom. Dug in along the Belgian frontier, the BEF held a 'front' where there was no fighting, no enemy, no activity. The miserable little villages dotted about the plains around Arras – seat of Lord Gort's GHQ – were packed with men wandering aimlessly about. There was nothing to see but sugar beet and rain, nothing to do at night but sit and talk. In Arras itself there were one or two cinemas and several brothels, but it was not often that the troops got to either. Dartboards and footballs were more precious than rations. Thousands were on their way but they did not seem to arrive. With so much time on their hands, the men took to writing letters home on a monumental scale, creating problems for the post office. As they dug their trenches, often with a foot of water in the bottom, and built their pill-boxes in the damp fields of northern France, the general grievance was, 'Why didn't the war start on a proper scale?'

Gloom was also deep in the bar of the Hotel du Commerce in Arras where the accredited war correspondents of the London press searched desperately for a war to report. They had to contend not only with the intense inaction, but also with the mutton-headed army censors, for whom a description of the weather was dangerous stuff, possibly of use to the enemy. Sometimes so many words and sentences were deleted from dispatches that verbs no longer agreed with their subjects. For months the correspondents could give no hint of the BEF's position, but had always to pretend they were somewhere they were not. They filled out their reports with descriptive passages in slow-moving prose.

Only a narrow vista meets the eye from the turf-banked block-houses that form the British front (wrote Kim Philby). A damp heavy atmosphere, foreboding copious rain, obscures the further horizons. Towns and villages, built of brick and set closely together amid the endless fields, are stained by persistent smoke to a mono-tonous reddish-grey. 'La Belle France' seems far away. Comfort-less skies follow one another in dreary procession ... 'Adolf' is the enemy, the infernal nuisance, the target of the private's wit and the goal of his endeavours. Adolf must go, cost what it may. Many express disappointment at the slow tempo of the overture to Armageddon. They expected danger and they have found damp.[1]

These sluggish weeks of non-war are, by an odd chance, among the best documented of Kim's life. Detailed descriptions of him – drinking in bars, poring over maps, commenting somewhat sententiously on the course of the campaign – appear repeatedly in diaries of the period, written and later published by colleagues in the press corps, who set down the minutiae of their daily life perhaps because they could say so little in their news dispatches. The best of these books, *War Reporter* by Bernard Gray of the *Daily Mirror*, was published posthumously in 1942 after its author's death in a submarine off Malta. Gray, a plain, honest fellow nicknamed Potato, who crashed after his stories like a bull-terrier, was Kim's in-separable companion. 'The lamb of journalism lying down with the lion,' their colleagues commented of this partnership between *The Times* and the *Mirror*. 'Philby and Bernard Gray formed a professional spearhead in search of news ... Each as a reporter was typical of the traditions of his paper, Philby writing coolly and meticulously in the third person, Gray mak-

1. *The Times*, 17 November 1939.

ing a hearty individual approach – neither more efficient than the other,' wrote F. G. H. Salusbury of the *Daily Herald*.[1]

The journalists were divided into parties of roughly six, each group travelling and working together under one conducting officer supplied by the BEF. Apart from Gray, Kim's 'syndicate', as the parties were called, included Evelyn Montague of the *Manchester Guardian*, a studious-looking fellow with a long face, a chin that stuck out like a rock, and a pair of big glasses, who once ran for England in the Olympic Games; and Philip Jordan of the *News Chronicle*, gourmet, connoisseur of wines and a rebel against all forms of authority, who had covered the Spanish War on the Republican side.

Kim at twenty-seven emerges from Gray's unsophisticated narrative as sturdy, boyish, keen, 'a useful amateur boxer', whose eyes tended to sparkle when allowed within range of the German big guns. Other contemporaries looked a little closer. The *Daily Herald* man detected something that 'suggested the ache of his tragic experience in Spain when he was the only survivor of a shelled motor-car' – his colleagues believed that this shock accounted for Kim's stutter; but, Salusbury added admiringly, 'the essence of him was deeply within his really first-class brain'. Not everyone took as flattering a view of him. John O'Donnell, an American journalist on a visit to the BEF, was affronted to see Kim failing to stand to attention when the 'Last Post' was sounded on Armistice Day, 1939, before the tomb of the Unknown soldier. 'Philby was on my left and from the corner of my eye I noted he was moving about. Just to be helpful, I muttered out of the corner of my mouth, "I think we should be at attention." Nothing happened. Don't think he even dropped his cigarette. Well, it was none of my business what a London *Times* reporter does but I made some crack on the way back and our London *Times* colleague overheard and made some observation to the effect: "I don't go for all this military rot." '[2]

Each day the various 'syndicates' led by their conducting officers used to visit various parts of the line, or call on some

1. *World's Press News*, 6 June 1940.
2. *New York Daily News*, 24 October 1955.

particular regiment in search of a story. Kim's group chose as
their conducting officer Captain Arthur Pilkington, a member
of the hunting, shooting and fishing class, known as 'Pilks'. As
competition between the syndicates hotted up, 'Pilks's circus'
took great pride in their ability to ferret out stories from a remarkably unpromising situation. Some were necessarily rather
thin: 'More Bakers for the BEF' was one headline in the
News Chronicle which earned the correspondent much friendly
teasing. But such mild fun did little to relieve the terrible
tedium.

Montague, Philby, myself and one or two more fellows were sitting
in the bar of the Commerce one afternoon feeling discontented
with the world in general (Bernard Gray wrote). Why did we have
to put up with such bad censors? Why did this darned bar always
smell so damned musty? Why was it called a bar, anyway, when
at best you could only describe it as a filthy old lounge with a lot of
wooden tables and bench seats?

In fact we were just in the mood to find fault with everything.
And at that moment I spied a little fellow in uniform heading our
way. A captain, too. 'Look at that little squirt,' I said. 'He's the
smallest officer I've ever seen. Wonder what he wants?'

We soon found out. The little man, who had heavy eyebrows
and rather an aggressive face, came straight to our table. 'I'm Captain McCormack from the War Office,' he said. 'I've come out here
to help Captain Reynolds in Public Relations. I'd like to hear any
complaints you may have.' ...[1]

Their boredom was abruptly ended when in the early morning of 10 May 1940 the Germans invaded Holland and Belgium
and bombed, amongst other French towns, Arras. The BEF
moved up into Belgium to check the German advance with
the press corps hot on its tail, dodging in and out of an almost
endless convoy of lorry-loads of troops singing their relief
that the war had started at last. Brussels airport had been
heavily bombed, but the city looked carefree. The streets were
packed with people, the sun shone, women wore their smartest
spring clothes. When the sirens sounded, gendarmes tried to
drive people off the streets and into air-raid shelters, but they

1. Bernard Gray, *War Reporter* (London, 1942), p. 34.

would not go, shouting and pointing into the sky as the anti-aircraft guns fired at the German planes clearly visible overhead.

Kim's 'syndicate' ordered a round of Munich beer in the café opposite the main station : 'But, sir, you can't drink that, it's German!' protested the waiter earnestly. 'It's still good beer,' Kim replied unmoved.

Probing closer to the fighting each day, the journalists were soon deep in the war. Pilks sometimes drove them up to the front through the night, his charges slumbering in the car, jerking awake at the sound of gunfire. Refugees fleeing from Belgian cities clogged the roads. Nearer the advancing Germans, British army engineers were digging trenches and laying mines. Louvain, emptied of its population, waited for the oncoming enemy tanks. Water and gas leaked into the streets from mains shattered by shells. Apart from the British and Belgian troops, the only occupants of the city appeared to be half-starved animals. Dogs left chained without food or water by their owners went mad and were put out of their misery by the troops. Kim, the group's permanent map-reader, charted their way back to base across the battlefield of Waterloo, giving them a history lesson on the way. As he stammered learnedly on, the honest sentimental Gray exclaimed over the beauty of the early summer. The lilac, heliotrope and white, was in full and glorious bloom and sprays of honeysuckle scented the hedges. 'Pity Beverley Nichols isn't here,' he said, 'at least he'd get some satisfaction from the flowers.'

On 17 May, seven breathless days after the start of the campaign, the war correspondents were, much to their disgust, ordered back to Arras. The great retreat had begun. There, many of the journalists found congratulatory cables from their news editors waiting for them. There was a telegram from *The Times* for Kim, distinctly an event for a newspaper which extended its sobriety to its relations with its staff; poor Bernard Gray's message from the *Mirror* asked bluntly for 'More facts, less flowers.'

But no sooner had the correspondents arrived in Arras than they found to their dismay that they were to retreat even further to Amiens. Kim's only recorded comment was, 'Good job we drank some of that Munich beer in Brussels, or the Germans would have got it all.' They took to the road along with what seemed the whole population of Arras, travelling with their goods and chattels piled high in a strange assortment of vehicles. But Amiens was no haven. People were fleeing from there too and most of the restaurants were closed. Kim and Bernard Gray eventually found a café well stocked with whisky and bottles of English Bass, where a small party took shape, ending in Gray's room at a second-rate hotel. They all went to bed at three in the morning, only to be awakened an hour later with the news that German tanks had reached the outskirts of the town. Feeling very angry with the enemy, very sorry for themselves, and completely bewildered by the rapid developments, Kim and Gray, unshaven, found their way round to the public relations headquarters where more bottles of Bass were emptied as they waited for orders. It was not till eight o'clock that the long broken line of cars moved out of the town towards the north-west. Nobody knew where they were heading for but sickeningly they realized that every kilometre they travelled brought them a little nearer England and a little further from the front. They passed through several featureless small towns. One possible destination after another dropped behind them, until in the end there would be only one, Boulogne.

Dutch and Belgian fishing boats crowded the harbour. British, French, Polish, Dutch and Belgian soldiers mingled in the streets. There were thousands of refugees – not only those from Holland and Belgium, but many more from Germany, Czechoslovakia, Italy, Spain, Poland and, of course, from those districts of France already overrun by the Germans. For all of them safety lay on the other side of a strip of water less than thirty miles wide. Very few of them were to cross it, despite attempts to bribe officials and to enlist the help of the war correspondents.

They had their problems too. From the moment of their arrival on 18 May they were floundering helplessly in the gigantic disorder around them. Telephone and telegraph lines to England were down and, insofar as the London papers were concerned, the correspondents might as well have been on holiday. GHQ refused point-blank to ferry all the correspondents to where the fighting was taking place but would promise transport for only one man per 'syndicate'. Beds were almost impossible to find and, worse still, both Kim and Gray found to their bitter rage that all their belongings had fallen into German hands at Amiens. The officer in charge of the 'rescue' operation had ordered his men, despite their protests, to get out with only 'half a load' when German planes appeared overhead.

Cut off from the war and from their news editors, the journalists spent most of the day eating and drinking and lying in the sun.

'Wouldn't it be grand to be in France in peacetime, on holiday, with weather like this?' Gray said.

'Yes, we'd go on from here to Le Touquet and play golf,' Kim said lazily. 'And then – we would have a car, of course – I'd like to drive to Brittany.'

He gazed reflectively at the smoke-clouds rising from his cigarette. He always insisted on smoking cheap Gauloises Bleus.

'Then, taking it easy, I think we'd follow the Breton coast, keep south, until eventually we reached St Jean de Luz ... A lovely place. I used to spend a lot of time there during the Spanish war. Come out of Spain for a rest, you know. I'd like to swim a race against you across the bay at St Jean.'

'It wouldn't be a race unless you gave me a nine-tenths start,' Gray interjected.

'Well, never mind. We'd swim. Then when we got tired of staying in St Jean – I know a lot of people there – we'd drive east along the slopes of the Pyrenees ... Then on to Marseilles – we'd have a look round the night life there, it's pretty sticky – and the Riviera. And sunshine all the way.'[1]

Air-raid sirens brought these reveries to an abrupt end. That evening Boulogne was attacked and the Imperial Hotel – the one building in the town taken over by the GHQ – was heavily bombed. How had the Germans done it, the correspondents

1. Gray, op. cit., pp. 104, 105.

speculated: brilliant target-spotting, or clever espionage? In fact, they learned, German agents had taken advantage of Boulogne's slackness with blackout regulations to expose two lines of lights across the town converging on the Imperial Hotel. The next night they were fool enough to try the same trick again, but were caught red-handed and shot there and then. But that Monday was another idle day for the correspondents. None could go to the front as all cars had been requisitioned by GHQ. Kim, Gray and Montague thought of playing golf at Le Touquet, but gave it up when they learned that the Germans were already in possession. On Tuesday, 21 May 1940, they left for England.

Pilks's Circus still had some life in it. Three weeks later, on 11 June, Kim, Montague and Gray, shepherded by Captain Pilkington, left Waterloo Station for a second spell in France. The evacuation from Dunkirk had taken place, but more British troops were being sent out to help the French hold the Weygand line north of Paris in a last bid to hold up the German advance. The old 'syndicate' found itself working for very nearly the whole British press. Kim now represented the *Daily Telegraph* as well as *The Times*. Evelyn Montague came on behalf of a curious partnership – the *Manchester Guardian* and *Daily Express*, while poor Gray had no fewer than four papers to look after: the *Daily Herald*, the *People*, the *Sunday Pictorial* and, of course, the *Mirror*.

The expedition was short-lived and a bit of a farce as the correspondents barely got out of Normandy. On landing at Cherbourg, Kim and Gray spent much of their first day in the NAAFI, getting drunk, which allowed them to sleep undisturbed through a massive air-raid. The next day they set off in glorious weather along winding country roads for Le Mans. Though their errand was serious – to meet the last trains from Paris, overflowing with refugees – they sang loudly and tunelessly most of the way, ignoring Pilks's despairing protests. 'God, I wish we were on holiday,' said Kim. 'I'd rather be hunting in Leicestershire,' put in Pilks from the front seat. A day later GHQ public relations announced, 'The British Army is going home and we go with it.' The press were given the choice of leaving from St Malo or Brest, but were warned that Brest would probably be bombed. Most plumped for it. Gray declared that he wanted to leave on the very last boat from France, a melodramatic announcement received with jeers and laughter; Kim ragged him mercilessly for what he called this 'display of exhibitionism'. A few hours later they were sailing for the British coast, and within twenty-four hours Marshal Pétain announced over the radio the French armistice with Germany.

Kim came home to a new domestic set-up. Lady Lindsay-Hogg, his Spanish girl-friend, was still in St Jean, Litzi Philby had returned to London but was already living with Georg Honigmann – but meanwhile Kim had found another girl.

He seemed to acquire his women almost by accident, but once a relationship existed, he was doggedly faithful to it, accepting its responsibilities with matter-of-fact thoroughness until forces clearly beyond his control cut him loose. His fidelity to these attachments matched the vein of solid consistency which was a feature of his espionage. A constant of Kim's character was commitment, and although very fond of women throughout his life, his instincts were husbandly rather than flirtatious. All his relationships suffered however from a disability which inevitably damaged them : he could not share with his wives and mistresses the secret of his work for Russia. An element of betrayal was built in. But this was not always hurtful – women sensed his elusiveness and liked him the more for it. In a more useful sense, his clandestine side made him a better rather than a worse companion, strengthening his character, injecting discipline into every moment of his day. For all the booziness of his middle life, he rarely missed an appointment, rarely neglected arrangements for his wife and family, and was hardly ever guilty of incompetence in running his private affairs. Espionage reinforced the careful virtues of the family man. It also directed into the single channel of his relationships with women much of the feelings for which other men find outlets in their work. The arid and dangerous desert of spying had to be compensated for somewhere, and caused Kim to pour into his liaisons all the sentiment of a life otherwise deprived – and he could be a very sentimental man.

Of all his amorous relationships, his early marriage to Litzi was the most candid in that his commitment to her was spontaneous and generous and there was nothing to hide. But after Litzi things could never be so frank again. The Spanish interlude with Frances Doble set the pattern of outward affection and inner withdrawal, and from then on none of the women with whom he was associated had much notion of the sort of man he really was.

To them he seemed a mass of contradictions: extremely gentle, and yet with a touch of animal roughness: gregarious and yet lonely; wanting to show off and be admired, liking his women to say 'Kimmy this' and 'Kimmy that', and yet never losing his independence. By 1940 Kim Philby at twenty-eight was a very attractive young man. He had articulate and intelligent friends acquired at Cambridge and in ten years of roaming around Europe as a student and journalist. He was invested with the glamour of having witnessed some of the key moments of the 1930s – Berlin in 1933, Vienna in 1934, the Spanish war, and now the retreat from France. He was likeable and personable. In the eyes of the middle-class girls he met, he scored a winning double – he was a nonconformist from a conformist background.

Aileen Armanda Furse, then aged twenty-nine, was not at all a wise or well-balanced young woman. It was astonishing that Kim took up with her, and their decision to live together on his return from France illustrated the almost reckless way in which this careful man contracted permanent relationships. He probably met her on leave from Spain, in 1937 or thereabouts, very likely through a mutual friend, Mrs Flora Solomon, head of Marks and Spencers' pioneering staff-welfare department in London. In 1934, when Aileen was twenty-four, she took the unusual step for a young woman of her class of taking a job in Marks and Spencers, and worked in their Reading and Oxford stores before being transferred to Mrs Solomon's department at headquarters. Mrs Solomon – kind, astute, efficient, whose welfare work has gone down in the history of the firm – made Aileen her personal assistant, taking her under her wing as she recognized that Aileen was a girl who needed a bit of attention. When Kim and Aileen (whom Kim nicknamed 'Miss Marks and Spencer') set up house together, Mrs Solomon was a frequent visitor.

In the Furse family there were three girls with mellifluous, anagrammatic-sounding names – Lilian, Melanie and Aileen. Their father, Captain George Armand Furse of the Royal Horse Artillery, died from wounds in the first month of the First World War, and their mother married a Mr Ernest Fleming who was killed in the last month of the same war. He was a rich man. On his death, his estate reverted to his family but the income from it belonged to his wife during her lifetime. Life was therefore well ordered and prosperous. The enterprising Mrs Fleming eventually married a third time, to become Mrs Alleyne, a highly respectable matron whose year was divided between the West Country, an enormous house in Queensgate Place, Knightsbridge, and a smart house by the seaside rented for August and September. The girls were sent to boarding-school and grew up in a manner proper to their station: Aileen was a good horse-woman and before the war used to be seen riding to hounds in West Somerset.

But she was her mother's despair, a constant source of worry and apprehension within the family circle. As a child she often gave herself quite bad bruises to avoid playing games. She had long, beautiful hair which she wanted bobbed in the style of the time, but her mother would not allow it. So Aileen set fire to her locks and had to be taken to the barber's to have the singed ends trimmed; and there were one or two other inexplicable and disturbing accidents with fire. Mrs Alleyne, who liked Aileen less than her other two daughters, could not face up to the problem and it was never talked about. It was a sort of guilty secret in the family where the explanation generally accepted was that the child did herself senseless injuries in order to attract attention or when she felt neglected. It was on her doctor's advice, however, that Aileen left her mother and in her early twenties went to live alone. When she first started living with Kim, she told him of her weird complaint and even asked her doctor to mention it. But her day-to-day behaviour was so normal that Kim did not realize the true position.[1]

Aileen had pretty blue eyes and well-marked eyebrows, a nice complexion and reddish-brown hair. She was not a beauty, being rather too thin, but she had good shapely legs. Her most attractive characteristic was a very pleasant and happy laugh. In her youth she was lively and talkative, always surrounded by young men but unwilling to settle down with any of them. On leaving home she had a mild flirtation with the Communist Party, took up briefly with a left-wing boy-friend and generally went through the paces of revolting against her background, but the revolt did not run deep. It never carried her out of her class or allowed her to surmount the harmless snobbery of airs, graces and connections. And yet it must have taken some courage for a girl of her sort to set up house with Kim, to change her name to his by deed poll and start bearing his children out of wedlock. Kim seemed plainly indifferent to whether his children were bastards or not. He was extremely fond of them as babies, and taught them chess as toddlers, but as they grew older they were a bit of a disappointment to him. With the coming of the children, Aileen's mysterious illness disappeared – at least for the duration of the war: she had been very jealous of Frances Doble but the children no doubt made her feel more secure. Another comfort was that Frances was older. Perhaps the children also helped Aileen over the constraints of living with Kim's mother, Dora, in the family home in Acol Road. Although glad to be quit of Litzi, Dora, worshipping the ground Kim walked on, sometimes let it be felt that she did not think Aileen good enough for him. Aileen was no less devoted. Nothing was ever too much trouble, and whatever Kimmy did she accepted. It was not, for example, the sort of household where he would feel under any pressure to come home at set hours. But Aileen never conquered a slight fear of him due to the fact that she had no real insight into his mind or character. She knew only that he

1. Mrs Melanie Learoyd, Aileen's sister, a personal communication to the authors.

was on a different plane from herself, and yet, when other people were present, she was argumentative, often talking a great deal of poppycock and constantly contradicting Kim. Her chatter was in great contrast to his sober, informed and balanced conversation, but he always went to great pains to win her round. He did not share her views or her values but he was patience personified.

All sorts of well-ordered lives were turned head over heels that summer of 1940, and for many people it was not an altogether unpleasant experience. There was a sense of liberation, after the doldrums of the Phoney War, in being forcibly freed from the routines of career and domestic arrangements, and being welded into a powerful national effort. Britain, threatened by imminent invasion, was defiantly preparing to fight. There was a tremendous to-ing and fro-ing from civilian life into war work, much pushing and shoving for the busy, glamorous jobs. It was a good time for women who now found themselves not only doing men's work but reaching the top. Children were evacuated from London and adults could feel independent human beings again.

On returning from France Kim joined the job-hunters. As far as he was concerned *The Times* had served its purpose. With Britain beleaguered, there was no immediate prospect of another foreign posting, wartime censorship had made a farce of reporting, and in any event the newsroom in Printing House Square must have seemed a cramped, even irrelevant, place to be when the war had suddenly thrown open the whole of government service – a career barred to him seven years earlier by his undergraduate Communism. Now, hardened by his years abroad and with his employment by the Russians giving him something definite to look for, Kim, like other undercover Communists, hunted for war work at home to avoid the risk of losing all control over his movements by an army posting overseas.

His natural target was the rapidly expanding intelligence, security and propaganda services. In terms of the crude business of getting in, he was far better off than most left-wing converts of his generation as his five years of careful camouflage had made him look 'reliable' to the summary vetting of the time, whereas former members of the ILP, Spanish war veterans, overt Communist Party members, and Marxist supporters of the myriad 'fronts' of the 1930s were often drafted into the Army Education Corps where it was thought they would not prejudice the fighting services. Others joined the BBC or the Fire Brigade. T. C. Worsley, for example, recounts in his autobiography how in 1940 he applied to join the RAF as an intelligence officer. After a short informal interview he was instructed to make arrangements to join up at once. But having done so, he was shattered to discover that his application was turned down. 'What had happened? Fortunately at the *New Statesman* we had the means of finding out. A friend of ours high up at the Ministry had a look at my papers. First there was the acceptance. Then, scrawled across it: "Not suitable for a commission. Works for the *New Statesman* and has been to Spain".'[1]

The security authorities were very slow at switching from a pre-war stance which identified bolshevism as the enemy to the realities of the threat from Hitler. One had only to be mildly socialist to be suspect. But the truth was that by the outbreak of war many of the old ideologies came to seem irrelevant as ranks closed against the Germans. Pacifists, although still fairly numerous, were stripped of all influence while the Communist Party suffered a disastrous loss of face owing to its vacillating policies on the war. The Party had first identified the war as an anti-fascist crusade and had thrown its weight behind it, only to reverse its attitude on orders from Moscow a few weeks later. Card-carrying membership slumped from 17,000 to less than 12,000 while the swarm of fellow-travellers who had been drawn to the party in the thirties now veered violently away. Before the war the CP had seemed the only firm base from which to oppose the Nazis, but old-fashioned, once reviled British democracy was now seen as a stronger citadel.

The events of the time must have posed Kim some delicate

1. T. C. Worsley, *Flannelled Fool* (1967).

problems of adjustment. On a superficial level the man who
for three years and in the most influential newspaper in the
country had put a sympathetic gloss on Franco's rebellion had
now publicly to rejoin the anti-fascist crusade. Kim was becoming adept at such surface corrections of aim, but deeper
down the problem was real. He had joined Soviet intelligence
the better to fight the fascists, but in September 1939 Russia
had signed a pact with Hitler and had opted out of the 'imperialist' war which Communist Parties everywhere were urging the workers to oppose. What could Kim think? No doubt
during the Phoney War he was fed the 'correct line' – that this
was just a tactical alliance to gain time – by his Soviet contacts on his occasional weekend visits to Paris from the front.
One small piece of evidence survives to hint that this battle-
hardened intelligence officer still had spontaneous left-wing
reactions. Another British journalist who met him during the
Phoney War was William Forrest of the *News Chronicle*, a
spare, cool Scot who joined the BEF press corps in 1940,
fresh from the Russo-Finnish campaign. Like Kim he had
covered the Spanish war – but on the Republican side. It was
normal for all newspaper veterans of the Civil War to get together, whichever side they had been on, but Forrest found
Kim very distant indeed. Was it because Forrest had just
broken openly with the Communist Party in revulsion against
Russia's brutal attack on Finland, and was then being abused
in the *Daily Worker* as a renegade and traitor – a view that
Kim no doubt shared? Such tiny lapses apart, no doubt his
discipline as a Soviet officer obeying orders helped him to
steer a relatively untroubled course through the personal and
moral dilemmas of the time.

In seeking an entrée into British intelligence in the summer
of 1940 Kim naturally sought the help of friends who had
been climbing career ladders in England while he travelled
abroad. An early hope was disappointed: he was interviewed
for a job at Britain's code-breaking establishment, the Government Code and Cypher School, by Frank Birch, a Cambridge
don and himself a wartime recruit. But Birch turned him
down, giving as his reason his inability to pay Kim a decent

wage. Kim was not in a position to protest too much: his Soviet contact must, as always, have counselled patience rather than the delivery of quick returns.

It was, as it happened, Guy Burgess who finally gave his career the boost it needed. Guy's life so far had been a noisy, less effective, echo of Kim's: Kim's quiet commitment to Russia and wary dropping of the left were paralleled by Guy's much publicized adherence to Communism at Cambridge and his flamboyant break with it in 1935. When both men had joined Soviet intelligence, Kim had spied on Franco, but Burgess had done no more than carry funds secretly to him on one or two occasions. Never much good in a job himself – he had settled into a minor post in the Talks Department of the BBC late in 1936 – Burgess still had the gift of impressing influential people by his wit and show of erudition. His acquaintance was legion and ranged from the upper echelons of the Athenaeum to guardsmen at such famous homosexual meeting places of the 1930s as 'The Running Horse' in Shepherd's Market off Piccadilly. He was more a climate than an individual, a jellyfish reacting to every intellectual, social and sexual current in his milieu.

At a cocktail party very shortly before the war Burgess had met a tall, lean caricature of a British secret agent called Colonel Laurence Grand who, in March 1938, had been appointed by the Secret Intelligence Service to set up a sabotage outfit – known as Section D (for Destruction) – to operate in enemy-occupied territory. Himself a man of imagination, the colonel was impressed by Burgess and took him on. Guy who was forever vaunting the intellectual and moral gifts of his friends – all his geese were swans – thereupon recommended Kim. So a compliment was repaid: Kim had got Burgess a job with the Russians; now Burgess got Kim a British job. In due course it came about that Ralph Deakin, Foreign Editor of *The Times*, received a telephone call from the War Office to inquire whether Philby was 'available for war work', and Kim was summoned for an interview with a formidable and charming elderly lady, Miss Marjorie Maxse, in the forecourt of St Ermin's Hotel near St James's Park Station. A

Philby

second meeting took place a few days later at which Kim was
told that, if he agreed, he should sever his connections with
The Times and report for duty to Guy Burgess at an address
in Caxton Street. A competent security check would have
labelled Kim either a Communist or a Nazi or, at different
times, both. He himself recounts that the only inquiry made
into his past was a routine referral to MI5, the security service, who came back with the laconic statement: Nothing
Recorded Against.

8 Britain's Secret Services

> A family with the wrong members in control –
> that perhaps is as near as one can come to
> describing England in a phrase.
>
> GEORGE ORWELL

An English lady of the empire-building class, tall, square-shouldered, clever, for whom the Roman virtues of duty and patriotism were as natural and inevitable as life and death, set out one December morning in 1939 on an unusual assignment. She travelled around London collecting messages from one unremarkable place after another. She was in fact emptying dead-letter boxes.

Admiral Sir Hugh Sinclair, chief of Britain's Secret Intelligence Service, had just died of a heart attack and his sister, Miss Evelyn Sinclair, was now clearing up his affairs. She alone knew the location of his DLBs, those hiding-places which spymasters use to communicate with their agents in order to avoid personal contact. The war which had broken out a few weeks earlier was soon to shatter the family-circle scale of the SIS, but in 1939 it was still small and intimate enough for the boss's sister to perform this vital task.

The SIS had been run for sixteen years on a pittance by Sir Hugh. 'Quex', as he was universally called, had taken over in 1923 from Commander Mansfield Cummings, RN, who first headed the service when it was created as an independent organization in 1911. The tradition was to have a serviceman at the top. During the First World War funds were plentiful and Cummings's principal achievement was to create a clandestine network in Europe based on passport control officers; but Quex's slender inter-war budget forced him to run the service down: only a handful of overseas 'stations' remained, and by the late 1930s the service was very small and very poor.

Its shabby headquarters at Broadway Buildings, just across the road from St James's Park Underground Station, was staffed mainly by former regular officers from the armed ser-

vices who tended to be drawn from honest middle-class backgrounds, not Guards officers or, in Anthony Powell's phrase,
'polo-playing sailors'. The agents abroad were civilians, operating under such cover as bank managers, shipping clerks,
newspaper correspondents, and the like. It was not a haven
for rich, well-connected young men, as has sometimes been
asserted. Of the twenty-three names which one officer of that
period recalls, three were members of the gentry, a couple
could boast of a private income of £400 a year, and only one
was a member of White's.

Quex's men were not intellectuals but young, daring, ingen-
ious-minded hobbyists, better at hiking through unmapped
Balkan mountains or navigating small boats up foreign creeks
than at analysing the ideological conflicts of the thirties. A
device for sabotaging Russian movies thought up by one of
them was to smuggle half-a-dozen moths into a cinema
which when released would cast black shadows across the
screen. Thus the threat of international Communism was
countered by practical jokes. In those days the SIS was more
independent of the rest of Whitehall than it is today. On his
staff Quex enforced and personally practised a solemn and
exaggerated secrecy. He went to elaborate pains to keep his
face hidden not only from the public at large, but also from
Whitehall insiders. A member of Naval Intelligence summoned one day to his Director's office found Quex there in
conference. To his surprise Quex turned his chair to the wall
and kept his face shielded for the duration of the interview.
No one was allowed to share with him the rickety lift in the
Broadway headquarters. His rigid conception of security for-
bade him ever to name a source – he ran his principal agents
personally – and as a result many of his 'scoops' were simply
not believed by the Foreign Office. On the whole it regarded
the intelligence service as a nuisance, whose boy-scout enterprise was liable to disturb the majestic workings of diplomacy.
Only its small scale made the nuisance tolerable, and the
Foreign Office therefore had a vested interest in starving the
SIS of funds.

In the 1920s and 1930s British preoccupations were focused

on the security problems of India, Egypt, the Persian Gulf and such overseas outposts. In Whitehall these overshadowed the principal secret intelligence targets of international Communism – a movement which the undermanned and underfinanced SIS only partially penetrated and imperfectly understood – and Latin America where an eye had to be kept on Britain's considerable business interests. British thinking was so MI5-minded and Empire-directed that attention was distracted from the threat of what was developing in Europe. When fascism arose on the Continent the SIS were appeasers, very slow to believe that the German Abwehr would ever mount operations against the United Kingdom. There was no British equivalent in the 1930s to the *Rote Kapelle*, Russia's European spy network directed against the Germans.[1] Even Swedish intelligence, with no colonial preoccupations, was better informed than the SIS about Hitler's Germany. But in fairness to Quex and his boys, it should be recorded that their Service merely mirrored the failings and vacillations of the governments to which they were responsible. The Munich scare in 1938 led to a belated reconsideration of SIS 'targets' and to a modest expansion of its staff. Men with experience of political intelligence in the Empire such as Indian policemen were natural recruits.

Such was the state of the Secret Service when in the chaos of the first weeks of the Second World War, its chief, Sir Hugh Sinclair, died suddenly. The Foreign Office appointed his deputy to succeed him, a serviceman like much of the SIS of the day, but differing from much of his staff in his Etonian, Life Guards background and his high-born, clubman connections. Maj.-Gen. Sir Stewart Menzies (1890–1968) was an honest, aristocratic soldier of fine physique who, after winning an early MC and DSO in France in the First World War, was seconded to intelligence and ran agents behind enemy lines. He stayed with the SIS and rose steadily within it, more because of his niceness and plain good sense than for his intellectual power or his grasp of international politics. His judgements of fascism and communism, the great contending ideas

1. *L'orchestre Rouge*, Gilles Perrault, Paris, 1967.

Philby

of the age, were uncomplicated to the point of innocence. His
mind had been formed at Eton in the first decade of the century under the tutelage of his housemaster, Edward Impey,
who passed on to his charges his own great admiration for Kipling by reading aloud to his boys long passages from *Stalky &
Co* and *Kim*. An Eton contemporary, Sir Rex Benson, remembers that 'On the playing fields Stewart was a beautiful athlete,
winning the steeplechase, probably the most coveted race to
win at Eton. As a football player he captained the XI. He was
also Master of the Beagles and President of 'Pop' – the Eton
Society. He had a friendly happy disposition, not easily
ruffled ...' Sir Rex adds that their housemaster 'never – and
quite justifiably – had a high opinion of our scholastic abilities,
but it was from him that we learned discipline, the value
of initiative and leadership'.[1] Throughout his rule over
the SIS, from 1939 to 1951, Menzies was noted for his probity,
fairness, consideration for others, but neither in his choice of
personal advisers nor in his three marriages did he step outside
the narrow boundaries of his social class. In his profession this
was a great handicap. His official title was CSS (Chief, Secret
Service), but in government circles outside the Service he was
always known as 'C', a legacy from days long gone when the
Secret Service's initials were MI1C.

Menzies was unhappy in the limitations of his two chief
assistants, Colonel Claude Dansey, ACSS (Assistant Chief),
and Colonel Valentine Vivian, DCSS (Deputy Chief), widely
known as 'Vee-Vee'. Under Menzies, Dansey was overlord of
the intelligence-gathering networks, whereas Vivian ran the
counter-espionage side of the Service as Director of Security.
The two men disliked each other, despised each other's operation, and by the early years of the war were almost literally
not on speaking terms. Dansey was ten years older than
Vivian and fourteen years older than Menzies. He had had
twenty years of regimental soldiering before 1914 and was a
real lieutenant-colonel, whereas Vivian had been only a temporary officer in the Indian Army during the First World War.

1. Lt.-Col. Sir Rex Benson, *The Times*, 6 June 1958.

Vivian, who vainly hoped for a knighthood, always wore a full colonel's uniform, while Dansey, who ultimately got (some would say an undeserved) KCMG, never wore uniform at all. He was after all already well into his sixties when the Second World War broke out.

The two men's incompatibility reflected their different backgrounds. Dansey, like Menzies, had been seconded to intelligence in France during the First World War, but left the Service in the twenties to try his luck in America where he launched a country club. This was an attempt to provide rich Americans with a setting allegedly like that of English country gentry, a class to which Dansey aspired. The project was not a success, and he returned to the SIS for service in Europe. No more than his chief could Dansey grapple with the rival ideologies of the 1930s: he was not just unintellectual, he was anti-intellectual. In the late thirties he created a network of agents in Switzerland directed against Germany and known as 'Z' Section. However, its effectiveness depended on secret communications through France, fatally disrupted by Germany's *blitzkrieg* victory in 1940.

Vivian sprang from a soberer intelligence tradition: when Dansey was gallivanting around Europe and America, he was in the Indian Police, working hard for little pay and acquiring the security-mindedness which was to mark his counter-espionage department. The son of a well-known Victorian portrait painter, he appreciated culture and the things of the mind and was not above the mild foppery of wearing a monocle. But in the top-level tussles of the SIS he was on the defensive, having neither the personal wealth nor the social status to shrug off Dansey's barbs. He always went on leave at the same time as Menzies so as not to have to take orders from Dansey. Lacking a sense of organization, Menzies could not get his two chief subordinates to work amicably together, nor could he call on other advisers of real merit. As a result he laid down no clear structure of command, and indeed the structure of the SIS was adapted to make allowances for the personalities in it, and the personalities were very bad. George

Orwell's description of England could at the outbreak of war be applied to the SIS under this elderly trio: 'A family with the wrong members in control.'

A rather more united family was MI5, sister service to the SIS and watchdog of British security. Just as the SIS had been benignly governed from 1923 to 1939 by Sir Hugh Sinclair, so the Security Service had a long-lived father-figure in Sir Vernon Kell whose rule lasted more than thirty years, from 1909 to 1941, linking the Edwardian era to the Second World War. At first glance the two organizations looked similar – both 'K' and 'C' were regular officers of the old school – but there were important differences. In Whitehall, MI5 was taken seriously, as it had to be, seeing that its responsibility was to keep Britain and the Empire safe from the machinations of foreign agents. Consequently it was larger, richer and a good deal more professional than the SIS. Although using War Office cover – whereas the SIS worked closely with the Foreign Office – it was very largely a civilian organization dealing with political intelligence in alliance with Scotland Yard. For these careful investigators poring over the files which are the heart of any security system life did not consist of make-believe in foreign capitals. They operated within British or colonial society and were subject to their laws and attitudes, and to the vigilance of public opinion in Parliament and press. Without police powers, MI5 used the Special Branch as a front when it wished to make an arrest or search a house. A Home Office warrant was necessary to tap the telephone of a private citizen. All these controls, which SIS operating in foreign countries escaped, made for a sensible organization.

Kell himself was the antithesis of the terror-wielding secret police chief of public imagination. In 1894, when he was twenty-one, he joined the South Staffordshire regiment from Sandhurst, helped to quell the Boxer Rebellion in China in 1900, learned Chinese, and came home to climb swiftly to the Committee of Imperial Defence. He was still a young captain when he was named the first director of MI5 in 1909. He was a public servant of the sort that pre-war Britain prided itself on producing: a man with a strong sense of duty, tact and discretion, who used his wide powers with notable restraint.

Both the Security Service and the SIS made a great point of secrecy: to the general public their chiefs were anonymous, their headquarters undisclosed, and their staffs sworn to discretion. Candidates for employment in pre-war MI5 would receive a handwritten letter on unheaded writing paper inviting them to call in for a talk on security matters. It was not made clear whether this meant securities of the stocks and shares variety or something more hush-hush. The only address to reply to was a box number in Whitehall. But for the SIS there was no address at all: with his agents at the mercy of foreign governments, Sinclair's practice of secrecy was understandably even stricter – hence his system of personally operated dead-letter boxes.

In spite of its virtues, MI5 at the outbreak of the Second World War was rather an old-fashioned outfit: most of the key men were fifty and upwards. It was quite efficient at keeping tabs on such allegedly subversive bodies as the British Communist Party, but its grasp of the ideas which moved men of Philby's generation was scarcely more sensitive than that of the SIS. There were however one or two able men lower down the MI5 ladder whom the war was to bring to prominence, and who are intimately involved in the Philby story. One was Guy Liddell, an inter-war recruit from the Special Branch, who by 1940 was the head of MI5's B Division where incoming intelligence was assessed in terms of possible action. He rose to be Deputy Director; another was Dick White, a schoolmaster who joined MI5 in the thirties and who eventually scored the remarkable success of ruling in turn both MI5 and SIS.[1]

1. The appointment of a civilian to such posts was not the break with tradition that it might appear to be. Dick White (later Sir Richard Goldsmith White) had gone into uniform in 1939 and retained the rank of Colonel after the war. But he was not enamoured of the military mind and never used the title.

The war put tremendous pressure on both MI5 and the SIS, painfully revealing their unpreparedness. But whereas the former had to cope with nothing worse than colossal muddle, the latter faced early disaster. The swift and ruthless overrunning of the Continent by the German Army in 1940 mopped up most of Dansey's agents before they became effective. The most spectacular setback came in November 1939 when Major H. R. Stevens and his assistant, Captain S. Payne Best, fell into a German intelligence trap. They were lured from their Brussels headquarters to a rendezvous at Venlo on the Dutch-German border with the promise that they were to meet representatives of the German opposition to Hitler. Both men were kidnapped, interrogated and dispatched to a concentration camp for the rest of the war. The German who masterminded the abduction was a Gestapo Officer, Group Leader Walter Schellenberg, whose boss, Himmler, claimed that the two Englishmen gave away the entire structure of the SIS. In a public speech Himmler named every member from Menzies down – a revelation which was marked 'Most Secret' even inside SIS headquarters. (Partly because of this early success at Venlo, Himmler put Schellenberg in May 1944 at the head of the new secret service which swallowed up Admiral Canaris's Abwehr, the disgraced intelligence machine of the German General Staff.) From the outset, therefore, the SIS was virtually crippled in Europe. For the new task of waging clandestine war in occupied territories, a different sort of organization was required. And so Special Operations Executive was created by Hugh Dalton, Minister of Economic Warfare, whom Churchill made overlord of all secret operations against the Germans in July 1940. From his ministry he brought with him into SOE such men as Sir Charles Hambro, the banker. To give Britain new ears and eyes on the Continent, SOE worked in close liaison with the resistance movements and secret services of Norway, Holland, Belgium and France. Defeated by the Germans in Europe and by SOE in Whitehall, Colonel Dansey's intelligence branch of SIS had few opportunities to regain its lost prestige and make a decisive contribution to the war. Dansey died in July 1947, aged seventy-one. To the end of the war he seemed more interested in fighting the hated SOE than the Germans.

But the outbreak of war meant upheaval at home as well as disruption overseas. To protect its precious archives from air-raids, the SIS moved its Central Registry to St Albans, while MI5 found temporary quarters in Wormwood Scrubs prison, evacuated for this purpose of its inmates. This was the moment of MI5's greatest confusion: in new surroundings, with new staff, the organization under the ageing Kell struggled to cope with a flood of rumour and misinformation about alleged German agents in Britain released by the British public's spy-mania of 1940.

Faced with near breakdown in the vital field of security, Churchill appointed a high-powered trio – Lord Swinton, William Armstrong (now Sir William), and Kenneth Diplock (now Lord Justice Diplock) – to take a hard look at MI5. The result was a far-ranging reform which led to Sir Vernon Kell's retirement and his ultimate replacement by Sir Charles Petrie who had gained experience of political intelligence in the Indian Police. The archives were rescued from Wormwood Scrubs, finding an elegant and orderly home in Blenheim Palace, near Oxford – in permanent wartime contrast to the untidy sprawl of SIS records at St Albans. Unlike the streamlined MI5, the SIS remained largely unreformed throughout the war under its old management of Menzies, Dansey and Vivian. What changes it underwent were due to pressure from its customers. The Service Departments insisted on the appointment of three senior officers to represent their interests, and in April 1942 the Foreign Office named Patrick Reilly (now Sir Patrick) as Menzies' private secretary with a brief to introduce some order into the chaos in which 'C' was working. Having just come from serving Lord Woolmer at the Ministry of Economic Warfare in that capacity, Reilly set out to behave like an ordinary Civil Service private secretary. He found it an uphill task, for this was a phenomenon hitherto unknown in the SIS, but Menzies came to appreciate his usefulness. Reilly worked and usually slept in a little office opposite his chief's who always returned to the office after dinner when a lot of work was done.

Perhaps the most shattering of all the wartime experiences of both MI5 and SIS was the massive influx of new men sucked into the two organizations by the enormous expansion of work. The recruits came from diverse backgrounds. There was a minority whose pre-war service in the Empire had given them intelligence and security skills. Then there was the horde of amateurs who were drawn in either because of international experience in banking, newspapers, the cable industry, shipping and such like, or because of academic brilliance – dons, schoolmasters, museum curators. From their peacetime careers they brought with them other values, other standards, other hierarchies. For them the war was not the supreme moment of their careers, but a nuisance to be got over as quickly as possible. They were impatient and highly critical of what they found in the old-fashioned bureaucracies of the secret world and were a sore trial to their professional bosses. But it is to the credit of the Security Service and SIS that they absorbed these independent spirits and put them fruitfully to work. In the end it was the amateurs who were largely responsible for the wartime triumphs of both services.

The myth that the British Secret Service was largely recruited from a high-born, socially isolated clubland élite is as poorly founded as the legend of a ubiquitous and invincible organization. The truth is that in the weeks immediately preceding the outbreak of war men already earmarked for secret work cast about for suitable recruits. 'If the balloon goes up, can you lay on a few chaps?' was the phraseology of the time. When suitable candidates were found for SOE or SIS they were often encouraged to join West End clubs, for the purpose of easy communication if for nothing else, and even this applied more to men from the City than from the Universities. Wartime MI5 was reinforced with such able men as the scientist Victor Rothschild who became its anti-sabotage expert, Anthony Blunt from the Warburg Institute, Herbert Hart, a barrister, later a distinguished philosophy don and Professor of Jurisprudence at Oxford, and Helenus Milmo, another clever lawyer who was to become a judge. A recruit with a less likely background was the art dealer Tommy Harris, who revealed an extraordinary skill for running double-agents and who in the context of MI5's highly successful deception programme, fed to the Germans an entirely false Allied Order of Battle at the time of the Normandy invasion – one of the great deception feats of the war. SIS absorbed such literary stars as Malcolm Muggeridge and Graham Greene. Even so exotic a figure as the late Nubar Gulbenkian was reportedly drawn for a time into the net.

Twenty-five years earlier, during the First World War, Compton Mackenzie as C's man in Athens poured British gold into Greek pockets. He drew on his experiences in *Water on the Brain* (1933), a satire on the Secret Service, peopled with stereotypes obsessed with secrecy, rank, and imaginary threats to the nation, in which two rival departments, M.Q.99(E) and the Safety of the Realm Department, forever throw spanners in each other's works. Many recruits into British intelligence during the Second World War discovered that Mackenzie's fairy-tale was not all that far from the truth.

Section D of the SIS to which Guy Burgess introduced Kim in July 1940 was tiny, ineffective and slightly comic. Although Kim did not know it, it was also about to be scrapped. As an intelligence-gathering organization operating underground in foreign countries and anxious not to draw attention to itself, the SIS had the gravest reservations about the acts of sabotage planned by Colonel Grand which were likely to be noisy and spectacular. Because of this lack of enthusiasm the colonel's Section D had been starved of funds and personnel ever since it was set up in March 1938, and even after the outbreak of war was rarely allowed to put its explosive plans into effect. In default of action, there was much talk. On Sundays Kim, under Burgess's wing, attended long and usually fruitless discussions at Grand's country headquarters. In such circumstances Guy's rococo imagination flowered. One of his more sober projects was a training school for saboteurs: it was curious that while large-scale subversion of German-occupied Europe was being considered, no one had so far given much thought to training the people who would do it. Burgess tossed the idea to Kim to work out. The result was Brickendonbury Hall, near Hertford, where some twenty-five Belgians, Norwegians and Spaniards were sent to be groomed as saboteurs. The syllabus was uncertain and the instructors largely at sea, under the direction of Commander Peters of the Royal Navy, the school commandant. They included a trigger-happy explosives expert called Clark; Major C. E. ('Pop') Hill, who had been a British spy in Russia during the 1917 Revolution and had been followed there by Sir Paul Dukes; and Kim.

Whatever its other failings, the cooking at Brickendonbury Hall was good. This was also to Guy Burgess's credit as he had induced Section D to take on two of his friends as house-keepers at the hall. The transplanting of Tomás and Hilda Harris from their London setting of art treasures and good living to the kitchen of a school for spies was one of the odder metamorphoses of the war. Both were stupendous cooks. Hilda was a pretty, rather conventional girl from Surrey, while Tommy was the handsome, colourful product of a marriage between a Jewish dealer in Spanish art, Lionel Harris, and a Spanish woman. In his teens Tommy had been a prize-winning artist and later became a collector and connoisseur. After the war he was one of London's most successful art dealers until his death in an accident in 1949. When Kim met them at the school, the Harrises were running the Spanish Art Galleries with a strong line in El Greco from their lavish house in Chesterfield Gardens. In their Bugatti it was a short-ish run from there to the kitchens at Brickendonbury – the mysterious establishment which those in the know referred to simply as 'the country'. Tommy Harris became one of Kim's closest friends, working with him professionally and providing later in the war a focus for much of the Philbys' social life. Kim and Aileen named their third child Dudley Tomás after him.

Hugh Dalton's broom soon swept Brickendonbury Hall out of the war. His SOE comprised three branches: SO1, concerned with black propaganda and later renamed the Political Warfare Executive; SO3, conceived as a planning body but soon defunct; and SO2 which now took over the subversion and sabotage interests of Grand's Section D. Commander Peters resigned, Guy was sacked, Tommy Harris returned temporarily to his El Grecos (before being taken on by MI5), but Kim sat tight and his pay envelopes – £50 a month 'and no nonsense from the Inland Revenue' – continued to arrive. Soon he was summoned by Colin Gubbins, one of Dalton's new men, and asked to produce a syllabus on the techniques of underground propaganda for use at a central school for saboteurs which Gubbins was setting up on the Montagu estate at Beaulieu in Hampshire.

Although still rather amateurish, Beaulieu was a distinct improvement on Brickendonbury Hall. It was conceived as a 'finishing school' for agents and saboteurs who had already completed their commando and parachute training. Having learned all the rough-and-tumble stuff, they came to Beaulieu for the intellectual gloss. Their three-week course included such topics as the recognition of enemy troops, police forces and officials; the use of codes, passwords and secret messages; how to keep alive in enemy-held territory; and finally the art of clandestine propaganda – a field in which Kim, on slender evidence, was considered an expert. Great emphasis was put on ingenious practical exercises devised by the staff. The students had to crawl through undergrowth without setting off booby traps or venture out to neighbouring towns like Bournemouth or Southampton to make secret contact with friendly agents, so as to practise the techniques of exchanging passwords and handing over messages. On occasions they would be hauled out of bed at three or four in the morning to face sudden interrogations on the doings of the day. What they thought was a watertight story could often be broken down. No torture was used, but they were sometimes made to stand in pyjamas for up to half-an-hour with arms stretched above their heads.

At the start the school occupied four or five houses on the Montagu estate – later it grew to twenty – given over to different nationalities. Each country section in SOE did its own recruitment of would-be agents, according to its own operational plans. The rule at Beaulieu was not to mix nationalities as it was thought they would not trust each other. In any event it was found to be impossible to give useful instruction to classes of mixed nationalities, if only because conditions differed so widely in the various countries of occupied Europe. Agents had to be taught to cope with highly specific situations. In Norway, for example, where letter-boxes are to be found by the garden gate, contact can be made without ringing the door-bell. The students were a motley collection of foreigners – poachers, convicts, priests and others of equally varied backgrounds. There were Dutchmen, Belgians and French, Norwegians and Danes, Poles, Yugoslavs, Czechs, and at least one German. The Scandinavian 'Vikings' were housed by the lake in the 'House on the Shore', in the belief that they would enjoy being near the water. The 'House in the Woods' was the officers' mess. Appropriately 'Vineyards' was the home of the French, and was run by a Captain Clark – 'Clarky' to everyone – who had been King George VI's gamekeeper and who taught the students how to pluck pigeons and trap rabbits as part of their instruction on how to survive in open country after a parachute landing. Based on the view that to be plausible a cover story had to be as close to the truth as possible, word was put about that the students at Beaulieu were men who had fled from occupied Europe and were being trained to fight in their respective national armies.

The school was under the command of James Munn, a young lieutenant-colonel in his early thirties who had started his career in the Indian Police. He shared his headquarters, 'The Rings', with two majors, six or seven captains and lieutenants, and one civilian – Kim Philby. This society was not exactly distinguished, but it was tolerant and intellectual. Most of the instructors were fair linguists and had knocked about the world. They included Hardy Amies, the dress-designer, who acted as liaison officer between the school and SOE headquarters in Baker Street, Paul Dehn, poet and script-writer, John Wedgwood of the pottery family, and Bill Brooker, the chief instructor, who later ran a similar training establishment in Canada. Instruction was given in French or German and otherwise through interpreters. Kim's stutter made him a poor lecturer, so, although he devised the propaganda course, most of the talking was done by his deputy, John Hackett, who came to the school from an advertising agency with Philby sitting in to answer questions. Hackett later headed a separate propaganda school for students who showed exceptional ability in this field.

Kim's definition of propaganda was 'the art of persuasion with a view to producing action'. He was an originator of ideas in what was then very much of a new subject, although he himself recounts how, to arm himself for the job, he consulted his old Vienna acquaintance Hugh Gaitskell, then Dalton's PPS, on the political content of the propaganda he taught his saboteurs. He also paid friendly visits in search of ideas to the 'experts' in 'black propaganda', such as Richard Crossman and Sefton Delmer, at their headquarters at Woburn Abbey. However, Kim was perhaps the first wartime propagandist to realize that propaganda was not a highly specialized activity to be left only to experts, but something which every saboteur could engage in if he had an idle moment. At Beaulieu he developed the notion of the 'subversive rumour' which, he insisted, should be both concrete and plausible. It was his idea, for example, to feed to the enemy the alarming information that French girls suffering from VD were being *encouraged* to go to bed with German soldiers – in contrast to the commonly held view that savage head-shaving was the penalty inflicted for such fraternization. Without camp-followers, the German Army in France relied on local girls, and in those pre-penicillin days syphilis took three years to cure.

Another of Kim's contributions had to do with the dissemination of propaganda messages, leaflets, and other subversive material in occupied territories. He realized at once that to be effective such messages had to be in print: print was always to be preferred to mimeographed, hand-written, or otherwise sloppily produced material. Print carried authority, it gave the impression of a big organization at work. But, with the Germans in control of every press, how was clandestine stuff to be printed? Kim hit on the idea that a friendly lino-type operator could, in the routine business of composing a column of print, knock out a line of propaganda every tenth line or so and slip it into his pocket. In an hour he would have twenty lines ready for printing. It was a simple and ex-, tremely effective scheme. Some of Kim's students developed great skill in a technique for underground communication, known in the jargon of the time as the 'innocent letter con-vention'. The idea was to bury a clandestine message in an otherwise seemingly innocent note by some such device as using the initial letter of every fifth word as a letter in the en-coded message. The art lay in making the note sound unstilted.

Kim also devised a course in leaflet writing which relied heavily on John Hackett's advertising techniques. A good subversive leaflet, he taught, should include three elements: a statement of grievance ('Your breath smells ...'); a message of hope ('Your breath need not smell if ...'); a call to action ('Suck so-and-so's lozenges.'). This was the model for propa-ganda leaflets of all kinds. Students were advised never to sign a leaflet with the name of an individual, but always with that of an organization. 'If an organization doesn't exist, in-vent one,' Kim used to say. Sir John Wedgwood recalls an aphorism with which Kim made great play at lectures. 'Truth,' he used to declare, 'is a technical advantage.'[1]

There was one aspect of training his mixed bag of Euro-peans which must have posed a pretty problem for a man of his ideological convictions. For historical reasons, many of his pupils hated and feared Russia as much as, if not more than, Germany. This was true of right-wing West Europeans, of Poles, of some Scandinavians, and of the few recruits from the Balkans. Poles, for example, when trained in sabotage and dropped into Central Europe, were as keen to turn their weapons against the Russians as against the Germans. This unfortunate tendency it was Kim's task to correct. Gracefully he used to begin his lectures with the words: 'Gentlemen, I

1. Sir John Wedgwood, a personal communication to the authors.

have no wish to prevent you blowing up the Russians, but I would beg you, for the sake of the Allied war effort, to blow up the Germans first.' His triumph was to devise the slogan: 'Germany is the *main* enemy.'[1]

To some of his fellow instructors at Beaulieu Kim seemed a pale Marxist, to others a faintly right-wing liberal, to all a somewhat disgruntled upper-middle-class intellectual, thoroughly anti-Nazi and reliable. Sir John Wedgwood who thought that Kim had been a 'C' agent in Spain – that is to say, a British secret agent – remembers his distinct bitterness against the British establishment which had concentrated all its guns on Communism, neglecting the fascist threat until the outbreak of the war. He was very scathing about the feebleness of the British war effort – perhaps rightly, until 1942. He claimed he had been classed as a suspicious person for subscribing to the *Labour Monthly* in the early 1930s. Sir John recalls that Kim gave still freer vent to left-wing views after Russia's entry into the war in June 1941. They had, for instance, a long argument on the labour theory of value, Kim inveighing against 'the fellow who gets a bloody good salary for doing damn all!' Wedgwood, in turn, pretended astonishment that such a 'Red' could have received a Franco decoration. Kim made good use of that Spanish episode in building up his liberal image. Paul Dehn remembers that with modesty and giggles he used quite frequently to mention the ruby cross that the Caudillo had given him, seeming ashamed of it in just the right way. The fact is that whether Kim was remembered as a Communist in 1934, or as a fascist sympathizer in 1937, by 1941 he was firmly a man of the centre, busily building up a repuation for hard work, integrity, wry humour and brains.

Thus his first year of government service at Brickendonbury and Beaulieu saw the emergence of the mildly unconventional bureaucrat which under all the masquerade he really was. Professionalism displaced the ideological stances of his past, whether of the right or of the left, which he now played down and reconciled in his new personage. As the only civilian at

1. Paul Dehn, a personal communication to the authors.

Beaulieu he was always very worthily dressed, in wide flannel
trousers and tweed jackets patched with leather at the elbows.
He sucked at a pipe. In Auden's phrase, 'He wore his stammer
like a decoration,' wrestling impatiently to get his words out,
with the blood rushing to his head, but never seeming embarrassed by this disability. Far from damaging his image, it
made him seem sympathetic and vulnerable. He had something about him – an aura of lovable authority like some
romantic platoon commander – which made people want to
appear at their best in front of him. Even his senior officers
recognized his qualities and deferred to him.

Kim's ambition from the late thirties had been to penetrate
the Secret Intelligence Service, and when he joined Laurence
Grand's Section D in 1940, he thought he had made it. But almost immediately he found himself shunted off into the newly
created SOE. Now he was eager to get back into the main
stream of wartime intelligence. For all its attractions, Beaulieu
was something of a backwater. Once again it was a friend who
gave him the entrée.

Tommy Harris, art collector and convivial host, had
escaped from the kitchens of Brickendonbury into the spy-
catching world of MI5, where his intimate knowledge of
Spain and Spaniards was put to good use. His house in
Chesterfield Gardens, where food and wine were generously
dispensed at all hours of the day and night, became an off-
duty meeting place for a small group of men in MI5 and
MI6, whose professional interest in Spain and spies brought
them together in working hours. The Chesterfield Gardens
gang called themselves 'the Outfit'. They met for drinks several
times a week, occasions that frequently developed into more
elaborate parties. Tommy Harris's boss, Dick Brooman-White,
then head of MI5's Iberian Section (not to be confused with
Dick White, also of MI5), was the Outfit's senior member.
An exception in this hard-drinking crowd, he neither drank
nor smoked. He suffered from stomach ulcers, looked thin
and pale, and was the only member of the group to be retiring
and introverted.

Kim, leaving Beaulieu whenever he could for a night out in

London, was soon on friendly terms with the Outfit, whose interest in Spain he shared. It was at Harris's house that he met Brooman-White, and thus the way was prepared for his decisive transfer from SOE to SIS. In July 1941 Harris put to Kim the possibility of a counter-espionage job in MI6 which called for a special knowledge of Franco's Spain. Philby was enthusiastic, and Harris set the wheels in motion by proposing his name to Brooman-White. Brooman-White then recommended Kim to Major Felix Cowgill, the head of MI6's counter-espionage division which was known to initiates as 'Section Five of 6'. By September 1941 these friendly manoeuvrings had borne fruit, and Kim found himself far from Beaulieu and deep in the sophisticated maze of counter-espionage.

Once again Philby vaulted effortlessly over the defences of the Secret Service. Such investigation as his career was given was cursory in the extreme, not because his employers were blindly negligent, but because nothing about him aroused suspicion. They knew about his youthful Marxism, but to have been a left-wing undergraduate in the thirties was so common as to be banal. The evidence of a generation of middle-class young men suggested that such undergraduate enthusiasms were short-lived. It was greatly to Philby's advantage that 1939–40 was precisely the moment when the security services were switching their attentions from Communists to Nazis. It was beginning to be recognized that pre-war routine vetting had been ludicrously obsessed with the left-wing bogey. In intellectual circles the authorities came under attack for their slowness in realizing that Hitler presented a graver threat than the Russian Revolution. An ex-MI5 officer remembers irreverent recruits from the universities – part of the great 1940 influx into war work – snorting with laughter over what they found in the files. Vetting which had been unimaginatively rigid now became incautious. Membership of the Labour Party was considered suspect in 1936: by 1941 there was no reason to worry, or even to notice, if someone were a fellow-traveller. If a Communist had not been found by then, there was a very good chance he would remain undiscovered.

Kim's appointment to Section Five of MI6 needed the approval not only of the Section head, Felix Cowgill, but also of Colonel Valentine Vivian, Deputy Chief of the SIS with special responsibilities for counter-espionage. Vivian's vetting took the form of a lunch invitation to Kim and to his father, St John Philby, whom Vivian had known in India before the First World War. 'When Kim went out to the lavatory, I asked St John about him. "He was a bit of a Communist at Cambridge, wasn't he?" I inquired. "Oh, that was all schoolboy nonsense," St John replied. "He's a reformed character now".'[1] Vivian summed up Kim's recruitment: 'He came to SIS from the "pool" [a list of potential recruits drawn up early in the war]. I was asked about him, and I said I knew his people.'

The lunch that saw Kim into the fold took place very shortly after St John Philby's release from five months' detention under Section 18b – one of the bleaker episodes in St John's eccentric political career. From his conversion to Islam in 1930, St John had lived almost continuously in Arabia, although without wholly losing his ambition, increasingly unrealistic as the years rolled by, of cutting a figure in British politics. Critical of Labour because of what he considered its undue absorption in home affairs, his Fabian connection nevertheless led him in 1939 to suggest himself as a parliamentary candidate to the Epping Labour Party. He was not adopted. But he had more luck with the British People's Party, a cranky little anti-war group, tainted with fascism and antisemitism, which had been founded in the summer of 1939 by the Marquis of Tavistock (later Duke of Bedford) to the great damage of his reputation. The party appealed for a 'Christian settlement' of the quarrel with Germany, criticizing the British government and press for having envenomed relations with Herr Hitler. The marquis's chief associate was John Beckett, formerly a leading member of Oswald Mosley's British Union of Fascists. St John was drawn into this dubious company by his anti-Zionism, fed by what he conceived to be the follies

1. The late Colonel Valentine Vivian, a personal communication to the authors.

of British Middle East policy and by his conviction that the British government was as guilty as Hitler for leading the world to war. The BPP put him up as its candidate for the Hythe by-election of July 1939, but he lost his deposit.

Defeat sent St John back to Arabia in still greater disgust with Britain. Certain that Britain would lose the war and not minding whom he said it to, he decided to leave for the United States and got as far as Karachi where, the story goes, he was lured to a cocktail party on board a British frigate and arrested. Alarmed by the defeatist reports St John had been spreading in Arabia, the British authorities were determined to prevent him from airing these views in America at a critical time. He was shipped back to Liverpool, 'and there consigned to the foulest jail in all England'.[1]

St John used to maintain in conversation that his arrest was the result of a personal vendetta waged against him by the British envoy in Jidda at the time, Hugh Stonehewer-Bird, to whom he had then to apply for the renewal of his passport. 'The trouble about you, Philby,' Stonehewer-Bird is reported to have once said, 'is that you're not British.' This was a reference to the fact that, for several generations, the Philbys had been born outside England. St John retorted, alluding to the envoy's Polish wife, 'Not only am I British, but my *children* are British too!' There was certainly no truth in the vendetta charge, but this story about St John, whether true or apocryphal, illustrates his solid attachment to Britain even at those moments when he was most critical of British government policy.

Even though unconventional, St John was at this time a distinguished and well-known figure, and the British mandarin class to which he belonged was tolerant of his crankiness. Indignant at his detention, his friends, such as Maynard Keynes, E. M. Forster and Donald Robertson, campaigned for his release. His case was reviewed and, as he recalls in *Arabian Days*, the tribunal that examined him not only set him free but unconditionally revoked the detention order. Rehabilitated, St John spent the war in London where he studied Him-

1. H. St J. B. Philby, *Arabian Days* (London, 1948), p. 316.

yaritic, the language of South Arabian inscriptions, sometimes rereating to his cottage at Festiniog in North Wales.

That Kim should have a father in the establishment, even if on the eccentric fringe of it, did his cover no harm. Whatever doubts such a background might have aroused, suspicion of Communist leanings was certainly not among them. With St John in the Athenaeum – even if, as he is remembered, 'pacing about impatiently looking for someone to quarrel with' – Kim sailed into the SIS through the main gate.

It was like going back to Cambridge: life and work, with no sharp barrier separating them, were once again on a collegiate basis; small intimate groups of friends lived closely together, paying each other's debts, protecting and defending each other, conscious of being bound up in a common activity. Off-duty mattered as much as if not more than working hours. Of the many in-groups of the time labouring away in blacked-out London, Kim and his friends spanned two of the most diverting – Chesterfield Gardens, the Harrises' home and social centre of 'the Outfit'; and Number Five, Bentinck Street, whose large protected basement served during the blitz as a superior dosshouse for a fluctuating population of men and women in one or another of the intelligence and security services. It was Victor Rothschild's flat, although he was away on MI5 business much of the time. People who turned up there on and off included Guy Burgess, the poet Louis MacNeice, Kim and Aileen Philby, Teresa Mayor who later married Rothschild, Richard Llewellyn-Davies and his present wife, Patricia, who was known as 'the Semiramis of Bentinck Street'. Varying permutations of Bentinck Street and Chesterfield Gardens would sometimes meet for dinner at the 'Madrid' in Greek Street. One dinner was called off because Patricia had measles: the restaurant was bombed that night and completely destroyed. In such an easy-going, free-living milieu, where drink and sex served to release war-time tensions, it might be supposed that secrets were poorly kept. The contrary was the case. Everyone worked in separate compartments. It was 'not done' either at Chesterfield Gardens or in Bentinck Street to talk about one's daytime job, or to question where others went or what they did. Security was observed with rather boy-scoutish self-consciousness. There was about such groups a touch of complacency and self-congratulation; they were constantly handing bouquets to each other's talents. But perhaps not without some reason: by and large they were a remarkable collection of people, hard-working, dedicated and very clever.

Guy Burgess was a founder member of both the Bentinck Street and Chesterfield Gardens establishments. Although he had been edged out of SOE as too boozy and too queer and was back at the BBC, he never missed a party, and they occurred several times a week. He would dominate an argument with a stream of fantasy studded with uncertain classical references. For the others, he was one of the principal links with the old days at Cambridge nearly a decade earlier, embodying the interminable ideological debate of the thirties and standing for, or so he seemed to proclaim, the values of love, honesty and personal relations preached by the Cambridge Apostles. It was his membership of this very special élite which made him seem of inestimable value, at least to his Cambridge friends, causing them to excuse the excesses of his personal life. Because he was thought to be brilliant, he was allowed to be garrulous, drunken, drug-taking, a seducer of page-boys. Women, repelled by his physical squalor – the sagging Old Etonian tie, the food-stains on his suits – were not always prepared to accept the high estimate of him, but put up with him out of loyalty to the men who admired him. Hilda Harris sometimes rebelled and threw him out of the house after some more than usually outrageous rudeness, whereupon Guy would stand on the doorstep with his finger on the bell until he was admitted again. On one occasion he took a handful of prawns from a silver dish and stuffed them into his coat pocket where they still were a week later: the stench was terrific. He was totally unpredictable, as likely at his own dinner parties to turn food on to the floor as to serve it to his guests. He appeared to have no sense of physical disgust, deliberately seeking out what was debased as if he felt a need to reject his mother's drawing-room and everything it

171

stood for. Burgess was an aggressive male homosexual and in this circle he did not have to conceal his sexual preferences. Without arousing any particular curiosity, he talked quite openly of hunting down some 'delicious boy' and was always trying to prove that Mussolini was queer. Guy occasionally slept with women, but usually because he had an eye on the man the woman happened to be with. Sex of all varieties played an enormous role in determining not only the friendships, but the loyalties and political alignments of the group.

For all these reasons – sex, Cambridge, intellect, Apostolic values, conversation – Guy Burgess inspired remarkably durable relationships, such as bound him to another habitué of Bentinck Street, the art historian Anthony Blunt. After being evacuated from Dunkirk Blunt, like so many clever men, was drafted into wartime MI5. At Cambridge where the friendship began he had taken a First in mathematics in Part I of the Tripos, switched to modern languages, and then to art history, a field in which he later made his name. He too was an Apostle. Guy converted him to Marxism but for Blunt it was an extension of his affection for Burgess rather than a real commitment. In the name of all the things they shared, Blunt continued to defend Guy, even when he had outgrown the spell Burgess exerted on him as a young man. When Burgess defected with Donald Maclean to Moscow in 1951 and was revealed as a Soviet agent, the effect on such friends as Blunt was shattering. It was not only the disclosure of treachery, but also the betrayal of complex personal values. Bentinck Street comradeship was seen to be a sham.

Unlike Burgess, Kim in the Outfit days was a neat, square-shouldered, physically clear-cut person, but he too found Burgess a boon companion. He got on admirably with homosexuals, perhaps because he was himself sexually well adjusted. He was utterly clean: there was no mustard on his lapels. He was gentle, responsive, nice to be with, although the stutter and his growing addiction to drink were already enough to put off some of the younger women. Kim first started to drink heavily when he joined Section D early in the war, and at Beaulieu his mess bill was, on his own admission, consistently the highest. Throughout the war he seemed to get hold of black-market whisky – at £4 a bottle – when nobody else could, and was often to be seen in such pubs as the 'Duke of York' in Jermyn Street and 'de Hems' off Shaftesbury Avenue, where he was friendly with the old chef in the tall white hat. In spite of the licensing hours he claimed to be able to drink round the clock in London. In retrospect this taste for alcohol in immoderate quantity is perhaps a signal of the tensions he was then containing. But then, of course, most members of the Outfit drank hugely. The party at the Harrises would often go on so late that everyone would stay on to breakfast off coffee and pernod. Liquor, served in gigantic tots, was one of the many things that united them. Although the Philbys saw a great deal of the Harrises, and the two men liked and admired each other immensely, Aileen had no such warm feeling for Hilda, and whenever possible cried off from the booze-ups. She preferred to stay at home during airraids to look after her two terriers, 'MI5' and 'MI6'.

Kim Philby was to become a counter-espionage expert. What does this mean? A few definitions might help to sort out the different activities lumped together in the public mind under the general heading of secret work. Security, the task of MI5, is a defensive operation concerned with catching spies and locking them up where they can do no further harm. In contrast the main task of the SIS is offensive: the collection of secret information in a wide variety of clandestine ways. Invariably there is a certain conflict in the practice of these two activities: MI5's duty is to close breaches in British defences as soon as they are detected, even if this involves letting the enemy know he has been detected, and thus drying up a potential source of further information about him. SIS's instinct, on the other hand, is to protect its sources of information about the enemy, so as to keep open the channels to him, even at the risk of a continuing leak. The basic clash, then, is between rival attitudes towards secret information: should such information be used at the cost of exposing oneself, or should it be hoarded in the hope that more will follow? These

173

are, of course, caricatures of extreme positions: an intelligence service is never wholly 'protectionist' where information and sources are concerned, nor a security service ever wholly 'free-trading'.

Counter-espionage is the most widely misunderstood of all secret activities. It is not a security operation like that of MI5: its purpose is not to apprehend enemy agents nor is its role defensive. But neither is it a straightforward offensive intelligence-collecting operation. It lies somewhere between the two, an arm of secret intelligence with a highly specialized target: the enemy's own secret service. The object is not merely to uncover political, military or other secrets: that is the task of conventional espionage. It is rather to build up a detailed picture of the operations, techniques, personnel, structure, and policy of the hostile service. Of course the most desirable information of all is what the enemy knows about oneself and, in a further sophisticated twist, what he knows that one knows about him. If the enemy's secret information about one can be discovered, it is by definition no longer secret, and his knowledge is powerless.

The classic technique for acquiring this highly coveted stuff is that of penetration. Penetration means planting an agent in the enemy organization, or 'turning' an enemy agent: that is to say, persuading a man working for the enemy to change sides and continue active in the conflict with all the added risks involved. One 'turn' makes a double agent, two 'turns' a triple agent, and so forth. The crucial question is which 'turns' are genuine, and which are false, manipulations which often involve delicate problems of psychology but if successful lead straight to the heart of the enemy service, providing reliable information about its actions and future intentions.

Thus the raw material of counter-espionage is secret information of a rather specialized sort, and its essential technique is painstaking, meticulous control of this information. This means keeping track of who knows what at any one moment, not only in the hostile camp but also in one's own. Such control is necessary since a main purpose of counter-espionage is to identify the exact nature and timing of any

leak to the enemy in order to exploit it. Whereas the role of a
security service is to stop all such leaks, counter-espionage on
the contrary depends for its success on constant, if controlled,
contact with the enemy. If, for example, an enemy network is
uncovered, security wants to obliterate it, pausing only long
enough to identify all its members, while counter-espionage
wants to keep it going in order to penetrate it, to exploit it, to
'play it back', to use it as a channel of tailored information to
the enemy so that his actions may be controlled and his judgements influenced. The ideal objective of counter-espionage is
to make the enemy service a docile extension of one's own.

In carrying out their duties, CE specialists not only keep
their eyes glued on the enemy, but spin a web round their
own service, checking and sifting, ready to pounce on any
discrepancy in their picture of who should know what.
Practitioners of this art consider themselves the queen bees
of intelligence: spying on spies, friendly or hostile. Their
knowledge of the whole range of secret operations is thus
necessarily both wider and more detailed than that of their
colleagues. 'It is not unnatural that men who specialize in
affairs of such complexity should regard themselves somewhat as the Cabots of the Intelligence world, speaking only
to God.'[1]

If his career is viewed as a whole, Kim Philby was beyond
question a queen bee. His penetration of the British Secret
Service is a textbook example of the art of counter-espionage:
for several years the sections in which he worked became unwitting extensions of the KGB.[2] Undoubtedly the fact that he
was himself a distinguished practitioner of the art – in the British interest, and for British pay, directed against Germany –
allowed him to remain so long undetected. He knew enough
about the control of information, which was after all his daily
chore, to leave no tell-tale trace and never to put a foot wrong.

1. Christopher Felix, *A Short Course in the Secret War* (New York,
1963), p. 147.
2. *Komitet Gosudarstvennoy Bezopasnosti* (Committee for State Security), the current name of the powerful Soviet espionage and security
service.

When after Munich Britain woke up to the possibility that German Intelligence might be mounting operations against her, there was an urgent need to expand British counter-espionage capability. Contact had belatedly to be made with the potential enemy to probe his intentions. This was the job of Section Five of MI6, Kim's wartime home. It did a better job than much of the SIS. As the targets of Churchill's offensive ambitions succeeded each other in rapid sequence from the summer of 1940 onwards – Norway, the Canaries, raids on France, Madagascar, Syria – the creaking structure of British intelligence was time and again found lacking. That the SIS could not meet the sudden and wholly unforeseen demands put upon it was not altogether surprising in view of the poverty of its pre-war resources and the cast of mind of its chiefs. In any event intelligence is not collected in a vacuum without any consideration of who will use it for what. Targets have to be defined by a 'customer' and requirements clearly spelled out before a service sets to work. Who between the wars could possibly have imagined that Norway would become an intelligence target?

The SIS was able to survive the severe buffeting it suffered from Churchill and the Chiefs of Staff in part because it was able to claim the rightful credit for its counter-espionage achievements; in part because its performance in the field recovered from the early débâcles. By 1942 a considerable amount of intelligence was arriving from agents in France and elsewhere, and by 1943–4 this had become a flood. There is no doubt of the effective support given to the French Resistance by SIS as well as SOE.

But Menzies was also able to resist attacks on himself and his service because of a fortuitous circumstance of more spectacular impact. Britain benefited throughout the war from a stream of highly secret, priceless information acquired by the deciphering of enemy radio traffic. Code-breaking and analysis were the work of a largely independent organization called the Government Code and Cypher School, nominally under SIS control. Due to this administrative accident, Sir Stewart Menzies personally carried to the Prime Minister the choicest

1a. Kim aged eight.
1b. Kim dressed as a King's Scholar of Westminster School, in the garden of his grandmother's house at Camberley.

From the Pyrenees to the Guadalquivir

by H. A. R. Philby

Chapter I - Irun - Burgos

After a tedious journey through that extraordinarily dull, flat country which some misguided people call 'la belle France', with a fat Frenchman in each corner, snoring loudly, and keeping every particle of air out of the compartment by shutting every ventilator and window, we cross the western limits of the Pyrenees and exchange the ceaseless bustle of the Frenchman for the calm gravity and noble bearing of the Spaniard.

The customs official is a stout bronzed individual who in the intervals of puffing out his 'fair, round, belly' chalks hieroglyphics on the packages, with the calm deliberation that exasperates the traveller in a hurry.

At last, however, everything is settled and we pass on to Irun platform and into a train marked 'Madrid.' After a long wait, the train, like all trains in Spain, moves out at a leisurely pace and saunters down the line as if dreading the looks of Cantabrian Mountains which looms ahead.

Our first big town is the famous San Sebastian.

2. A page from the diary which Kim wrote aged twelve on a visit to Spain with his father in the summer of 1924.

re is one great difference between religious + economic groups. When once religion
s escaped from the state into society, it remains there untroubled because its
ctivity is preached by spiritual conviction. No economic group can escape so entirely

(K) From Hegel to Lenin. English development suggests that society grew round
he state. Marx and Engels built on Hegel's foundation. Lenin built on Marx + Engels.
egel - Bourgeois society supervenes on the old natural kin-group as a system of.
rocuring subsistence. It therefore becomes a series of classes. (i) immediate product-
xtracting class (ii) distributing class (iii) incipient state (class concerned with general
terest). B. Soc. develops laws which represent the de facto rules, uniform tendencies.
ese laws consecrate existing order. It develops a police, an armed, professional force
rther to consecrate existing order. Hegel is giving key into the hands of Socialism.
it he went further. He argued that under proper conditions (Prussian?) there comes
om above a system of state protectionism, supplementing defects of B. Soc (education)
e also argues that from below comes a use of corporations. Under such conditions
Soc. is moralised by the state, and by itself. On this basis the true state
an develops its own system of social ethics. Under other conditions (particularly
ngland), where B. Soc is left to act unchecked there develops (i) an
unregulated accumulation of wealth + (ii) proletariat or rabble, depressed below
ubsistence level.

2

. Kim, the high-minded young Communist just down from Cambridge,
1933.
. A page of Kim's Cambridge notes, written in his minuscule hand.

4a. Frances Doble, Lady Lindsay-Hogg, Kim's mistress during the Spanish Civil War

4b. King George VI meets war correspondents at Lord Gort's Headquarters outside Arras during the phoney war. Left to right: Lieutenant Colonel B. T. Reynolds, Major Roger Machell (both of Army Public Relations), Kim Philby (*The Times*), Philip Jordan (*News Chronicle*), Skene Catling (Reuter's), Raymond Franklin (French press), Hal Denny (*New York Times*).

Kim bathing in the Damour River, Lebanon.

6a. Taken in Anzac Harry's Bar, Beirut, in the late 1950s. From left, Colone Slade-Baker of the *Sunday Times*, Theo Larsson, Eleanor and Kim Philby, Olga Hyka.

6b. Extreme left, Eleanor and Kim at a Beirut cocktail party.

. Kim on a visit to his father and stepbrothers, Khalid and Faris, Riyadh, Saudi Arabia.
. St John Philby, Eleanor and Harry, Kim's youngest son, on the terrace of the flat in Beirut.

8. Eleanor Philby after her separation from Kim.

morsels from these 'most secret sources'. Much scorn has been poured of late on British intelligence, but its brilliant and so far largely unrecorded work in the field of cryptanalysis rescued its reputation as it helped to win the war. Kim Philby never broke a code, nor was he directly connected with the GC and CS although, as will be seen, he owed to it some of his successes in the SIS. His rise and fall in the British service depended very largely on radio intercepts, a fact not hitherto revealed. Properly to understand his career and its background of modern espionage, light must be thrown on the ultra-secret world of the code-breaker. The next chapter therefore interrupts the narrative of Kim's life to tell for the first time[1] how Britain developed this most valuable arm of her intelligence.

1. This claim was true when the present book was first published in 1973. Since then the history and activities of the GC and CS, and its contribution to the Allied victory in the Second World War, have been extensively documented, notably in *The Ultra Secret* by F. W. Winterbotham, London, 1974.

9 The Golf Club and Chess Society

> It may not show the whole truth; it can even
> provide material that is false or misleading; but
> it is the enemy speaking.
>
> DONALD MCLACHLAN, *Room 39*

Teatime at a country house in the depths of rural England was
a daily occasion to forget the war against the Germans for an
assault on a lesser enemy – *The Times* crossword puzzle. For
Alastair and Dorothy Denniston it was a point of self-respect
to dispose of the puzzle before tea was over. They were both
addicts, this small spare tight-lipped Scot and his rather taller
wife whose Eng. Lit. course at Oxford had equipped her with
a fund of useful quotations.

Bletchley Park in Buckinghamshire, a large house rising
uncomfortably above a sprawl of huts and prefabs, was
Britain's main code-breaking agency. Officially known as the
Government Code and Cypher School or GCHQ, and to its
inmates as the 'Golf Club and Chess Society', it was the most
clandestine, the least acknowledged and arguably the single
most important outfit in wartime Britain. Its job was to read
other people's secrets, or rather their coded cables and radio
communications, thereby culling a rich intelligence harvest. It
was a paper-and-pencil, mind-twisting war with figures and
alphabets, a war waged with the help of computers in the upper
reaches of applied mathematics. It was arid, demanding work,
locked in the toils of a fiendishly difficult crossword. Success
demanded that the GC and CS live and dream codes. It also
demanded a secrecy so absolute as to bury Bletchley without
trace. Denniston presiding over this establishment was himself discreet to the point of total silence and his children,
Margaret and Robin, played rounders in the grounds without
the slightest clue to what their father was up to. Turned in on
itself for compelling security reasons, the small community of
the GC and CS was rather donnish and upper middle-class in

ethos, and permeated by an overpowering sense of duty and a total submission to the war effort – a climate influenced perhaps by the fact that the Dennistons were old-fashioned Christians: Dorothy used to collect like-minded people from the huts in the park to hold prayer meetings.

Like other Second World War think-tanks, in other obscure parts of the country, Bletchley assembled amateurs and professionals, servicemen and civilians, technicians and intellectuals. As households were made up at random, this mixed population had a chance to observe each other at close quarters. One lady, a veteran of the Secret Service, was billeted rather grandly with two old gentlemen, professors at Oxford and Cambridge. Meals for this trio were served with great punctuality by a parlourmaid in streamers. The Oxford professor took the same walk round the village green each evening, stopping for a single glass of beer at the local, while his Cambridge colleague always retired to the solitude of his room immediately after dinner. Late one evening – it was shortly after the great German bombing raid on Coventry – the house was alarmed by a powerful explosion: the Cambridge professor, who was fond of shooting, had bagged a rabbit from his bedroom window. For others there were tamer sports, such as writing and performing sketches for the amateur dramatic society.

> There'll always be a Bletchley
> As long as there are bricks.
> So here's to every billeter
> And every billetrix.

No secret has been better kept than the contribution of the cryptanalysts to the winning of the war. Official histories do not record their triumphs, and to this day, over thirty years on, it is hard to find an ex-billeter or billetrix who will talk about the esoteric goings-on at the Park. But there cannot be a proper appreciation of the conduct of the war, of the role of intelligence in it – or of Kim Philby's war-work for Britain, the basis of his whole career – without some understanding, however fragmentary because of the taboos still surrounding the subject, of what was done at Bletchley. It can however be said that, in the Second World War, no source of intelligence yielded more or better information than the interception, deciphering and reading of enemy radio traffic. Communications intelligence surpassed every other form of intelligence – whether captured documents, air reconnaissance, prisoner-of-war interrogation, the old-fashioned agent on the ground, or whatever. In fact all these sources had to be judged against what the cryptanalysts provided, as their source was, so to speak, the horse's mouth.

The war blew cryptology up into a major international industry. Before, it was a poor relation of intelligence, even a slightly dubious one, only one source of secret information among many; by 1945 its primacy was universally accepted and it was well and truly launched as a permanent feature of international relations. Every newly independent nation now wants a cipher of its own as badly as it wants a seat at the United Nations or a national airline; each of the major powers sinks uncounted millions in intercepting and deciphering the secret radio traffic of other countries. The National Security Agency, for example, the organization which does this job in the United States, dwarfs its better-known CIA sister in size and importance. Communications intelligence has moved its global snooping into a stratosphere in which code-makers and code-breakers no longer play with hand ciphers but with artificial satellites, advanced radar, guided missile systems, spy ships bristling with electronic equipment, and other telemetric gadgetry for detection, interrogation, identification and control. Attempting to break codes and read secret messages is, of course, as old a form of human endeavour as the sending of such messages. But the central position which cryptology has today is due to two modern inventions and their use in warfare – telegraphy, which gave enormous impetus to the making of codes, and radio, which by vastly expanding military communications provided the code-breakers with their chance. In Britain this modern science had humble beginnings.

On the outbreak of the First World War in August 1914, the British Post Office found itself listening to mysterious signals of which the only thing that could be said was that they were not British. Nobody quite knew what to do with them. They were sent to the Director of Intelligence at the Admiralty and he, for lack of a better inspiration, passed them on to his old friend Sir Alfred Ewing, then Director of Naval Education, but with little prospect of educating the Navy in wartime. Ewing was an engineer by training with a mind drawn to puzzles, acrostics and other such brain-twisters. He had become intrigued by codes when testing submarine cables off the coast of Uruguay in 1875. His first move was to call in four of the Navy's language teachers, one of whom was Alastair Denniston, professor of German at Osborne College, and put them to work in his own office. None of this group knew anything about wireless telegraphy or codes, or for that matter warfare, naval or otherwise, but with the help of a manager of the Marconi Company the mysterious signals were identified as coming from Germany – probably from Nauen, the powerful radio station outside Berlin – and seemed to consist principally of weather reports and other official communications to German colonial governments in Africa. Very soon German coded military messages were flowing in from the Western Front to add to the confusion. The first light on a cloudy subject was provided by the French, far and away the best cryptographers at the time. They gave the British War Office the method and key for solving the German military ciphers and at last some sense began to emerge from a fog of guesswork.

The next move was a piece of fruitful amateur meddling such as British history is full of. Two radio hams, a barrister, Russell Clarke, and his friend, J. B. Hippisley, a Somersetshire land-owner, came to Ewing with the news that they had managed to pick up large quantities of German naval signals on their amateur receiving sets (which had unaccountably escaped being closed down by the police on the outbreak of war). They persuaded Ewing to let them set up interception facilities with the help of the GPO at Hunstanton Coastguard Station – well placed for tapping the Flanders air – and this was quickly followed by other interception centres all round Britain's coasts.

The volume of German intercepts, nicknamed 'Black Jumbos', grew to a flood. It soon became apparent that the Admiralty cryptographers would have a round-the-clock job listening to the communications of the German fleet. More men were recruited, but with the added numbers conditions in Sir Alfred's room, still the team's only quarters, were increasingly uncomfortable. Work was complicated by the crowd, the need for secrecy and the equal need for charwomen. Sir Alfred had a certain amount of naval education to look after and people to see in his office, and occasionally it was necessary for the cryptographers suddenly to pack up their papers as innocently as possible and scuttle into the small box-like room occupied by the secretary. In November 1914 the section moved to a new room in the Old Building of the Admiralty – Room 40, which was to give Britain's cryptographers their wartime name and create a legend. But at this point cryptanalysis as a profession did not exist. A mathematical mind was thought to be the best foundation for the work, but the new recruits, mainly educated in the classics, were chosen largely for their good German and their reputation for discretion. They were aided by 'ladies with a university education' and by wounded naval officers unfit for active service. They themselves knew nothing of the German fleet and very little of the geography of the German coastline, while their ignorance of either English or German naval phraseology was profound: the First Lord, Lord Fisher, had cause to point out that warships did not 'run in' and begged the staff to adopt the word 'proceed'. To supply the necessary professional knowledge and to assess the importance of the intercepted messages, Commander Herbert Hope RN was put in charge of Room 40, although he always alleged of himself that he knew no German, no cryptography, nor why he had come. The staff in its early innocence made some errors. British destroyers were sent fruitlessly in search of German ships at Inner Gabbard, because the very similar code sign for Heligoland was misread. It is to be imagined that when he arrived each morning Hope anxiously checked the overnight work of his amateurs, always ready to issue a hurried correction: 'In our number xyz, for so-and-so please read such-and-such.'

Apart from this assembly of amateur ingenuity and talent, Room 40 was launched on three pieces of good luck. On 20 August 1914 the German light cruiser *Magdeburg* was destroyed in the Gulf of Finland by the Czarist Russian navy. A few days afterwards the body of a German signalman who had belonged to her was washed ashore with a copy of the Imperial German Naval signal book still clasped in his arms. The Russians recognized its tremendous value and sent it over to Britain where it ended up in Room 40 in mid-October. (The practical Russell Clarke turned himself into a photographer and his private house into a studio to produce three additional copies.) The second find was the German Mercantile signal book, the *Handelschiffs Verkehrsbuch* or HVB, seized in Sydney, Australia, from a German merchant vessel on the outbreak of war and sent to England. Room 40 were happy to discover that the whole High Sea Fleet and especially outpost vessels, airships and submarines used the HVB very extensively – of course, like the Naval signal book, always in reciphered form whose decoding was by this time not beyond the skill of Britain's cryptographers. At the end of 1914 Room 40 got its third windfall: an English trawler fishing in the North Sea brought up in her trawl another book of naval codes from a German destroyer sunk in action. This was a most secret code book used by the German Admiralty in correspondence with senior officers and naval attachés abroad. It proved to be of the greatest immediate value in dealing with the German cruiser fleet.

By New Year 1915 Room 40, already about fifty strong, was a cheerful party. Everything the German Navy said was contained in one of the three books they had secured. All German naval signals which the stations could intercept were read and circulated.

In those days the possibility of a change in the cipher key was prophesied with bated breath and the authorities were informed that such a danger should be reckoned with. Should it happen it was generally considered that this valuable source of intelligence would dry up for several days at the very least. At last one evening early in January 1915 the watch was confronted with signals which would not yield to the ordinary treatment. The dreaded change had come. All the available staff were summoned by telephone and, after a night-long struggle, the new key was obtained to the joy and admiration of all concerned. The First Lord called early next morning and congratulated the experts who had solved the key so promptly. In the course of the day it was discovered that the key had *not* been changed, but that the existing key had been 'slid', and that the actual work involved need not have taken five minutes.

This discovery Room 40 kept to itself and when, a few days later, the key really did change one morning, the new one was produced quietly and without much trouble in a few hours. Two years later, when the key changed every night at twelve o'clock, the night watchmen were greeted by the cold contempt of their relief, had they failed to evolve the new key.[1]

So, throughout the rest of the war, Room 40 was able to pinpoint for the War Room the exact disposition of the U-boats and Zeppelins, and of the High Sea Fleet which was usually kept out of harm's way in the river estuaries of the Heligoland Bight behind the German minefields. German raiders would occasionally sally forth into the North Sea, but from 1915 onwards they made no sortie in force without Room 40 warning the Admiralty beforehand. Even the British admirals at sea did not really know the jealously guarded source of this intelligence: no attempt was made to discourage the view that it was the work of highly active British spies in Germany. After the Battle of Jutland in the early summer of 1916 the German warships never dared leave their base again, and as Churchill put it, 'Without the cryptographers' department there would have been no Battle of Jutland.'

For the first year of the war the men of Room 40 had their gaze fixed almost exclusively on German naval movements. They had no thought of extending to the field of politics and diplomacy the amazing intelligence weapon which the interception and reading of enemy signals had so unexpectedly provided. But the interception stations were of course picking up

1. The late Commander Alastair Denniston, private papers.

from the start vast numbers of signals in unknown codes and languages, many of which had clearly nothing to do with naval affairs. The art of reading other people's telegrams was still in extreme infancy. These intercepts were labelled 'NSL' – 'neither sent nor logged' – and stored unread in cupboards where they remained until, in April 1915, Room 40 got yet another windfall. The India Office had obtained (by sandbagging said one, by payment said another) the effects of a German consul in Persia and, knowing nothing of such things as code books, had turned the lot over to intelligence. Room 40 examined the books and found them to contain not naval but diplomatic codes. The cupboards of unread telegrams were made to disgorge. It was the end of the age of innocence.

Up to this point Room 40 had been strictly speaking a cryptographic bureau dealing only with naval matters. Now it was reorganized into an intelligence department, codifying and appraising the material it gleaned from the air, rather than just passing it on to Naval Operations. As part of the new deal Alastair Denniston, who had joined at the very start, became head of the naval cryptographers and George Young (later Sir George) head of the diplomatic cryptographers. Finally a naval commander was appointed to administer the fifty-odd Intercepting and Direction-finding stations round the coasts and the 800 members of the Shore Wireless Service who manned them. Cryptanalysis was already becoming big business.

The man who in Britain first properly exploited cryptographic snooping for political ends, with all the elaborate deception which protection of the source requires, was Admiral Sir Reginald Hall or 'Blinker' Hall, as he was universally known on account of a ferocious facial twitch. He took over as Director of Naval Intelligence in October 1914 and so was Ewing's immediate superior in the naval contest of the early years of the war. When Ewing left the Admiralty in May 1917 to become Vice-Chancellor of Edinburgh University, Hall took direct control of Room 40, immediately gaining further scope for the exciting forays into international affairs which he so relished.

Reading diplomatic wireless traffic put great power into

Hall's hands, particularly as the Foreign Office, unlike its Continental counterparts, was still squeamish about taking under its wing a *chambre noire*. But the diplomats had to endure Hall's invasion of international politics for the duration of the war as he alone had the intercepting stations and the skilled cryptographers.

Among Hall's more spectacular *coups* was the arrest in April 1916 of Roger Casement on his being put ashore from a U-boat on the west coast of Ireland. This was made possible by a Room 40 intercept. In much the same way information about German efforts to raise revolt against British rule in India and about German sabotage plans in America and the Far East was noted in time and acted upon. Early in 1917 Room 40 read secret messages from Berlin to Abdel Malek in Morocco whom the Germans were helping rebel in order to pin down French troops and keep them away from the Western Front. On this information French aircraft were able to sink a U-boat landing arms and ammunition. But Hall's greatest triumph was his handling of the Zimmermann Telegram.

On 16 January 1917 the German Foreign Minister, Arthur Zimmermann, sent an explosive secret message to his ambassador in Mexico. He gave him advance notice that, in order to bring Britain to her knees, Germany intended from 1 February to launch submarine attacks on all shipping, neutral or otherwise, heading for the British Isles. He instructed his envoy that if this course brought America into the war he was to propose to Mexico an alliance directed against the United States, with as a reward for Mexico the reconquest of Texas, New Mexico and Arizona.

Room 40 intercepted the message (and took five weeks to crack it) but Hall's problem was how to persuade the Americans that it was genuine without giving away the secret of the cryptographers' existence. To dispose of the problem of his possession of it, he got a British agent in Mexico to steal a copy from the telegraph office. As it happened, the American State Department had its own copy – undecoded and unread – because the message from Berlin to Mexico had travelled over

American wires, a courtesy extended by President Wilson to the Germans in the cause of peace. Hall got the Americans to produce their copy and showed them how to read it. Its authenticity was thus established. It was released to the press and caused an immediate and profound sensation, swinging American opinion in favour of war. So America entered the conflict, helped to secure an Allied victory, and embarked on her own destiny as a superpower. As David Kahn records in his massive history, *The Codebreakers*, 'No other single crypt-analysis has had such enormous consequences. Never before or since has so much turned upon the solution of a secret message. For those few moments in time, the codebreakers held history in the palm of their hand.'[1]

The four linguists whom Sir Alfred Ewing had called in to puzzle over the 'mysterious signals' of August 1914 had by the end of the First World War swollen into a curiously assorted band of some eighty skilled cryptographers. They included such aces as Nigel de Grey, a young publisher, and the Rev. William Montgomery who together deciphered the Zimmermann Telegram; Ronald Knox (later Monsignor) and his brother, Dilly, whose cryptanalytic talents reached their peak in the Second World War with the cracking of Germany's machine code; Oliver Strachey, elder brother of Lytton; Frank Adcock (later Professor Sir Frank Adcock of King's College, Cambridge); F. Fetterlein, a Russian cryptographer whom the British snapped up after the October Revolution; and, of course, Alastair Denniston whose lifework cryptanalysis was to be.

A month after the Armistice, this team celebrated their war-time triumphs – some 15,000 German messages deciphered and read – with a concert party in Chelsea. Denniston and a colleague sang a duet:

> While some say that the boche was not beaten by Foch
> But by Winston or Ramsay MacDonald
> There are others who claim that the *coup de grâce* came
> From the Knoxes (our Dilly and Ronald)

1. London, 1966, p. 297.

Philby

> It was Tiarks and Thring who with charts and with string
> Gave the U-boats their oily quietus
> Yet without the Lord Mayor in his diplomat's lair
> The Huns *might* have managed to beat us.
>
> There are Zeppelins about, the key isn't out
> And Lord knows what's afoot in the Bight now
> When the tube basket's crammed and each message is jammed
> Operations want all the news right now ...

For most of the audience and performers there, that night marked their demobilization. With the end of the war Room 40 was being wound up, and with it, its clandestine excitements. Together they sang:

> No more delights like these for us
> But *Denniston* will *never*
> Desert his solitary post.
> *He* will go on for ever.

For the next twenty years, from one German war to the next, the burden of keeping alive Britain's cryptanalytic capability fell mainly on the shoulders of this small taciturn Scot whose dogged fidelity as a public servant was only equalled by his horror of publicity. His son, Robin Denniston, recalls: 'My father was the most secretive man I knew. I learned more about his work from his colleagues than I did from him. Our whole family life was dominated by the fact that my father could not and would not talk about his job. "The less said the better" was the ruling principle of his life.'[1] Such secrecy, an essential prerequisite of effective cryptanalysis, was from every other point of view a handicap and a source of frustration. In the long lean interwar years the fact that so few people, even in Whitehall itself, knew about or fully appreciated the war-winning work of Room 40 meant that cryptanalysis lacked supporters. In the interdepartmental wrangles and the scramble for staff and funds Denniston was not well placed. Working on a shoestring, virtually unrecognized in their civil service limbo, his codebreakers spent grinding years of puzzle-solving,

1. Robin Denniston, a personal communication to the authors.

their efforts frequently frustrated by Treasury tightfistedness and the blunders of their political masters. But in spite of these handicaps, it was Denniston's achievement that by 1939 Britain was cryptanalytically, if in few other ways, prepared.

Even Whitehall insiders thought that Room 40 had died with the peace. In fact within weeks of the 1918 Armistice the Cabinet quietly decided that a handful of volunteers from Room 40 and from the Army's cryptographic bureau – which had done useful work on the Western Front, notably in frustrating the German offensive of spring 1918 – should be kept on the payroll. They were given the respectable sounding name of Government Code and Cypher School with the avowable task of providing secure codes for British official communications. What was buried in secrecy was their equally important function of reading everybody else's coded traffic. This was the side of the business which Denniston nursed with loving care.

Throughout those two decades from 1919 to 1939, Denniston's overlord was Admiral 'Quex' Sinclair who in 1919 took over from 'Blinker' Hall as Director of Naval Intelligence, was midwife to the birth of the GC and CS, and then rose in 1923 to the exalted post of 'C', head of the SIS. It was in this capacity that, recognizing the unique intelligence-gathering potential of cryptanalysis, he moved Denniston's boys into SIS headquarters at Broadway Buildings. There they stayed in the heart of London until on the eve of the Second World War the Admiral bought Bletchley Park in Buckinghamshire to keep his 'most secret sources' out of harm's way. Sinclair was Denniston's principal champion in the troubled years of peace, but it was 'Blinker' Hall's portrait which hung above Denniston's bed – the man who, in politics and war, had first and best put the weapons of cryptanalysis to aggressive use.

From the very beginning the effectiveness of the GC and CS was greatly curtailed by political mistakes at a high level – blunders which cut the cryptanalysts off from the secret traffic of Germany and the Soviet Union, the two powers Britain wanted most closely to watch. The German setback occurred on the very morrow of the first war. Knowing that its wartime codes and ciphers had been cracked by the British, and still smarting from the international scandal of the Zimmermann Telegram, Germany immediately started developing spy-proof communications. It had missed winning the war by a hair's breadth, and it was Room 40 – responsible for breaking the naval stalemate and for hurtling America into the war – which had provided the difference. The Germans were determined not to be caught napping again. They became the first nation in the world to put their communications on an impregnably secure foundation: the one-time pad. And what is more the victorious Allies let them do so. The terms of the Armistice ignored the subject of ciphers altogether, a breathtaking lapse of political judgement. As a result British codebreakers working in the wings of the Versailles Peace Conference drew a total blank. They could read all their Allies' secret traffic but what passed between Paris and Berlin defeated them.

The one-time pad is a random key scrapped every time it is used, an unbreakable system in theory and in practice. It is most useful for stable diplomatic (or espionage) communications rather than fluid military ones as the real disadvantage of this totally secure system is its cumbersomeness. If traffic is heavy, enormous quantities of keys have to be produced and distributed. (Even without taking into account the appetite of the OTP system, part of the vast Oxford University Press was kept busy printing code books and keys throughout the Second World War.)

Perhaps because of these physical problems, the German code-makers were not satisfied with OTP alone. From the early 1920s they developed a diplomatic code book so complex that it took the British more than fifteen years to crack and in addition wrapped this code in a thick blanket provided by a machine cipher. Thus, from 1919 to the middle of the Second World War, Germany's secret communications stayed secret – a remarkable achievement. Had the British leaders been able to read Hitler's telegrams in the 1930s, would they have given him the benefit of the doubt for so long?

The frustrations suffered by the British cryptanalysts in connection with Soviet Russia were if anything even sharper because in this sector everything had seemed to be going swimmingly. Like Germany, the Soviet revolutionary leaders had in 1919 to build their codes from scratch. The defection of cryptologists like Fetterlein to the West would have been enough in itself to throw the Tsarist codes they inherited into disrepute. But less experienced than the Germans, they began with simple methods which the British successfully attacked, so that the first moves in diplomacy of the young Soviet régime were followed step by step in Broadway Buildings. In particular, and naturally of special interest to the Foreign Office, the traffic between Moscow and Soviet envoys in London was read by the GC and CS.

This state of high privilege lasted until 1927, when the British learned from intercepts of a spy network which the Russians were attempting to set up in Britain under the cover of Arcos, the Soviet Embassy's commercial agency. The Security Service demanded and secured prompt action: the trade mission was raided, evidence uncovered, and the offending diplomats expelled. But at what cost? The Russians immediately realized that their codes had been compromised and switched to the dreaded and impregnable OTP for all their diplomatic and commercial traffic abroad. The British cryptanalysts were shut out. It was a classic illustration of the permanent conflict of interest between security and intelligence: MI5 wanted to put the spies out of action, the SIS wanted to keep its window open to the East. The government chose security and sacrificed unknown quantities of secret intelligence – surely a short-term view.

Against these setbacks, bitter and disappointing as they must have been to Denniston's backroom boys, should be set the real achievements of the painstaking inter-war years. By 1939, the GC and CS was able to read – even if it did not always do so for lack of staff, money and incentive – the secret traffic of all countries, friend, foe and neutral alike, with the sole exceptions of Germany and the Soviet Union. For instance the British cryptanalysts intercepted and cracked the Comintern's worldwide network of secret communications in the 1930s; they penetrated Japanese diplomatic and naval traffic; they read all Middle East communications from the War Office's busy intercepting station at Sarafand in Palestine; and from a station in north-west India they helped to preserve the frontiers of the Empire.

Britain's code-breakers served her well, but the record suggests that she was less blessed in her code-makers. The Germans, as was later discovered, were reading British codes from the mid-1930s until well into the war, possibly as late as the summer of 1943. No doubt the Russians did as much. It is astonishing that the British, having learned so much about other people's codes during the First World War, should have failed to design fool-proof codes and ciphers of their own. The reasons are hard to come by. Very probably in the transfer of the GC and CS from Admiralty to civilian control in 1923 awareness of the need for operational security was to some extent lost. But the Navy itself was also to blame: until the outbreak of war, the conservatism of its upper echelons resisted the introduction of machine ciphers which the Germans had been using for more than a decade and which even the Americans, at that time notoriously innocent in intelligence matters, had adopted in the mid-1930s.[1] More generally the reason for this lapse may have been a by-product of excessive secrecy, the code-making left hand not knowing what the code-breaking right hand was doing. Possibly the GC and CS as a whole was less interested in defence than in attacking the signals security of other nations.

This priority of offence over defence was disastrously illustrated by the Italian invasion of Abyssinia of the mid-1930s. For Denniston's team the flurry of Italian naval activity was a gift: it enabled them to make a thorough and successful study of Italian codes and ciphers. Little did they realize that this same international incident enabled the Germans to make a thorough and successful study of the codes and ciphers of the British Navy, then in the Red Sea watching the Italians. In the pecking order the Germans came out on top.

The Abyssinian crisis laid the foundations for the spectacular wartime feats of the German Navy's cryptanalytic

1. Donald McLachlan, *Room 39* (London, 1968).

agency, the Beobachtungdienst, B-Dienst for short – Germany's revenge for the triumphs of Room 40 in the First World War. Admiral Karl Doenitz's fifty-strong team of cryptanalysts in Berlin, working in total secrecy, were directly responsible for the loss of hundreds of Allied ships during the Second World War and the failure of a dozen operational plans. Captain Stephen Roskill, in his official history *The War At Sea*, reports that at the climax of the great Battle of the Atlantic Germany very nearly severed Britain's sea-links with the Americas in March 1943 – the high point of B-Dienst's activities. If after surviving these perils Britain emerged on the winning side, it was in good measure due to her cryptology. Only in 1942–3 were Britain's codes secured and Germany's cracked, a twin development which contributed powerfully to the turning of the tide.

Germany's technological lead had been due to the early and widespread use by her three armed services of the Enigma machine whose wired code-wheels poured out cipher alphabets in such random profusion as to defeat any code-breaker. The battery-powered portable version was about the size of a big typewriter and German signals officers were confident it was the best in the world and totally secure. It had foxed the GC and CS since the 1920s and given Denniston's chief code-breaker, Dilly Knox, many a sleepless night. He had diagnosed its existence and its nature, but right up to 1936 he had been starved of evidence of its powers through a lack of German service traffic. Its use by the Italians in the Spanish civil war gave the British the chance to study machine encipherment – but they still could not read Enigma. Solving machine codes involves no less than reconstructing the actual machine and Dilly Knox's years of effort to reconstruct Enigma were boosted by several pieces of good fortune. The first was a reconstruction of the basic Enigma machine, built by Polish intelligence before the fall of Poland and smuggled back to Britain by Denniston. But a replica of the enemy's machine did not of itself reveal the enemy's messages: behind Enigma's keyboard were in addition a number of electrically connected revolving drums printed with the letters of the alphabet, pro ducing between them an astronomical number of possible variations which it would take a school of mathematicians, or a computer, to sort out. Consequently Denniston's team at Bletchley turned to the new science of electronics and designed themselves a computer which was ready and waiting for the first German signals intercepted in the spring of 1940.

Between 1940 and 1942, further complications, predictably nicknamed 'the Enigma variations' by GC and CS, were introduced in the functioning of the machine. Here Dilly Knox had another lucky break, with the arrival in Britain in January 1941 of the Russian-born American, William F. Friedman, one of the greatest cryptologists of all time, who had lately crowned his remarkable career in the United States by cracking Japan's top machine cipher, the Purple (an eighteen-month effort which ended in a nervous collapse). He immediately got down to work on the Enigma with Knox. Their success was assured first by the smuggling into Britain by the Polish resistance of a page of German ciphers, and then in May 1941 by the capture intact of a German U-boat – the U110 – with all her codes and ciphers on board. By 1942 the last problems were solved – the year in which the Enigma also fell to the cryptanalysts of Soviet Russia. To the end of the war the Germans could not believe that their machine had been cracked, but attributed Allied intelligence scoops to the work of traitors and spies.

Denniston's small and undervalued outfit of the inter-war years had by 1942 grown into a formidable wartime establishment, some seven thousand strong, crowded into the prefabricated suburb of Bletchley Park. From being a poor and barely acknowledged relation of the Foreign Office and the SIS, the GC and CS moved to the very centre of Britain's war machine, providing a stream of vital intelligence to the Army, Navy and Air Force whose sections at the Park now called the tune. Denniston's strength had always been his skill in nursing to achievement the work of a small band of brilliant men: Dilly Knox and Oliver Strachey who had been with Denniston from the start and now headed separate code-breaking sections named after themselves; Fetterlein, cryptographer to the

Tsars; Professor Adcock, brought back from Cambridge to fight his second cryptanalytic war; and a number of other sharp-witted dons whom Denniston had recruited at Oxbridge on the eve of the conflict. One of the most brilliant of them was a woman whose sudden insights in the middle of the night required her to be billeted near the office so that she could run over when inspiration struck.

But Denniston was not a born administrator and the job of running the war-swollen establishment proved too much for him. Bletchley may have outgrown his capacity to use it. So many powerful men and agencies now had an interest in its output that the man at the centre came under severe pressures. He grew abrasive and difficult to get on with. He quarrelled with the men Whitehall sent down to help him run the place. He was always having minor rows with one or another of his team of wayward sceptical professors as they kicked against the elaborate tradition of secrecy, the dreary routine, the battery-fowl life that inhibited free-wheeling intellect, demanding painstaking ingenuity in its place. To a man they dreamed only of being liberated to their colleges.

Late in 1942 Denniston became seriously ill and was replaced as head by Commander Edward Travis, later knighted for his wartime services. Travis's career had been in code-making, not code-breaking, the security side of the GC and CS's activities which was under Foreign Office supervision, just as the cryptanalytical side fell naturally within the intelligence-gathering scope of SIS. With Travis's appointment as head, the GC and CS was taken under the FO's wing where it is today.

Denniston left Bletchley for a small office in London where he worked on intercepts dealing with German diplomatic and Abwehr activity. He retired in 1945 with a CMG and a pension of £591 a year, returning to teach French and Latin at an Epsom prep school to eke this out, and coaching the village boys at cricket. There was no official recognition, not even an obituary in *The Times*, when he died aged 79 on New Year's Day, 1961. His family asked his former colleagues if they would write a brief memorial, but they felt that the less said the happier Denniston would have been. They were probably right.

William Friedman, the ace American cryptanalyst who had worked closely with him in the dangerous early war years, wrote to Denniston's daughter (nicknamed 'Y' before her birth, as she was an unknown quantity):

Dear 'Y',

... Your father was a great man, in whose debt all English-speaking people will remain for a very long time, if not for ever. That so very few of them should know exactly what he did toward achievement of victory in World Wars I and II is the sad part of the untold story of his life and of his great contribution to that victory. His devotion to the supremely important activities to which he gave so much of himself unstintingly, and with no thought to his own frail strength and physical welfare, will never be forgotten by those of us who shared the pleasure of knowing, admiring and loving him.

10   Bureaucrat of Intelligence

Secret intelligence work, like Grand Opera, is
a breeding ground for jealousy.

STRIX, the *Spectator*, 19 July 1963

Kim's intelligence war began in the late summer of 1941. He
left his rather comic school for spies at Beaulieu to enter the
more professional world of the SIS at a time when British intelligence was struggling to go over to the offensive after the
early reverses of the war. Most SIS stations in Europe had
been overrun by Hitler's armies and mopped up by the
Abwehr; intelligence gathering by agents on the ground in
Occupied Europe hardly existed; SOE's hit-and-run organization was still largely at the training stage, trapping rabbits
and letting off home-made explosives in the English country-
side. What information about the enemy was available came
almost solely from the GC and CS scanning German radio
traffic. It was these intercepts, providing direct access to the
mind of the enemy, which enabled the SIS to plan its counter-
attack.

Reaching for the enemy, the SIS sought him out in the
neutral capitals of Europe, the only places where physical
contact was still possible. These became the arenas for the
elaborate, often ritualistic, jousting which rival counter-
espionage services engage in. Competition was fierce. The SIS
and the Abwehr, each with its supporting cast of lesser organizations, threw up smokescreens, put out feelers, probed each
other's intentions, tried to turn each other's agents, and sometimes even took pot-shots at each other on dark nights in the
streets. There were half-a-dozen major centres for this constant if controlled contact with the enemy – each in turn gaining and losing importance with the movement of the war –
such as Switzerland, that railway junction for plotters of all
nations, or Stockholm, close to the Baltic and a good place
for mounting operations in occupied Norway and Denmark.

Istanbul, strategically placed between the Balkans and the Middle East, was an even more active centre as both camps struggled to tilt Turkey into the war on their side. It was moreover German intelligence headquarters for Rommel's North African campaign, whereas Britain's Middle East and Balkan intelligence was based in Cairo. Another place for diplomatic duelling with no holds barred was Madrid because Franco's neutrality was vital to the Allies. Finally there was Lisbon, the main jumping-off point for Axis agents against Britain as for British agents into Occupied Europe – and for both sides a haven from the rigours of the war. In Lisbon there was gaiety, luxury and food, and not all the trips there were directly connected to the war effort.

Kim's Spanish expertise now found scope for employment. He owed his appointment to the fact that MI5, desperately trying to plug holes in British security defences, was then pressing SIS for more and better information about German plans to send spies to Britain. Befriended at the Tommy Harrises' by Brooman-White, MI5's Iberian specialist, Kim found himself at the age of twenty-nine posted down to St Albans where Section Five – SIS counter-espionage – had retired from the blitz under its chief, the ex-Indian policeman Felix Cowgill. Kim was put in charge of the Spain and Portugal subsection, known as Section Five (d).

It is a classic principle of intelligence that the men who ferret out secret information should not also be the ones who assess its importance and decide what action should be taken on it. This principle was built into the structure of the SIS. Half the organization in London ran the intelligence-gathering stations overseas and were known as G Sections. The other half, known as Circulating Sections, processed the information provided by the G Sections and passed it on to the relevant 'customers' in government departments. Whereas the G Sections were organized on a country-by-country or regional basis, the Circulating Sections were organized on the basis of subject matter. There was a political section, an economic section; there were army, navy and airforce sections – and there was Section Five. But, unlike all the other Circulating Sections, counter-espionage was not limited to assessment and distribution of other people's information. To protect the overseas agents of the G Sections and to warn MI5 of hostile operations against Britain, it needed men in the field as well as research analysts at home. So at St Albans Kim found himself in charge of a little counter-espionage empire which included three or four men junior to himself as well as undercover agents in Madrid, Lisbon, Gibraltar and Tangier.

It just so happened that this little empire's concerns were of prime strategic importance at that moment. Spain was a major preoccupation of the Chiefs of Staff from the collapse of France in May 1940 right up to the landings in North Africa in November 1942. Throughout this troubled period, and particularly after it had become clear that Hitler had abandoned any plans for invading Britain, the British were obsessed with the fear of Germany's overrunning Spain and taking Gibraltar. The loss of Gibraltar and the closing of the Mediterranean would have been disastrous. It was known that from 1940 to 1943 a German plan existed for the seizure of Spain, and that troops for this mission were being given special training at a small town near the Swiss frontier. The British of course had counter-plans. In the event of a German invasion a small expeditionary force stood ready to capture the Canary Islands and so cover the Atlantic shipping routes, while a sabotage unit was being prepared in 1941 to put Spanish ports and railways out of action.

There was also the possibility that Franco might of his own accord choose to throw in his lot with the Germans because of the help they had given him in the civil war. But with the passage of time this seemed increasingly unlikely. A far more actual worry was that Franco would be neutral on paper but lean Germany's way in practice. There was a lot at stake. There was the fear that prowling U-boats on the Atlantic and Mediterranean beats could call in to refuel, restock and repair at countless points along Spain's extended coasts. Precious iron ore, even Spanish fruit and vegetables, could be shipped to Axis-held Marseilles and Genoa. A more serious anxiety was that Franco would give the Abwehr free rein in Spain,

excluding British influence and allowing German agents to
build up such a position of strength that no British ship would
be safe in the Straits, and that no Allied naval operation could
be mounted from Gibraltar without the Germans knowing
all about it. Abwehr officers were thick on the ground in Spain
and their chief, Admiral Canaris, whom Hitler had charged
with special missions to Franco, was personally deeply im-
mersed in Spanish affairs, priding himself on close friendships
in the immediate entourage of the Caudillo.

Such was the unpromising picture confronting the British.

Some service chiefs in London believed that the only safe
course was immediate preventive action. In 1941 they wanted
to seize the Canaries before the Germans did. In 1942 they
urged sending in commandos to flush out German detection
posts overlooking the Straits of Gibraltar so that the North
African landings could be planned undetected. At all times they
called for a tough line with General Franco. Fortunately wiser
counsels prevailed. Men who knew Spain well argued that
nothing was more likely to drive Franco into Hitler's arms
and bring German troops roaring over the Pyrenees than crude
strong-arm tactics. Instead Spanish national pride should be
cosseted, every British asset in Spain mobilized to bring
friendly pressure on the régime, and an unremitting diplomatic
effort made to keep Franco on the narrow path of true
neutrality.

Britain was not without friends in Spain. There were many
well-placed Spaniards in industry, banking and shipping
whose sympathy to the Allied cause drew them into an intelligence network operating on an old-boy basis. The Admiralty
in London also ran an elaborate vice-consul organization in
Spanish ports whose chief task was to keep a sharp eye on the
movement of Axis ships. A real trump in the British hand
was Commander Alan Hillgarth, Naval Attaché in Madrid,
who as British Consul in Palma throughout the 1930s had
built up unrivalled personal contacts with Spanish naval
officers. The Spaniards liked and trusted him and he knew
how to handle them. So influential was his position that Secret

Service funds were put at his disposal and he was given direct access to the SIS chief, Sir Stewart Menzies, and to the Prime Minister himself. His official brief was to protect British ships from German sabotage, in which cause he had built up useful friendships among stevedores, dock watchmen and the local police in every major port in Spain. But his real value was as a diplomatist, cajoling the Spaniards into believing that strict neutrality was in their best interests. There was a touch of iron in his velvet-glove approach: the Spaniards were well aware that Britain's control of the sea routes gave her a stranglehold over Spanish imports of oil and wheat. Generally however Hillgarth resorted more to protests than to threats, vigorously complaining of German mischief-making and forcing the Spaniards to take action by supporting each complaint with fully documented evidence. It was Kim's job in Section Five (d) to produce this evidence.

He thrived on the work. Kim was not an intellectual in the All Soul's sense; he was not drawn to abstract ideas at a high level of generality. But he had a fine memory and a great ingenuity of mind – a formidable combination in intelligence work. The aptitude required for counter-espionage is a minute study of the subject on which one is working. His desk was deluged with telegrams from his men in the field, with pressing requests for tip-offs from MI5, with situation reports on Abwehr strength from other SIS specialists, and – most precious of all – with the vital raw material of the radio intercepts from GC and CS. From 1940 the code-breakers had been reading German intelligence hand-ciphers, so producing a stream of information. To make sense of this mass of detail, detecting the significant patterns in it and sifting out the dross, demanded method, precision, tolerance of boring routine: a mind like a filing system. Kim's reports were models of lucid, well-ordered prose and his briefings were excellent. He was proud of his neat small handwriting and had a special, rather affected, way of holding a pen between only two fingers. The same junior-officer qualities of charm and integrity which had so won over his trainee saboteurs at Beaulieu now attracted the affectionate respect of his subordinates at St Albans, especially of his secretary. She gave him a wallet which twenty years later he took with him to Moscow.

Within a few months of his taking over Section Five (d), the Abwehr in Spain had few secrets from the British, so complete was the mosaic which Kim and his section pieced together from the intercepts. They had penetrated both the Lisbon and the Madrid headquarters, as well as their numerous dependent out-stations. They learned that Lisbon controlled the Azores and Portuguese East Africa, while Madrid oversaw Bilbao, Vigo, Algeciras, Malaga, Seville and Barcelona. The detailed briefs containing names, addresses and targets of German agents in Spain with which Section Five (d) supplied the British Embassy in Madrid allowed the Ambassador, Sir Samuel Hoare, and his staunch Naval Attaché, Hillgarth, to put pressure on the Spaniards to turn these agents out.

Possibly the biggest success of this Spanish operation took place in the early months of 1942. Word reached Section Five (d) of a major Abwehr project code-named Bodden, the gravest threat so far to Spanish neutrality. The German plan as pieced together by the British was to rig up powerful infra-red cameras and radar apparatus on the Spanish and African approaches to Gibraltar which would allow no vessel to pass through the Straits undetected, even at night. As these stations would be linked by radio with Berlin and with U-boat Command the Allied supply position in the Western Mediterranean was in immediate danger. The worst British fears seemed confirmed, and the Admiralty was all for a preventive strike against the stations.

Hillgarth saw that his policy of 'vigilant appeasement' was in peril, and sent off a flurry of telegrams urging that diplomatic channels, successful in the past, should once again be tried. The problem of how to deal with Bodden travelled rapidly up the Whitehall ladder – from the Joint Intelligence Committee to the Chiefs of Staff to the War Cabinet which, on 19 May 1942, decided to let the Madrid Embassy try its hand. Sir Samuel Hoare was instructed to raise the matter personally with Franco, and, to provide him with ammunition, Philby drafted a powerful memorandum outlining the full scope of the German plans, with chapter and verse, drawn from the incontrovertible evidence of the GC and CS intercepts. The Caudillo was impressed and within a month confronted Admiral Canaris with the evidence, ordering him to dismantle his stations and remove his men. The collapse of the ambitious Bodden operation freed Allied strategy in the Mediterranean for the great North African landings which took the Abwehr completely by surprise. Credit for bringing off this spectacular diplomatic *coup* must be shared between the codebreakers at Bletchley, Hoare and Hillgarth in Madrid, and of course Kim's Iberian desk at St Albans. Goering later admitted that the greatest mistake Germany made during the war was to heed Franco's insistence on remaining neutral and to fail to take Gibraltar.[1]

These were the great days of 'the Outfit', the small group of friends from counter-espionage and MI5 whose job was to defeat the Abwehr in Spain and Portugal and whose unofficial club was Tommy Harris's big house in Chesterfield Gardens. Kim was often up from St Albans to crow over the latest arrest of some Axis agent, betrayed by the infallible intercepts even before he set out. With the GC and CS weapon in their hands and the enemy's mail arriving daily on their desks, the Outfit was well on top of the job. Harris, much experienced in Spain and Spaniards, was a key man in London, grilling suspects at the 'tough' interrogation centre on Ham Common, playing back turned agents, acting as 'cutout' between them and B Division of MI5 (the division where information was assessed and action initiated) run by the formidable pair, Guy Liddell and his assistant Dick White. By the end of 1942 few operations mounted against Britain from Spain or Portugal had much chance of success; the Spanish Embassy in London had been successfully penetrated; potential mischief-makers in a wide arc from the Pyrenees through Lisbon and the Canaries to Portuguese East Africa had been docketed and

1. Maj.-Gen. Sir Kenneth Strong, *Intelligence at the Top* (London, 1968), p. 72.

filed. Kim paid regular visits to his stations in the field, returning with a steadily growing reputation from these adventurous wartime trips to Madrid and Lisbon (where MI5's chief agent, run personally by Dick White, was none other than 'Klop' – Russian for 'flea' – Ustinov, father of the actor Peter Ustinov). In the event of Spain's entering the war on the German side, the Outfit had up its sleeve a rebel Shadow Cabinet which Kim from his extensive knowledge of Spanish personalities constantly reshuffled.

So far the work of Cowgill's Section Five had been largely defensive but with the North African landings in prospect it prepared for a more offensive role. The areas of interest expanded. Spain whose neutrality now seemed more or less assured was downgraded in favour of the active theatres of war. First North Africa, then Italy, came into Kim's net, involving surreptitious visits in the guise of a war correspondent to Cairo (where the counter-espionage staff worked in a house known as Dracula Villa). To meet the new demands of a fluid military situation, Section Five set up Special Counter-Intelligence units, attached to the army staffs to carry the intelligence war to the Abwehr in the field. Their complicated task was to penetrate the Axis espionage networks in order to feed false military information to the German High Command, an endeavour that met with particular success during the Italian campaign. Later in the war these methods were put to work on the Western Front. The usual technique was to uncover enemy wireless operators, run them under control until an Allied substitute could replace them without detection – then jail them. Increasingly the teams involved in these subtle manoeuvres with double and treble agents looked to Kim at headquarters for the flow of information they needed. He was the man whom Cowgill and above him Colonel Valentine Vivian, the DCSS, listened to, the man who could get you an extra wireless operator or more money. Kim was the one to whom everyone – juniors, seniors, and American allies – deferred.

In 1943 Section Five's inconvenient exile in St Albans was ended and Cowgill and his growing staff were shunted back to offices in Ryder Street, London, within easy access of their chief customers, MI5, and of the SIS high command in Broadway Buildings. Kim was always to be found at his desk after working hours – or if not in the office at least with the duty officer in the pub. When Cowgill went on an official visit to America in late 1943 he named Philby as his deputy for the whole section on intelligence matters. Clearly this wartime recruit was firmly on the ladder moving up.

In Cowgill's absence occurred the case of the German Foreign Ministry papers which helped give Kim's career a further boost. A German defector smuggled a suitcase of secret documents into Switzerland and handed them over to Allen Dulles, then head of the American Office of Strategic Services in Berne. Dulles passed them on to the SIS but both Cowgill and Colonel Dansey, the Assistant Chief, took them to be a plant. Asked by Cowgill to look into the matter, Kim showed a selection of telegrams to Alastair Denniston of GC and CS to see if they tallied with radio intercepts. They did. Moreover they gave the codebreakers valuable leads in their work on German diplomatic codes. Denniston pronounced the material genuine beyond doubt and Kim circulated it to the gratitude and enthusiasm of the Foreign Office and Service 'customers'.

The favourable impression Kim was thus able to make no doubt owed something to the fact that his boss Cowgill was notorious for sitting on information rather than circulating it. Indeed so excessively discreet was he that some saw his mission in life as the suppression of intelligence. This son of a missionary, whose mind had been formed on highly disciplined lines in the Indian Police, found himself during the war in exclusive control of the whole stream of German intelligence radio traffic, intercepted by the GC and CS and handed to him on a plate to do with as he saw fit. At times he seemed to drown in the precious stuff, staying up all night in his office and working himself into a state of hopelessness. He used to be found in the morning asleep with his head on the blotter. His miserly attitude to the treasures at his disposal enraged the customers of Section Five, and in particular MI5 who would dearly have liked sight of all the Abwehr material rather than having Cowgill release to them only what he felt concerned British security. The rationale of Cowgill's restrictiveness was the overriding and sacred need to protect the source. In the classic intelligence debate between 'protectionism' and 'free trade', he was fanatically on the protectionist side.

Not only did Cowgill make enemies in MI5, but in most places. Leonard Palmer (later Professor of Comparative Philology, Oxford) and Dennis Page (later Master of Jesus College, Cambridge), the two GC and CS specialists in Abwehr code-breaking, were critical of his hoarding of their hard-won material. Colonel Vivian, who shared his Indian background and had brought him into the SIS at the time of the Munich scare, grew to distrust him: as he later remarked in a private communication, 'Cowgill was a very ambitious chap, going straight to the Chief in an attempt to dislodge me.' Cowgill even had to face a rebellion within his own empire, mounted by a clever wartime recruit, Hugh Trevor-Roper (later to become Regius Professor of Modern History at Oxford). Trevor-Roper served in another part of Sir Stewart Menzies' empire, the Radio Security Service (RSS) which was run by a splendid brigadier called Gambier-Parry. A large organization, RSS intercepted all enemy intelligence traffic, and was responsible for radio communication with SIS stations, officers and agents abroad, more especially with those officers who conveyed Enigma material to commanders in the field. (Incidentally, it was from this organization that the very efficient Diplomatic Wireless Service developed after the war, giving Britain an unmatched global communications network at the time.) From 1941 Trevor-Roper was Cowgill's liaison officer with RSS. The row between them was triggered off by his uncovering among the Bletchley intercepts a series of deciphered communications labelled ISBA – Intelligence Service British Agents – which Cowgill had ordained should not be circulated. It was a collection of all the messages which mentioned, however marginally, the names of British spies, even announcements of their deaths. Trevor-Roper wasted no time in letting it be known that Cowgill's obsessive discretion was once again leading to a large-scale suppression of intelligence. The Colonel hit back by asking Commander Travis, then head of GC and CS, to take Trevor-Roper off the list of recipients of secret material. In the trial of strength that followed, Cowgill went so far as to get the SIS to produce a document for MI5 hinting that Trevor-Roper was in touch with Germans: the evidence was a hunting expedition he had made to Ireland – where there was a German mission.

Invited to tell his side of the story to Lord Swinton, Trevor-Roper poured out his disenchantment with the SIS and its senior officers. For talking out of school he was hauled up in front of 'C' himself, with Vivian as prosecuting counsel urging that in view of what had happened Trevor-Roper should be sacked. But Cowgill lost the battle. Trevor-Roper made amends with a letter of apology and, to get him out of Cowgill's hair, he was allowed to set up his own section within RSS, but reporting directly to Menzies, the Radio Intelligence Section (RIS), to which he recruited a sharpwitted trio of dons, Gilbert Ryle, Stuart Hampshire and Charles Stuart. Its job was to produce signals intelligence in order to help RSS interceptors improve their performance. Much of its material was not decoded texts at all, but call signs, data on procedures and suchlike. In studying Abwehr traffic, Trevor-Roper's team – perhaps the most brilliant in the whole wartime intelligence world – saw that it contained a mass of information about the Abwehr itself and about much wider subjects. They produced a series of extremely valuable papers which brought renewed and constant conflict with Cowgill: RIS naturally wanted its findings circulated, Cowgill, from concern for 'the security of the source', bitterly opposed the circulation.

What these skirmishes achieved, without anyone being fully aware of it, was to prepare the way for Cowgill's fall and his replacement by his talented junior, Philby.

Trevor-Roper had done more than score off Cowgill. He had won a battle of principle – the right to build up a picture of the German secret service as a whole. The extraordinary fact was that the SIS had no specifically German section.

SIS stations abroad were attached either to diplomatic missions or to armies, and these stations were in turn run by G Sections at home. As there was as yet no army or diplomatic mission in Germany, there was no German desk. The German intercepts were broken up according to subject and sent to Circulating Sections, but no one put all the bits together for an overall view. In fact the SIS had lost the opportunity to do so at the very start of the war, when it was already clear that the chief source of operational intelligence was going to be radio intercepts and code-breaking. The Armed Services conceded that these functions should be organized centrally but they did not want the raw material to be filtered to them through an SIS interpretative grid. They wanted it fast and they wanted it direct. As a result the construction of the mosaic on operational matters for the Army, the Navy, the Air Force and the Ministry of Economic Warfare was taken out of the hands of the SIS and given to the ministries concerned. GC and CS was confined to the role of a cryptographic agency rather than an intelligence department, being treated by the three Services and the MEW as a source of raw intelligence and not as a body for assessing it. It is possible that the reason that the SIS remained unreformed throughout the entire war and the top of its pyramid undisturbed was precisely that its functions had so dwindled. The only way to rescue the SIS from its relatively marginal role would have been the creation of a civilian-staffed central intelligence directorate to collate and evaluate intercepted German communications – an organization such as was campaigned for after the war by Sir Kenneth Strong, the first Director General in 1963 of the integrated Defence Intelligence Staff. In the absence of any such ambitious possibility, Trevor-Roper's wartime RIS did at least give the SIS an overall view of the Abwehr in all its guises.

By late 1943 Hitler's defeat was clearly only a matter of time. For the clever band of dons, stockbrokers, museum curators and so forth, whom the war had turned into intelligence officers, a happy release to civilian life was in sight. To the percipient it was obvious that Germany's collapse would put the Abwehr experts out of a job. Those who wanted a post-war career in intelligence – and who wished to be well placed on the day – now started to consider what the next target would be. Already looming large was the problem of how to handle Russia, as, with Germany knocked out and France enfeebled, Soviet power would after the war be unchallenged on the Continent. The bogy of Soviet imperialism – old Tsarist ambitions to recover former territory now reinforced by revolutionary ideology – was too real to be ignored.

In SIS and other government departments, committees were set up long before the end of the war to chart future policy. Even at the height of the wartime alliance, 1941 to 1943, relations with the Russians on the intelligence side were far from close. Russia had been a prime SIS target up to and beyond the Nazi-Soviet pact, but on the German invasion of the Soviet Union Churchill had ordered a moratorium on British spying in an attempt to build up Soviet confidence in the alliance. He wanted the Russians to be told everything, and the only argument for restraint which he would listen to was that Russian security was so bad that anything told them would probably reach the Germans. Some secrets were therefore kept from them because of their supposed inefficiency, notably British success in the allegedly impossible task of cracking German ciphers. But without knowing the source they were not prepared to take information on trust, and not for a moment did they believe that Britain had given up spying on them. Their suspicions were soon to be proved correct. In late 1943 or early 1944 the SIS, reverting to its pre-war preoccupations, turned its attention once more to the problem of penetrating Russia.

Needless to say Philby gave this renewed SIS interest in the Soviet Union his closest attention. The twenty-three-year-old lad recruited into the Russian service in 1935 was now, nine years later, an agent in place and very close to target. In the small world of Section Five, and in the even smaller band of intelligence professionals who would be staying on after the war, Colonel Felix Cowgill was the main obstacle to Kim's access to the new anti-Soviet activity. But, difficult to work with, the ex-Indian policeman had undermined his own position by making so many enemies among his colleagues. The MI5 chiefs in particular had put up with a great deal of obstructiveness from him and were quite prepared to voice their grievances in the higher echelons of the SIS, and it was child's play for Kim to give the tottering Cowgill the *coup de grâce*. Playing on Colonel Vivian's fears that Cowgill was out for his own job, Kim arranged for MI5's grievances to be channelled through Colonel Vivian to Sir Stewart Menzies. When, therefore, the question of what to do about Russia had to be solved institutionally within the Service, 'C' decided to set up a small separate Soviet counter-espionage section outside Cowgill's jurisdiction and offered Kim the job of running it. On the announcement of Philby's appointment, the by-passed Cowgill tendered his resignation which, to his surprise, Menzies in the interests of good relations with MI5 cheerfully accepted. Cowgill was ultimately shunted off to a security job in Germany, and Kim, in the autumn of 1944, left his old desk in Section Five for the mysterious, and to insiders highly prestigious, task of picking up the threads of anti-Soviet operations.

In 1945, riding high in his new role, he visited France, Germany, Italy and Greece to brief SIS stations on what his new section, Section IX, would require. In Paris Malcolm Muggeridge, then one of his underlings, recalls Philby taking him after a convivial dinner on a nocturnal stroll to the gates of the Soviet Embassy in the rue de Grenelle – a target to whose penetration, he said with drunken solemnity, they must now bend their efforts. Later that year in Berlin he was seen at an intelligence party downing a glass of V2 fluid in the belief that it was hock. His heavy and somewhat indiscriminate drinking habits were already an acknowledged part of his persona.

The end of the war brought a drastic scaling down of Section Five's staff and activities. On the ground in Germany all C-E operations were under the control of MI5's Dick White, now with the rank of Brigadier, while in Ryder Street a single home desk wound up the struggle against the Germans by editing the 'Purple Primer' – a list of some ten thousand agents in all parts of the world, compiled from captured Abwehr and SD (Nazi party intelligence) files. On the fly-leaf of the volume the editors wrote. 'They come not single spies, but in battalions . . .' As an intelligence problem Germany existed only for the historian. Russia was now claiming the active resources, and it was not long before Kim, the new Russian expert, merged the dwindling German rump with his Section IX to emerge in the autumn of 1945 as head of a revamped counter-espionage division pointing eastwards.

For Kim and Aileen and their growing family the immediate post-war period seemed the crest of the wave. They were by now installed in a large handsome house of their own, 18 Carlyle Square, Chelsea, and professionally Kim's qualities and promise were widely recognized. On the surface, 1945–6 was the year of fulfilment, the year in which after the training and the testing he emerged on to the plateau of successful adult life.

The good times began in late 1943 with the move up to London from the quiet of St Albans where the Philbys had shared a house a little way outside the town with the Milnes. Tim Milne, the friend from Westminster School with whom Kim had explored pre-war Europe, had preceded him on the Iberian desk and was now his number two in the anti-Soviet section. On first coming back to London the Philbys crowded into a basement in Drayton Gardens, a street off the Brompton Road which was long to remain on the family map: Dora Philby took a flat in Grove Court, Drayton Gardens, in 1949 and lived there until she died. The interlude in the basement lasted a year or so. Then Aileen's affluent mother, Mrs Alleyne, lent them the money to buy a twenty-year lease on the house in Carlyle Square where, in the first home they had ever owned, they immediately began living in wild and joyful style. Aileen was very clever at finding strange but efficient servants and life seemed an endless succession of excitements. In the upper storeys a lodger (at one time the London editor of the *Manchester Guardian*) helped meet the mortgage payments while in the ground-floor dining-room Aileen and a friend, Mrs Patsy Collins, ran a nursery school with the help of a hired teacher for their own and half-a-dozen other children. What with one thing and another, the house was not particularly elegant: neither Kim nor Aileen cared much about their visual surroundings. But they lived in cheerful disorder amidst children, friends, books, music and alcohol. Kim was very moved by Beethoven, especially the Quartets.

His image as an Establishment eccentric was becoming fixed – competent and valued at his job, giving an impression of robustness and energy, but with the ragged edges tolerated by English convention. He could work for twenty-four hours, drink for another twenty-four, and still be on his feet. He drove about in a broken-down taxi-cab, still wore a shabby tweed jacket patched at the elbows and cuffs, was a well-known figure at his local, the Markham Arms. He loved pubs, newspapers, gossip. He cooked well and ate largely. Like St John, he kept up his membership of the Athenaeum and cultivated a degree of fastidious aloofness. 'He doesn't like anybody,' Aileen, who was forever building him up, would say, and this aura of inaccessibility only made people want to please him more.

On 25 September 1946 Kim (34) and Aileen (35) finally got married. Most of their friends had long supposed that they were already man and wife and Aileen turned up for the ceremony in Chelsea Register Office in an advanced state of pregnancy with her fourth child. But there was nothing furtive about the occasion which was followed by a great celebration in Carlyle Square. The witnesses of the union were Tommy Harris, art dealer turned MI5 ace, and Flora Solomon, Aileen's early protector from Marks and Spencer. Almost seven weeks later Miranda was born. She was their second daughter. Josephine, the first child and her father's favourite, was born in 1941, followed by John in November 1942 and by Dudley Tomás in December 1943. He was a seven-months baby and spent the first weeks of his life in an incubator. A fifth child, Harry George, was born in Washington in 1950. Kim was a tolerant and affectionate father, with no firm principles about child-rearing except total hostility to religious education. He was a militant atheist, not an agnostic, a position his friends thought inappropriate in a man of his reasonableness.

Aileen's admiration was clearly not irksome to Kim and theirs was on the whole a good marriage. She was quick-witted and not unintelligent but rather argumentative and politically not always well informed. Kim continued indulgently to put up with her interruptions and contradictions. In her favour she helped create an atmosphere of permissiveness which was precious to him. She did not mind what he did. If on a binge he were to tear down the chandelier she would have laughed as uproariously as anyone. She provided him with a relaxed domestic setting and a cover of scattiness, valuable to him at this period of his life, but to an acute observer the relationship was not solidly founded. It was not proof against the strains to come.

In the great post-war shake-out of the SIS Kim stood out as intellectually more distinguished than most of the professionals who stayed on in the Service after the amateurs had returned with relief to their civilian jobs. The SIS was then run by a 'top floor' general staff of four or five men, supported by a second echelon of some twelve heads and deputy heads of departments. Kim, as head of counter-espionage, had now reached this second echelon. He had found his *métier*: his war work was rewarded on his thirty-fourth birthday with an OBE in the 1946 New Year's Honours List, while his transition from wartime recruit to peacetime professional was given official cover with his appearance in the Foreign Office list as a First Secretary (Temporary). Acquaintances not in the know understood him to be compiling a daily news digest for his FO colleagues.

The reputation of Britain's wartime Intelligence Service rests on two achievements – the code-breaking operations at Bletchley and the Special Counter-Intelligence units, both of which made a significant contribution to victory on all fronts. Section Five stood at the very intersection of these two currents, exploiting the first to promote the second. Although he had not made a remarkable personal contribution, Kim's emergence at the end of the war as head of Section Five put him in a highly regarded spotlight. Particularly ready to admire were the American intelligence officers who, coming over to learn the trade during the war, thought the Section Five team a very exceptional body of men.

The Americans had started arriving in London after Pearl Harbor: first Arthur Thurston, an officer sent by J. Edgar Hoover to liaise with MI5, then a code-breaking party led by William Friedman, followed in due course by an OSS (Office of Strategic Service) mission headed by Norman Holmes Pearson (later a professor of English literature and collaborator with W. H. Auden in compiling a poetry anthology). On the counter-espionage side James Angleton, later a senior CIA official, and Andrew Berding (the biographer of Cordell Hull) were among the first officers to be housed in 1943 in Section Five's Ryder Street headquarters for an intensive six-weeks course. Co-operation between Section Five and OSS X2, its American equivalent, was close and successful, both in London and in the field. The Americans recognized that the British had far and away the better records of German intelligence activities, and to the end of the war the SIS provided communications through London for the American counter-espionage men. After training in England the Americans moved out to Italy as a field service, there to co-operate with the British SCI units which were busy interrogating suspects, playing Axis radio operators back to the Germans, and relating field operations with information from London. Relative newcomers to the game, the Americans were impressed by what they learned of Kim's early work in the school for spies – British training centres of this sort enjoyed a prestigious reputation among her Allies – and they saw him as the victor of an SIS 'palace revolution', the outlines of which they only dimly discerned and whose significance they possibly exaggerated. His house was often full of high-powered American visitors.

So much for the overt side of his domestic and professional life. What about his covert career as a Russian secret agent? In the three years, June 1941 to mid-1944, the unclouded years of the alliance with the Soviet Union, a British Communist would have found no conflict of interest in loyally serving the British overtly and the Russians secretly. But they were also years in which Philby had nothing of vital interest to communicate: Churchill and Roosevelt were doing the job far better than he could hope to. His real career as a spy may be said to have begun only in 1945. It has been pointed out that at this turning point of his life, Philby chose Stalin's murderously repressive Russia in preference to Attlee's humane Britain. But to what extent did he have a real choice? Could he have gone back to *The Times*, where his reputation as a correspondent was high, just as so many of his colleagues returned to their civilian careers? Could he even have made a clean breast of his Soviet attachments to the SIS? The damage he had so far done might well have been forgiven him had he agreed to be 'turned' and played back against the Russians. In his methodical way he must surely have explored where these paths would lead him. Fidelity to the romantic Marxist ideals of the 1930s can at this point have counted for little in the careful calculations of this bureaucrat of espionage.

But there were powerful and compelling arguments on the side of the Russian intelligence service. For one thing he was already deeply implicated by the few jobs he had been able to pull off during the war. He had plundered the Russian source books from the SIS Central Registry at its wartime home in St Albans (although it should be said that these lists of British contacts and agents in the Soviet Union were out of date). When on night duty at Broadway, he had monitored cables from the War Office to the British Military Mission in Moscow, no doubt passing on their contents. Very possibly he had told the Russians what German ciphers the British were reading – in particular the ones they said they were not. But here too a corrective is necessary. Security at wartime Bletchley was fierce and there are reasons for believing that Philby knew only in broad outline what was going on there. He would not have dared make a direct inquiry outside his field of interest, confined for much of the war to Spain. Perhaps because the holy of holies of the GC and CS proved so impenetrable, he appeared to develop a certain envious resentment of the code-breakers, referring to them unflatteringly as *voyeurs*. All things considered his greatest gift to the Russians was to manoeuvre himself into the job of head of the anti-Soviet Section IX. This was clearly a triumph of penetration, even if he had nothing explosive to report: from the British point of view the section was not very effective in the immediate post-war period, as its information was largely pre-war and needed extensive updating. But no doubt the Russians were glad to know how weak it was.

These still quite modest but highly promising achievements had won Philby the praise of his masters, and this, given his rather schoolboyish appetite for approval, meant a lot to him. But there was a darker side to the coin. The Russians can have left him in no doubt that they would tolerate no defection: Philby knew too much. His contact with the Russian service had been too extensive. To get out would have been a sentence of death, as Walter Krivitsky, the ex-Soviet intelligence officer found dead in a Washington hotel four years earlier, had discovered. Unlike Communist intellectuals not engaged in covert work, Philby was denied the opportunity for public recantation, even had this corresponded with his intellectual development. The Communist fall-out among intellectuals of his generation had been colossal, precipitated by seemingly cynical changes in the Party line. Changes of heart had taken place, notably at the time of the Nazi–Soviet pact and of the Russian invasion of Finland, and were to occur again when the Russians broke with Tito in 1948, and yet again on the crushing of the Hungarian Revolution in 1956 and of the 'Dubcek spring' of 1968. But a Soviet agent cannot afford such luxuries of independent thinking.

Kim had his measure of human frailty. Although he may have enjoyed excitement and there can be no doubt of his courage, he was physically squeamish, hating pain and violence. He could not bear to see anything killed, on one occasion fishing out of a lavatory a mouse flushed down by a maid. He was frightened of horses. Above all he had a terrible dread of physical torture, knowing that he could not stand up to it. This was not the steely secret agent of popular fiction, but an averagely sensitive, averagely vulnerable human being.

There was one other facet of his character which militated with perhaps equal force against withdrawal from the Russian service: this was the intellectual and moral arrogance inherited from his self-willed father. 'You've got to live with yourself,' the old man would say, 'and be true to your own moral inclinations.' In manner Kim seemed a rather unassuming person, an impression reinforced by his stutter which was clearly a severe physical and mental burden to him, a hurdle he always had to clear, particularly with new and official contacts. But those who worked with him and knew him understood that vanity and even self-regard were the keys to his character. More than most people he liked to be surrounded by men who respected him and thought well of him. Beneath his surface politeness was a reluctance to concede that anyone was his intellectual or moral equal, and this flattering self-indulgence was built deep into his character. To admit now that he had been wrong would have been too self-destructive even to contemplate.

And so, almost independently of his will, the choice was taken, a course of continued treachery made inevitable by a combination of fear, egotism and guts. From the start it was a double life which entailed formidable risks. It is not surprising that it resulted in heavy drinking and a high state of neurosis. The strains were relieved only by a greedy grasping for the everyday pleasures of life, what he called 'living life to the full'. It was the attitude of a soldier on leave, a man permanently at war.

In counter-espionage everything eventually comes out in the wash. However careful one may be – and Philby was very careful – it is virtually impossible as a secret agent to avoid brief moments of exposure, tiny inconsistencies, the scattering of microscopic clues which one day, perhaps years later, a counter-espionage officer will piece together into an incriminating pattern. Above all, one cannot be proof against the unpredictability of others, against slips, defections and betrayals in one's own camp. In the agonized calculations of every spy must be the near certainty that such hidden timebombs are ticking away and will one day blow him into the open. The nice and dangerous judgement he must make is how long he can work in the shadow of this threat before he must jump clear. Philby, a C-E specialist himself, knew more exactly than most agents the nature of the risks he was running, and that somewhere, sometime, a C-E man would be waiting for him. He also knew better than most how far he could push his luck.

By end-1944 he had been obliged to leave in his trail a number of clues which he must have known any future investigators of his career would ponder over. There was the suppression on two occasions, late in 1942 and again in the spring of 1944, of evidence suggesting that a conservative opposition in Germany wished to make contact with the British in their struggle against Hitler. On the first occasion Philby refused point-blank and without explanation to allow the circulation of a paper prepared by Trevor-Roper's RIS pointing to rivalry between the Nazi party's secret service and the Abwehr, whose chief, Admiral Canaris, was angling to meet 'C'. And on the second, he dismissed as unreliable a warning of the July 1944 Generals' plot against Hitler given by the German defector Otto John.[1] Why did Kim stifle at birth these two reports which time was to prove correct? A possible explanation is that the Russians feared the success of a rightwing *coup* against Hitler and were reluctant to see the Reich break up before their armies were on the spot to impose a postwar settlement. But this interpretation of Kim's motives hinges largely on hindsight, and must even now be considered too ambiguous to be damning.

A third possible clue to his culpability, a harder but still not conclusive piece of evidence, planted a nagging doubt in the mind of James Angleton, a wartime trainee in Ryder Street who had taken over American Special Counter-Intelligence.

1. Otto John, *Twice Through the Lines* (1972).

Angleton's early esteem for the SIS had not survived his wartime experiences. He had developed a grudge against British counter-espionage and against Kim in particular when his attempts to recruit an Italian prince and former Axis agent into his own organization were foiled by a Section Five officer. But what had been a mere grievance is thought to have hardened into a suspicion when Angleton learned of the *Rote Kapelle* case. As the Allied armies advanced into Germany, the British Special Counter-Intelligence unit there received a letter from a Mrs Schmidt whose son had been executed as a British spy by the Gestapo. The mother was demanding compensation. The head of the SCI unit cabled London about the case but received no answer, and it appeared that his telegram, of which no copies were kept, had been lost. There was no record of it in Ryder Street. When, however, captured Abwehr archives came under scrutiny after the war, it emerged that Schmidt had been not only a British agent but also the main Russian agent in the German Air Command. Was this why the telegram about him had been 'lost'? Had someone in Ryder Street suppressed it in order to head off investigation of a Russian espionage network? Was this a bid to protect the mauled but still resilient remnants of the *Rote Kapelle*, Russia's Europe-wide net directed against Germany, whose foundations had been laid in the 1930s? Such were the puzzles which must have led Angleton to wonder whether the SIS were harbouring a traitor; and it was the slow maturing of such suspicions which, in 1951, hardened American hearts against Philby after the flight of Burgess and Maclean. More importantly, it was these worries about British reliability which, among many other factors in the early post-war period, encouraged American intelligence to break free from British tutelage and go its own way.

But these uncomfortable question-marks in Kim's otherwise unblemished success story were as nothing compared to the peril which emerged in the summer of 1945, threatening to blow his whole carefully constructed career sky high. As with the danger posed to him in 1937 by the Soviet defector General

Krivitsky, this time too the hazard came from within his own Russian service.

Konstantin Volkov, an NKVD officer[1] attached to the Soviet Consulate General in Istanbul, had in August approached the British Vice-Consul to ask for political asylum for himself and his wife. Among the secrets he promised to bring over in return were the names of three Soviet agents working in Britain: two, he claimed, were in the Foreign Office, and the third was head of a counter-espionage section in London. When Volkov's cry for help reached London it was natural that 'C' should hand this top-secret case to his anti-Soviet expert for immediate action.

There in the papers on his desk Kim saw destruction staring him in the face. His only hope of salvation was to tell the Russians as soon as possible of this mortal threat to himself and make sure they had enough time to deal with Volkov. He was lucky. Volkov, alleging that the Russians could read some British ciphers, had pleaded that all communications about him should go to London by bag. As a result a full week passed before Kim learned of his approach to the Vice-Consul. There were to be more delays. It took three days for 'C' to dispatch Kim to Istanbul via Cairo to handle the case on the spot, and another twenty-four hours were lost when bad weather diverted Kim's aircraft to Tunis. As a result he arrived in Cairo too late to catch the onward plane to Istanbul, and another day was wasted. In Istanbul itself a further day went by because the British Minister wanted to consult his ambassador in Ankara before authorizing action. As it happened, the Ambassador, Sir Maurice Peterson, had known Kim in Spain during the civil war and invited him aboard his yacht on the Bosphorus. Only there was he given the go-ahead to contact Volkov, but by this time there was no Volkov for him to meet: the Russians had spirited him away.

How did Kim get away with it? Of course there was an inquest and all aspects of the case came under scrutiny, including his handling of it. The thesis he advanced in his official

---

1. *Narodnyi Komissariat Vnutrennikh Del* (People's Commissariat for Internal Affairs), a forerunner of the KGB.

report to 'C' was that Volkov's own insistence on bag communications may have given the Russians time to catch up with him – after all, nearly three weeks had elapsed since the first contact. A crucial factor then intervened to mislead the investigators. A member of the British Consulate General in Istanbul admitted mentioning Volkov's name in a telephone conversation with the Embassy in Ankara, and as the telephones were tapped, it was assumed that this was how the Russians learned of Volkov's intention to defect. This stroke of luck provided Philby with a permanent loophole.[1] However incriminating the Volkov case later came to seem, the evidence could never be judged conclusive.

So the immediate danger passed. By a mixture of luck, swift communications with his Russian friends, his own skill in juggling and the trust he enjoyed from his British superiors, Kim had successfully negotiated a very nasty corner. But he could never be sure that the case would not be reopened and his own role examined more closely. It was certainly time to tie up any remaining loose ends.

Perhaps it was some such fear that his early life might come under investigation which prompted him to choose just this exposed moment to put a final end to his long-forgotten marriage with Litzi. If this Communist connection were about to be unearthed by MI5, it would be as well if Kim were seen to do the job for them first, thus giving himself the opportunity of putting his own gloss on this association. He had parted from Litzi ten years earlier in the autumn of 1936 when he was posing as a German sympathizer and, except for a furtive meeting in Paris in 1939, they had probably avoided each other since. But the fact remained that they had not been divorced – most probably because any reference to Litzi during the war would have drawn attention to Kim's Communist past at a time when he was seeking to consolidate his position in the SIS. But by 1946 she had become a dangerous burden to be jettisoned. Moreover, the interests of his SIS career dictated the need to regularize his situation with Aileen. To Kim it

1. The late Colonel Valentine Vivian, a personal communication to the authors.

must have seemed that there was only one thing to do: he must briefly resurrect Litzi, who had by now joined her war-time Communist lover, Georg Honigmann, in East Berlin, and sever his link with her forever. Boldly he asked his boss, Colonel Vivian, for leave to go to France to meet Litzi and get her to divorce him, so that he could marry Aileen. It was another perilous hurdle. Calculating that frankness was the best policy, he disarmed the honest Vivian by pointing out that his youthful escapade with a left-wing refugee (whom he had not seen for years) now prevented him from making an honest woman of the mother of his four children. Vivian was won over, and put in a routine request to MI5 for a 'trace' on Litzi. The reply (on information from 'Klop' Ustinov, via his boss Dick White) was that Litzi was a Soviet agent.[1] It is a measure of the confidence and affection in which Philby was held by his colleagues that this revelation should seem to add nothing to what he had already confessed to Vivian. So Kim went to Paris, and we can only speculate on the interest of that meeting. In due course Litzi Philby petitioned for a divorce on the grounds of her husband's adultery, and the decree was made absolute on 17 September 1946, a week before the second Philby wedding in Chelsea Register Office.

Dangerous though they were, the *Rote Kapelle* case, the Volkov affair, the tainting association with Litzi, could do no more than provide circumstantial evidence against him. The case which finally drove him from the Service was not directly concerned with him at all. It began on another continent, in circumstances quite outside his sphere of action and involving information and agents he had nothing to do with. The clue that started the deadly ball rolling derived from the surest source of all – the enemy speaking – overheard by Britain's code-breakers, Kim's despised *voyeurs*. In the summer of 1945, for a few brief exhilarating weeks after the defeat of Germany, the experts at Bletchley were able to crack Russian intelligence traffic between the Soviet Consulate General in New York and the Centre in Moscow. These precious intercepts pointed

1. The late Colonel Valentine Vivian, a personal communication to the authors.

decisively to two security leaks in the Western camp which in the fullness of time were to lead to the arrest of atom spy Klaus Fuchs in 1950 and to Donald Maclean's flight to Russia when he was threatened with exposure in 1951. It was this time-bomb ticking quietly away ever since 1945, long before Philby even knew of its existence, which was eventually to bring him down.

11   The Microbe in the Blood

After the Volkov affair Philby never felt secure again. In the seven years 1944 to 1951 on which his reputation as a Russian super-spy rests, he was in fact occupied as much with defence as attack, as much with protecting himself as betraying Western secrets. His achievements for the Soviet Union were paid for expensively in anxiety.

The immediate post-war year had been a very difficult one, bringing him to the very brink of exposure. His nervous system had suffered a bad shock. A spy in a position such as Kim's is sustained by his total confidence in his masters: it is his belief in their power, their competence and their concern for him which keeps him going. The officers who run him become in effect his only real friends, the only persons to whom he entrusts his deepest fears and most vital interests, and the result is an intimate relationship not unlike that between patient and psychoanalyst. But when the masters prove fallible, what loneliness and despair the spy suffers! Imagine Kim's state of mind when, with the immediate threat from Volkov disposed of, he had leisure to reflect on the vulnerability of his situation. He had confided the secret on which his life depended to a faceless organization in a distant country, and now a man he did not know and over whose efficiency and loyalty he had no control had erupted out of this anonymity to destroy him. He must at that moment have cursed his Russian friends whose inadequate security had so put him at risk. It is routine in these circumstances for the spy's masters to spare no pains to reassure him. The psychological dependence necessary for his effective control must be restored. Kim would be assured of the esteem in which the Centre held him and of the great value put upon his work; a contingency plan for his eventual escape would be unfolded to him; he would be urged to work hard for his British employers in order to repair any damage his image may have suffered in those quarters. He would in effect be given a holiday from active spying, and to throw the counter-espionage bloodhounds off the scent, contact would be interrupted for a time.

During this period of convalescence after the Volkov affair, the SIS posted Kim to Istanbul as Station Commander for Turkey, that is to say, as head of British intelligence operations in that country. Up till that moment his career had been in C-E and on this side of the business he had risen to a position of seniority second only to Colonel Vivian. But the end of the war brought great changes to SIS. Because of its poor wartime record, the Chief, Sir Stewart Menzies, had to fight for the Service's existence in the face of scepticism from the new Labour government and rivalry from other agencies, such as SOE. In the autumn of 1945 Kim himself sat on a committee for SIS reorganization. Colonels Valentine Vivian and Claude Dansey were eventually retired and the upper echelons were strengthened with an influx of senior army and air force officers. Careful limits were put on their activities. Even in colonies acceding to independence, where the SIS could have expected to move in, the British government decreed that MI5 should keep its old monopoly. Known as the Attlee Doctrine, this drawing of the frontier between SIS and Security Service operations overseas was to break down when Commonwealth countries such as Cyprus or Ghana became involved with foreign powers – and so entered SIS territory. The British were often slow, however, to change gear from MI5 to SIS, sometimes encountering resistance from senior British diplomats on the spot for whom espionage had a bad odour.

So Kim, the bureaucrat from head office, was posted to Turkey in February 1947 to widen his experience and give him a taste of operations in the field. Moving out from the centre of the web, and from the privileged vantage point which C-E confers on its practitioners, was a net loss: he would now be at the total mercy of another Volkov. But the posting was an important one and a promotion for him. Situated on Russia's southern flank and with the Truman Doctrine about to sweep it into the American orbit, Turkey was in the front line of the Cold War, an ideal vantage point for peering over the Iron Curtain into the Soviet Union. Directing such probes was a natural extension of what Philby had been doing as head of the anti-Soviet section in London. It was a posting which both his masters must have rated high. For Kim himself there was piquancy in returning to the scene of Volkov's liquidation by the Russians: the local SIS station had fiercely resented London's mishandling of the affair, and he was no doubt looking forward to the opportunity of tying up any compromising loose ends in the files.

Having handed over his C-E responsibilities to his successor and brushed up his anti-Soviet expertise at a training course, Kim flew east. He broke his journey to call on his father in Saudi Arabia, his first visit to the country which St John had made his home. After spending the war years impatiently in London, St John had returned to the desert as soon as he could, leaving his wife in Drayton Gardens and his mother in Camberley, but not before celebrating VE Day *en famille*. For the occasion old Mrs Philby produced a quart of whisky which she had been saving for years. Dora's enthusiasm for living in Arabia, never very great, cooled after the war, particularly when St John acquired a house in the small, severely Muslim capital of Riyadh, cut off in the middle of Arabia from contact with the outside world. There was talk of his keeping Arab concubines. Such goings-on cannot have been easy for Dora to accept but, although she developed a strong penchant for gin, she was not the sort of woman to crumble in the face of her husband's eccentricities. Warm-hearted and tough, she was a considerable personality in her own right and, left to her own devices for much of the year, contrived to make a life for herself in London. In the immediate post-war years and before the Palestine War of 1948, the Arab embassies did much entertaining: it was as if the Saudi flag were always flying over the Dorchester, and Dora used often to be seen at such entertainments.

On his return to Arabia St John negotiated the sale of his

company Sharqieh and its local agencies to the City firm of Mitchell Cotts, who, largely because of his great influence at court and knowledge of local conditions, kept him on as a consultant. As usual St John was optimistic about the business prospects, but before money from oil started flowing in large quantities in the early 1950s, trade was slack. Mitchell Cotts had the Rootes agency and hoped to build up a market for British cars, but the Saudis preferred Chevrolets in glaring colours with lots of chrome. When Kim arrived on his brief visit in 1947 Jidda was not much different from the primitive place St John had found in the twenties. Fresh water piped from Mecca had only that year reached the town, and, fearing the water would not last, a great crowd of people carrying every conceivable sort of container had queued for the first week or two at the terminal tap in the square outside St John's Green Palace.

From Jidda, swathed in Arab headdress, Kim was taken up to Riyadh for an audience with the king. It was not a very successful occasion. St John was keen to show off his son, now an important British government official, and he was equally anxious that Kim should admire his hero Ibn Saud. But the king was tired and disgruntled and conversation faltered, and Kim could not hide at least from his father how unimpressed, even bored, he was by the Saudi court and its petty self-importance. On his way to a big job in Istanbul, the son's prestige seemed for the first time to have outstripped the father's. Kim found his father's precious Arabia alien, bleak, unbeautiful – and dry, and he did not mind saying so. Drinking, even in Jidda, was possible only behind the closed doors of private houses and in Riyadh unheard of. Before lunch one Sunday at the Jidda home of a British businessman, Kim asked for a cognac. An unopened bottle of Cyprus brandy was produced and in a short while he had very nearly emptied it. Even his father was startled.

The truth was that alcohol had become an essential bromide and Kim's consumption of it, always liberal, now vastly exceeded anything that could be considered normal in a man just thirty-five. This abandonment of himself to it betrayed the state of his nerves. Later in Istanbul at lunch in a colleague's house, he arrived drunk, drank the best part of a bottle of Bols gin, following this up with several glasses of red and white wines. He asked to be excused and went to the bathroom, returning a moment later smacking his lips. 'What's that stuff you've got in there?' he said. He had been drinking *eau de cologne*. And there were many other occasions. His staff were beginning to wonder how a man who behaved so extravagantly could be trusted with highly confidential information. But these queries were the expression of affectionate concern rather than suspicion: Kim was popular, approachable, thoughtful of the welfare of his colleagues, an easy-going man to work for.

Disguised rather thinly as a First Secretary, he ran his five-man intelligence office from the ground floor of Barrie's majestic Consulate General building, which the SIS still preferred to the embassy in Ankara. The SIS job in Turkey was both offensive and defensive – that is to say, it involved the running of agents against specific targets and liaising with the Turkish Security Inspectorate on counter-espionage matters. On the offensive side the main targets were the Soviet Union and her Balkan satellites. To penetrate these countries suitable agents had to be recruited, and much of this immediate post-war period was spent combing the *émigré* communities in Istanbul itself for talent. As boss of the outfit Kim had little direct contact with agents, a task left to his staff, but he made no secret of his contempt for the wretched right-wing refugees from Communism who were his potential recruits. His suspicion of these people and his offhand treatment of them – a ruthlessness greater than the job required – led at least one member of his staff to wonder where Kim's sympathies lay.

Operations planned against the Soviet bloc also involved extensive exploration of the border areas to see whether suitable agents could be found there and to pinpoint the best places to put them across. Two luckless young Georgians, furnished with weapons and gold, were sent over during Kim's tour of duty but, as might be expected, were never heard of again. Such preoccupations gave Kim a pretext to do a good deal of roaming about Central Anatolia in a jeep, often accompanied by his faithful secretary, a young woman who served him devotedly and admiringly (as his secretaries tended to do) right up to the end of his active career in 1951. His journeys into the wastes and mountains of the hinterland – bird-watching on Lake Van, he called them – were his best therapy, more effective than alcohol in releasing him from the pressures of his double life. He was a lively travelling companion with an amateur interest in botany, geology and wild life. He collected samples of rocks and plants and tried to identify them, almost self-consciously aping his father's explorations of the Arabian desert. In the same spirit Kim initiated on behalf of the War Planning Directorate of SIS a photographic survey of the Turkish–Soviet frontier which he dubbed 'Operation Spyglass', but which he never completed. These camping expeditions in the pre-war English tradition of the gentleman spy were of limited value to anyone but himself: by 1948 vast teams of Americans were already engaged in aerial surveys of the whole of Anatolia, planning airfields, road systems and military installations. A far more trying side of Kim's work in Turkey was the necessary liaison with the fiercely anti-Communist Turkish security services. The Turks were deeply suspicious of their age-old enemies, the Russians, whose embassy was kept under constant surveillance. People seen entering or leaving the building were photographed from an apartment block across the street. To profess any form of socialism in Turkey in those days was a crime ferreted out by an army of informers and punished by all the rigour of a police state. It was Kim's unattractive duty to entertain the officers who applied this policy.

So his first uneventful, reasonably recuperative, year in Turkey passed. Almost certainly his Russian masters, who had a healthy respect for Turkish counter-espionage, reduced contact to the minimum.

The cure was not complete, however. His colleagues in the office may have thought him no more than averagely unconventional, and London may have been well satisfied with his work. However, Patrick Reilly who had worked with and thought highly of him in 1942-3, met him again at this time and remembers 'a vague feeling of discomfort, an impression that this was not quite the man I had known, and some surprise that given our previous relations he was not more friendly'. To the most intimate observer of all, his wife, it was increasingly obvious that he had something on his mind. He appeared to find life in Istanbul irksome, leaving her alone with the nanny and the children for weeks on end. When he was at home there were bouts of depression which found relief in heavy solo drinking, very different from the convivial celebrations of wartime London. Knowing nothing of Kim's commitment to Moscow, she could not have comprehended, even had he tried to explain, the ambiguity of his political loyalties, and therefore had no insight into what was tormenting him. Politically her mind was conventional.

Aileen and her four little children had followed Kim out to Istanbul by sea, to find that they were not to live with other diplomats on the fashionable European side of the Bosphorus, but on their own at Vanikoy across the water on the Asiatic coast (a lonely spot evidently chosen to facilitate Kim's contacts with his Soviet case officer or cutout). A cobbled path led from the rough, tortuous road through trees and undergrowth down to the house, an old Turkish structure standing alone right on the shore and commanding a fine sweep of water: to the left the minarets of Aya Sophia stood on the distant skyline, and to the right, on a bend of the Bosphorus, was the massive pile of the Anadolu Hisari fortress. The Philbys' garden was luxuriant and overgrown, thick with untended apple and almond trees. In this wilderness the children played practically naked, splashing about in a paddling pond and inventing families in their Wendy house called 'Copper-Nob Villa' (later shipped to England where it stands in the garden near Oxford of one of Kim's former associates). A few hundred yards downstream was the boat station from which Kim caught the ferry over to Istanbul. Both he and Aileen were always ready to help the villagers by giving them lifts up from the ferry in their car. Anxious to be liked and yet not speaking a word of Turkish, Aileen would smile nervously at everyone. Again in contrast with life in Carlyle Square, they entertained very little.

Aileen was lonely. She had not lived abroad before and nothing in her background had prepared her to grapple with an unfamiliar environment stripped of all the friendly props of London life. A characteristic product of the English middle classes, her intuitive understanding of foreign countries was limited. The posting to Turkey had imposed fresh strains on her, seeing that she now had for the first time to play some public role in his life as a British intelligence officer. Men working at headquarters in London generally keep to office hours and leave their work behind them when they go home. But the moment an officer goes into the field, his wife must become involved in his work and a decision has to be taken about her. In extreme cases she may not even be made 'conscious', that is she may not be told the nature of her husband's activities. Aileen of course knew full well what Kim's job was, but whereas in London it had not affected her, she now had to shoulder some of his responsibilities, she had to act out his cover, she had to live a lie. An intelligence officer has to instruct his wife whom she may and may not invite to the house. He has to be able to tell her, for example, 'Tonight you must go alone to the National Day celebrations, as I have work to do.' Some women take enthusiastically to these cover roles; to others duplicity is anathema. Aileen belonged more to the second category than to the first, and with such a wife in Turkey Kim entered into a new area of risk. Indeed, the situation caused him to enter into a new relationship with her.

Aileen knew a lot, at once too much and not enough for her peace of mind. As well as the hateful cloak-and-dagger situations in which she knew him to be involved as SIS chief in Turkey, she may well have noted that there was something else in this strange country, something in Istanbul itself (to which Philby had flown at the time of the Volkov affair), which had badly unnerved him. But he would not share his anxieties with her. Left much alone and missing the friends, affection and fun of Chelsea, she supposed her husband to be having an affair. A visit by Dora to her beloved son that first year at Vanikoy did little to cheer up her daughter-in-law.

Another visitor depressed her still more. Early in 1948 Guy Burgess, a man she had always detested, arrived to stay with them. After being turned out of SOE early in the war, Burgess had been taken on as talks producer by the BBC where his gift for picking up useful people and impressing them served him well. He predicted a Labour victory after the war and had the opportunity of presenting some up-and-coming politicians to a radio public and so grooming them for stardom. One of his stars was John Strachey who became a very effective wartime broadcaster, perhaps second only to J. B. Priestley. Another was Hector McNeil, a Scotsman of modest origins who was perhaps dazzled by Burgess and his Cambridge cronies, clever boys out of the top drawer. In spite of McNeil's great qualities, his career was ultimately to founder on drink – a tragedy perhaps not unconnected with his disreputable protégé. When Labour came to power in 1945, McNeil was made a junior minister and appointed Guy his assistant private secretary. He tried to get the FO to establish Burgess in what was then Branch A of the service; they compromised by establishing him, but in Branch B (Executive). As late as autumn 1947 McNeil was continuing to press for his transfer to Branch A, a proposal which the FO countered by demanding that Burgess must first show a capacity for Branch A work. To test his abilities, he was moved to the Far Eastern Department, although remaining in Branch B.

'I've got sitting in my jeep outside one of the most disreputable members of the British Foreign Service.' This was how Kim announced Guy's arrival to some Turkish friends, and his lighthearted tone suggested that Burgess's reappearance had done much to raise his spirits. But was Guy really a welcome guest? From an intelligence point of view the visit seemed to contravene all the rules.

In *My Silent War* Kim claims it was on his introduction that Burgess was recruited in 1936 by the Russian secret service and that a year or so later Burgess carried Russian funds to him in Spain. If we are to believe it, this evidence suggests that at least at the start of their careers the two agents were 'inter-conscious', that is to say that they knew each other to be engaged in clandestine activities. It is a basic principle of intelligence procedure that two men in this situation be kept strictly apart lest they endanger each other. Perhaps in the 1930s, when Soviet espionage techniques were relatively unsophisticated and when Kim was of little account, a certain amount of hobnobbing would be allowed; but by the late 1940s such slackness was unthinkable. Kim was by now probably the Russians' most valued British spy. He had just completed a stretch as head of the anti-Soviet section of the SIS and was clearly rising in the service. His would be considered a most sensitive case, to be hedged around with the most stringent security precautions both in Moscow and in Turkey. His case officers and controllers would have jealously guarded him against outside threat. What place had the blundering Burgess in such a delicate web?

There is certainly nothing to suggest that after the Spanish civil war Burgess had been kept informed of Kim's continued career in the Russian service. If he had been 'conscious' early on, the presumption must be that thereafter he was given no more secrets. Indeed how much work he himself did in the Soviet cause is unclear, and doubt remains whether he did anything of significance. And yet he could not be dropped. He was a contact of the 1930s who knew too much and who could be silenced only by playing him along. This seems the only plausible explanation of Guy's visit to Istanbul and of Kim's ambivalent attitude towards him, then and later. He did not share Guy's homosexual tastes, nor his personal indiscipline, nor his flamboyant recklessness. His undergraduate admiration for Guy must have been wearing thin, and yet he sought his company and made much of him.

For Aileen the visit brought only a further sense of neglect, as Kim carried off his guest for long, solitary walks or whole days away together. What she could not abide was the suggestion that the two men had something unfathomable in common from which she was excluded. Guy, she felt strongly, was a bad influence. This unwholesome slob had turned up and, without so much as a by-your-leave, had kidnapped her husband, taking him away from her and bringing him home stupid with alcohol. One night at the Moda Yacht Club, a centre, fashionable as its name suggests, for the richer levels of Anglo-Turkish society, Kim and Guy dined with two sisters. Aileen stayed at home. The evening was prolonged with the men talking and drinking into the small hours. When the bill was settled it was discovered that they had drunk fifty-two brandies. Guy shocked the rather correct members of the Moda by turning up in an open-necked shirt and sandals (he borrowed shoes and a tie from a waiter to be allowed in), and by spending much of his time in Istanbul in a shamelessly disorderly fashion. One day at the Philbys' house he threw himself out of a window into the Bosphorus. He paid not the slightest consideration to anyone, least of all Aileen, as if aware that his ascendancy over Kim gave him *carte blanche*. However dimly she analysed it, it was this suggestion of emotional blackmail which she found distasteful.

As a child Aileen had reacted violently when she felt hard done by, and would inflict wounds on herself to attract pity and attention. This mysterious complaint, which had lain dormant during her life with Kim, now reappeared, triggered off perhaps by Burgess's visit and her sense of grievance. Burgess had departed and Kim was as usual away on a trip. In his absence Aileen had been advised not to drive by herself on the lonely roads behind the house, but disregarding this advice she took the car out one night and some time later arrived at the house of one of Kim's colleagues, shaken and covered in blood. Her head was badly cut. She claimed she had been assaulted. She had stopped, she said, to let another car pass on the narrow road, and someone had jumped on the running-board of her car and attacked her. The details of the accident were never fully established, but nearly thirty years later the fact that Aileen grazed her head in suspicious circumstances is still remembered at Vanikoy. Had she engineered the accident to bring Kim back to her?

She was placed in the care of a Dr Quinke at the German hospital, but her wound became infected and there was talk of 'a microbe in the blood'. Her condition worsened and a few weeks later she was flown out on a stretcher to a clinic in Switzerland. Kim, badly upset by the incident, went with her and stayed three weeks in Berne in the house of the SIS officer there, an old friend of his. It was with these friends, who liked her very much, that Aileen spent her months of convalescence. The choice of a Swiss clinic must be counted a curious one. Why was Aileen not flown back to England where the SIS have arrangements with discreet Harley Street specialists? For obvious reasons all intelligence services insist that in cases of psychiatric disorders only approved physicians are consulted. Moreover Switzerland was expensive. In 1949, with Britain deep in financial trouble, foreign exchange was hard to come by. Did Kim have a reason for keeping his wife out of England? Was he afraid that under treatment she might talk compromisingly to her doctors? Did he prefer a neutral Swiss to the informed ear of an SIS psychiatrist? In any event he would have taken advice from the Russians on where to send her. The SIS must have queried his choice of Switzerland, and his explanation may well have been a wish to confer with his friend and colleague in Berne.

Kim would not live again in the old Turkish house at Vanikoy. Before leaving for Switzerland he parked his four children and their nanny in the ground-floor flat of a large villa in Moda owned by their friends Zeki and Hazel Sporel, and it was there that Aileen rejoined them. But while she was away Kim sank into a sea of alcohol and depression not seeming to have the strength to pull himself out of it. There was an awkward scene at the Moda Yacht Club one night when he got so drunk that, to the shame of his friends, he had to be carried bodily to bed. Contrite, he vowed the next day not to touch a drop again, but such resolutions were short-lived.

Barely six weeks after Aileen's return from Switzerland in the winter of 1948, Kim was called to London on office business. One evening their hosts went out to dinner, leaving Aileen alone in the house. As is often the custom in Turkish houses, the Philbys' sitting-room was equipped with a charcoal stove placed under a table. To warm themselves on winter evenings people squat under the table wrapping themselves in a warm quilt. Mr and Mrs Sporel returned home about midnight and, thinking Aileen had gone to bed, retired as well. An hour later they heard screams. Rushing downstairs they threw open the door of the Philbys' sitting-room to see the room in flames and Aileen ablaze in a nylon nightgown. She had lain down under the quilt, stirred the embers in the stove and no doubt a piece of glowing charcoal had fallen on to the quilt. She was badly burned and was immediately taken off to hospital while servants carried furniture into the garden and brought the fire under control. Kim was summoned by cable. Although Aileen's wounds once again became septic, she refused at first to leave Kim, but was eventually persuaded to return to the clinic in Switzerland. Seeing that she had suffered two such traumatic accidents in Turkey, her doctors advised her not to return to live there. Some months later she came back only very briefly to help Kim pack up.

12 Beaten by the Intercepts

Wireless intelligence does not come in a steady continuous stream, but in fits and starts, deceptive, irregular, exasperating. It is made up of all sorts of disjointed fragments. Above all, it can be cut off when the enemy changes his codes with the suddenness and finality of a light fusing. Today, with the almost universal use of one-time pads and machine ciphers of hideous complexity, the code-breaker's task, unrewarding at the best of times, is truly thankless. Knowing the enemy's coded traffic to be unbreakable in principle, he must tirelessly monitor it, waiting for the split second of human frailty which alone can give him a clue to its secrets: the cryptographer's error is the cryptanalysts' only hope. It was just such an error, made by normally efficient Soviet cipher officers in the summer of 1945, which put the time-bomb under Kim's career. By some confusion of code-books, a low-grade cipher was used by the Soviet Consulate General in New York to transmit top-secret intelligence traffic to Moscow. This lapse lasted a very short time, but long enough to show Western security that a spy was delivering to Moscow secret documents from the British Embassy in Washington.

When the first messages to Russia were deciphered at Bletchley, the SIS was astounded to find that they were texts of personal telegrams from Winston Churchill to President Truman, transcribed with meticulous accuracy even down to the numbers on the cables. Fortunately for the SIS Moscow pressed for details: how had this precious material been secured? At this point in the exchanges the Russian telegrams became far more difficult to read. Whole sentences could not be cracked by the code-breakers, and in others only a word here or there could be read, leaving gaps to be filled in by guesswork. But there was one glimmer of light: from these fragments British security inferred that the Washington Embassy spy came to New York to see his Soviet contact twice a week. This was the only clue the spy-catchers had to go on. It was to be a crucial one. For the next six years British and American security men worked on the case – but with the Federal Bureau of Investigation in overall control since the leak had occurred in the United States.

Rudely awakened by a whole series of security shocks, the FBI in the late 1940s was increasingly turning its large resources to Communist spy-hunting. There had been the British atom spy Alan Nunn May (given away to the Canadians by a Russian cipher clerk, Igor Gouzenko, in September 1945), whose treachery had helped Russia build her A-bomb. Then in America itself there had been the case of the Harvard-trained State Department lawyer Alger Hiss, revealed to have a Communist past. Far worse was the discovery that a young woman in the Justice Department, Judith Coplon, had been passing to Moscow top-secret reports on Soviet espionage in America, allowing the Russians to watch the FBI watching their own agents. Coplon's arrest in 1949 put an end to this Russian privilege.

It was through Coplon that Moscow had been able to follow the Anglo-American investigation into the Washington Embassy leak uncovered in 1945 by Britain's code-breakers. But when she was removed from the scene, the Russians needed another inside informant and turned to Philby in the hope that he could help them although he was then still in Istanbul and a long way from the SIS counter-espionage files in London. This was the first hint Kim was given that somewhere in the world-wide apparatus of Russian espionage another slip had been made, another investigation was proceeding which on its way through the files might lead, however indirectly, to himself. It was a new anxiety on his hardly peaceful mind.

At this point providence took a hand. Headquarters cabled to offer him the job of chief SIS representative in the United States, with the special duty of liaison with both the FBI and the CIA – a job of the first importance which would among other things take him to the heart of the Embassy case under investigation. He came to London in August 1949 for a month's briefing on the whole complex range of Anglo–American intelligence relations – and learned what the Russians wanted to know. It confirmed his worst fears. The leak from the British Embassy, he was told, involved high-grade diplomatic communications and had taken place in 1944–5, details which were enough for him to be pretty sure in his own mind about who the spy was.

Donald Maclean had never been a close friend of Kim's but had attracted his attention as one of the stars of Cambridge Communism. Over the years they had had little to do with each other. Encouraged by Soviet intelligence to enter the British Foreign Service, Maclean had been posted to Paris in 1938 where he met and married a young American girl, Melinda Marling; but on the German invasion of France in 1940 he was transferred back to London where he spent the greater part of the war. In May 1944, three weeks before his thirty-first birthday, he was posted to the Washington Embassy. His years in America, 1944–8, were just the years when Russia, struggling to develop her own atomic capability, badly needed to know if and how the West intended to exploit its temporary military dominance. As acting head of Chancery and secretary of the Anglo-American Combined Policy Committee on Atomic Developments, Maclean was well placed to keep them informed, and it is on the secrets he passed to Moscow then that his reputation as a top Soviet agent rests. In the transition from wartime alliance to Cold War enmity he was no doubt able to keep Moscow abreast of exchanges between London and Washington on the all-preoccupying subject of what to do about Soviet Russia. Lewis L. Strauss, a member of America's Atomic Energy Commission from 1946 to 1950 and its chairman in 1953, reports in his book *Men and Decisions* that he withdrew from Donald Maclean a permanent pass to AEC headquarters after learning 'that this particular alien was a frequent visitor in the evenings after the usual working hours'.[1]

1. London, 1963, p. 256.

The pass was of a character that did not require Maclean to be accompanied in the building. Luckily for the Allies, the damage he could do was limited by the fact that many of the major issues affecting Anglo-American relations were dealt with by other departments, geographical or functional. However he was considered a high flyer of promise and, as in Kim's case, what distinction he achieved was at some cost to his peace of mind. He began to exhibit the tell-tale symptoms of overstrain – heavy drinking, irresponsibility to his wife and children, homosexual affairs – which were in Cairo in 1950 to lead him to total crack-up. When in August 1949 Kim first learned of the Washington Embassy leak, Maclean was already in Egypt and heading for collapse.

The threat to their security inherent in the Embassy leak brought out the interdependence of Philby, Burgess and Maclean as fellow agents in the Russian service. Their British careers had, from the Russian angle, led to a certain division of function. Maclean was the top-level atomic and political news-gatherer; Burgess, having lesser secrets to betray, was mainly useful as a courier; while Philby, the counter-espionage specialist, reported to the KGB on its Western rivals and was now well placed to play a defensive, protective role with regard to Maclean. This task was to be his major preoccupation for the whole of his Washington tour of duty from 1949 to 1951. Maclean was in danger and if he were caught and interrogated, who knew where the investigation might lead? The security of all three rested on Kim's shoulders, a responsibility which his nerves, already frayed by the tragedies of his domestic life in the aftermath of Volkov, were in poor condition to bear.

One of his briefs from the British was to work closely with the FBI in its pursuit of the mysterious Embassy spy; his parallel brief from the Russians was to tip them off in good time so that Maclean could make his getaway. At all costs his capture and interrogation had to be avoided, not only to protect himself and the others, but even more important to protect the fruits of his work. Information about an enemy is power only insofar as the enemy does not know you have it: if London and Washington were to learn exactly which of their secrets Maclean had passed to Moscow, the Russians' knowledge would be neutralized.

Before he left London to take up his post in America, Kim knew that within the next two years, depending on the progress of the investigation, he would have to act to save Maclean's skin – and possibly his own into the bargain. As if this was not enough weight on his mind, he had another anxiety. Both he and his Russian masters knew well that the next year or two might see the end of his active career. Moreover, in Washington he was bang on target. From now on there would be no time for rest, recuperation, the cosseting of a much-tried nervous system. He would have to deliver the goods. It would be strenuous work all the way.

Kim arrived in America at a moment of renewed intimacy in Anglo-American relations. As the Cold War blew colder there were moves on both sides of the Atlantic to revive the wartime alliance and this was naturally reflected in closer working co-operation between the SIS and the CIA: there is no better barometer of the international political climate than the state of relations between intelligence services. After the war the Americans had determined to build a powerful intelligence machine of their own, independent of all foreigners including the British, but the rise of the Soviet menace and the world-wide confrontation this led to caused them to appreciate once more the contribution allies could make.

The post-war years saw the American government driven inexorably along a path from optimism about the chances of peace with Russia, to President Truman's attempt to 'contain' international Communism by propping up friendly governments, and finally to vigorous counter-attack against a now acknowledged enemy. But the American public did not docilely follow these fundamental changes in its country's international posture. For most citizens it was an article of faith that 'the business of America was America', and that involvements abroad, if they had to occur to quell some troublesome foreigner, should be short, sharp and successful. They did not find attractive the idea of 'containment' because implicit in it was the notion that Communism was there to stay, could not easily and swiftly be defeated but at best could only be held in check. It seemed a life sentence to embroilment overseas.

However, 1949 brought still more violent shocks to deep-seated American attitudes. Far from being contained, international Communism, the great bogy of the period, seemed to be sweeping all before it in Europe, where Czechoslovakia had fallen a year earlier, and even more portentously in Asia where China, vast China, had been overrun by Mao's armies. The explosion of Russia's first atomic bomb in September 1949, wiping out America's nuclear lead, lent a touch of hysteria to an already deeply troubled nation. It was as if confident, generous America had been knocked off balance by these set-backs, and its judgement deranged, a corporate neurosis finding expression at home in the Communist-haunted nightmares of Senator Joseph McCarthy. A handful of spies there certainly was – Nunn May, Coplon, Fuchs and his associates – but the Federal Employee Loyalty Program, an FBI name check on four million government servants, testified to the depths of the national obsession with Communist plots. From one end of America to the other leftists were hunted out of public life by those who, in bitterness and confusion of mind, sought revenge at home for the reverses their country was suffering abroad. The rapid and disorderly growth of the intelligence agencies reflected these national fears.

In the mood of wholesale demobilization of September 1945, President Truman had disbanded General 'Wild Bill' Donovan's OSS, the American wartime cloak-and-dagger outfit that had equalled and even outdone its British counterparts in sabotage, black propaganda, counter-espionage and general skulduggery. Only four months later the obvious and urgent need to keep an eye on Communist developments had prompted the creation of the Central Intelligence Group which for twenty months formed a bridge between the defunct OSS and the CIA, established in 1947 by Act of Congress. But at the start, the CIA's targets were limited and its activities restricted to intelligence gathering on a narrow front. 'I don't care what the CIA does,' General George Marshall is reported to have said, 'All I want from them is twenty-four hours' notice of a Soviet attack.' Others made rather wider demands on it which it sometimes failed to meet: Washington got no advance warning of the revolution in Colombia in 1948, or more traumatically, of the Soviet A-bomb blast of 1949. When in June 1950 the agency failed to foresee both the Communist invasion of South Korea and Peking's massive intervention in the war, it became evident that American intelligence needed a thorough overhaul. An overriding object of this exercise was to weld the various proliferating agencies, civilian and military, into an integrated 'intelligence community' able to provide truly national intelligence estimates. Thus 1950 saw the CIA, under the hard hand of its new director, General Walter Bedell Smith, and his deputy, Allen Dulles, shed the last vestiges of its wartime amateurism. The 'misfits, the Martini set and the OSS leftovers'[1] were booted out. Even the best of them were thought of as having too many suspicious foreign contacts, as having gained their experience and established their loyalties in an era that was now over. And so began the CIA's evolution into the powerful professional bureaucracy it has since become. Kim had a ringside view of these convulsions.

Summoning up his reserves of discipline and self-respect, he had arrived in Washington early in September 1949. He was sustained by a good deal of private satisfaction. In spite of everything he had gone through, in spite of the narrow squeaks and Aileen's mysterious collapse which might yet damage his prospects, he had pulled off a job at the very heart of the enemy's intelligence apparatus. His posting to Washington was a counter-espionage success such as the textbooks prescribe but life rarely provides. A *coup* like this does great things for one's morale. From every point of view he could afford a little self-congratulation. The British had given him one of the top dozen jobs in the SIS: as chief British intelligence representative in the American capital, liaising with and representing British interests to the burgeoning agencies of the American intelligence community, he was a key man. He had ten or a dozen people working under him and, of all the Embassy, his

1. Sanche de Gramont, *The Secret War* (New York), p. 131.

office had the fastest and most secure communications with London. All most immediate, top-secret traffic passed through the hands of his cipher clerks.

He was preceded to Washington by a considerable reputation. Some of the senior Americans with whom he was to work had passed through London during the war and knew him as a rising star of British counter-espionage; victor in the SIS 'palace revolution'; a specialist in anti-Soviet operations, the subject now occupying American minds almost to the exclusion of any other. Some had even served their apprenticeship with him. His heavy drinking was no secret but at work he impressed by the cutting edge of his mind, his bureaucratic orderliness, his precision, perhaps even by the felicity of his writing. He had qualities of discretion (to which his crippling stutter contributed), charm and skill which made him something of a legend. The fact that after his father's wartime internment under the 18b regulations, Kim had been admitted to the British Service and had worked devotedly there seemed a measure of the political sophistication both of the British and of himself. Altogether he was an object of very considerable interest to his American colleagues who regarded him with admiration – but also wariness, as he was thought to be an unusually wily and resourceful character. It should be stressed that the Americans knew nothing of the many ordeals, professional and private, which he had endured in the years 1945–9 and which had shaken the nerve behind the laconic front. For them those four years did not exist and they based their judgements on the skilful wartime operator. Moreover, they assumed that he had been sent to America, the biggest foreign job available, as the personal representative of 'C', Sir Stewart Menzies, and this seemed both flattering to themselves and an indication that Kim – still only thirty-seven – was a bright boy, someone to watch, marked out for prominence.

In spite of the rapid post-war build-up of American intelligence, when Kim reached Washington Britain's world-wide communications were still superior – facilities which had been carefully salvaged from the wholesale disposal of overseas assets during the war. The United States did not then have its present superb global networks. As speed of communication is paramount in intelligence work, Kim had a small advantage over his American opposite numbers. At their regular meetings he used to enjoy producing an operational report from a British source which the Americans could not match: their despatch had not yet arrived. A CIA man recalls Kim calling on him one day. 'What do you make of this development?' he asked, with a tiny smile on his lips, laying a typewritten field report on the American's desk. The American scanned it hungrily, knowing that nothing comparable had come in from his organization. Savouring his embarrassment Kim murmured: 'Of course, we'd be delighted to handle your communications for you ...'

This sort of irony pin-pointed the less than unquestioning trust that existed between SIS and CIA in spite of the friendliness of personal relations. Kim found, for example, that James Angleton, who had early shown scepticism about British virtues, was now a leading figure in the CIA's intelligence gathering division, the Office of Strategic Operations (OSO) headed by Colonel Robert Schow. Bedell Smith himself, whose driving personality and sharpness of mind Kim admired, made mistrust a working principle. 'When you see a visiting Britisher being overwhelmed with hospitality in Washington,' he remarked, 'it does not necessarily mean that we trust him; hospitality is an excellent device to avoid serious discussion.'[1] So, for this and other reasons, Kim had to be a diplomat. If his appointment flattered the CIA, it seemed a slight to J. Edgar Hoover's FBI, robbed by the rise of the CIA of its investigative monopoly, and ousted altogether from counter-espionage work in such former FBI preserves as Central and South America. Now Kim's brief was to promote more aggressive Anglo-American intelligence operations – which meant upgrading SIS – CIA relations.

The first of these operations was, as it happened, a largescale fiasco. It was an extraordinary plan, unimaginable in a

1. Quoted in Strong, op. cit., p. 235.

later climate of coexistence, to take Albania away from Joseph Stalin. In spirit this venture was a hangover from the war, involving the smuggling into Albania of bands of armed *émigrés* who were to spread over the country, subvert the population and overthrow the Hoxha régime. The Communist takeover of Czechoslovakia in 1948 had persuaded Washington of the need for a violent riposte in kind, and when Tito was kicked out of the Cominform the same year, cutting Albania off from the rest of the Soviet bloc, an opportunity too good to be missed seemed to present itself. The fact that the Albanians were also meddling in the Greek civil war, then drawing to its close, was only a further reason for teaching them a lesson.

But the CIA was still only an intelligence gathering operation and had no apparatus for delivering such paramilitary lessons. Frank G. Wisner, an ex-OSS man, was brought in from the State Department hastily to set on foot a suitable organization which he christened with the innocent-sounding name of Office of Policy Co-ordination (OPC). It soon rivalled the OSO in size and independent status. Remote control of the Albanian escapade was exercised from Washington by the OPC – and Kim. In London Sir Stewart Menzies was far from enthusiastic but he agreed to British participation as a way of keeping happy the ex-SOE 'stinks and bangs people' who still enjoyed some influence in the clubland fringes of intelligence.

Needless to say, Kim's command of the operation doomed it to failure: as he later boasted in an interview in *Izvestia* (19 December 1967), 'little did the CIA suppose that a staff officer of Soviet intelligence was privy to their plans'. But even without his treachery the enterprise's chances of success were slim. For one thing the Albanian *émigrés* who were to do the fighting were a motley and colourful collection of widely differing political allegiance, spread over half-a-dozen Western centres from New York to Belgrade, with little in common except their anti-Communism and their dream of entering Tirana in triumph. For another, although the Americans were free with funds, very few of them had more than a vague acquaintance with the exotic complexities of Balkan politics. An ex-officer

of OPC, who shared command of the operation with Kim, has
written:

I was summoned to a conference in Washington. On entering the
room I remarked an intricate organisational chart on the wall. One
of my colleagues – I didn't know he was even interested in the
operation – rose and then started his discourse by pointing to the
chart and saying, 'I have now worked this all out, and, as you will
see, you need 457 bodies for this operation.' He then spoke for
forty minutes, without once even mentioning the country with
which we were concerned. I confined myself to remarking that I
didn't think we could find 457 'bodies' and that I would happily
settle for six brains.

By way of contrast, I went to London a week later and observed
the British approach to the same problem. After sitting around a
table in desultory fashion for an hour or two, one Englishman
finally said, 'I say, why don't we get old Henry up here? He knows
about this.' A day or two later old Henry showed up from down in
Sussex, and when the problem was put to him, finally agreed to
undertake the task, although, as he said, 'This will wreak havoc
with the garden, you know. Just getting it into trim.'[1]

'Old Henry' had fought with the Albanian Partisans in the
war, but the cards were stacked against him. Quite apart from
the major sponsors, Britain and America, other powers –
Greece, Yugoslavia, Italy – had their favourite Albanian exiles
whom they wanted to see in the leadership of the enterprise.
There were great difficulties in recruiting and training suitable
men and in shipping them to Albania by night from their
secret base in Malta. It was open season for counter-espionage
officers of all nations – and even for the press, so poorly was
the secret of the attempted invasion kept. As the guerrillas
landed, Hoxha's men, alerted by all this publicity and put on
target by Kim's more precise information, were able to mop
them up with ease. There was considerable loss of life. Those
who were not killed on the beaches were later brought to trial
in small batches and executed.

1. Christopher Felix, op. cit., pp. 55, 56.

Kim had been in America a bare couple of weeks when the explosion of Russia's first atomic device in September 1949 threw the whole intelligence apparatus of the Western world into a fever. For three or four days and nights Kim and Peter Dwyer, his predecessor who had not yet left his post, hardly slept as they struggled with the vast volume of secret traffic which passed between Washington and London.

Although no one had expected a Russian explosion so soon, scientists were already standing by to evaluate any fission products picked up by American aircraft in their ceaseless monitoring of the Soviet Union's borders. In the team was Dr Wilfrid Mann, an SIS expert on radioactivity whose brief was to make sure that London was fully and speedily informed of anything that might happen. When the airfilters provided incontrovertible evidence of Soviet fallout, Mann sent the news to the Prime Minister, Mr Attlee, over Kim's SIS communications network.

The shock was very great on both sides of the Atlantic. The Americans set up a 'war room' to sift intelligence on the bomb, to which two British representatives, William Penney (now Lord Penney) and Lord Tedder, were summoned. For nine anxious days the two governments debated whether to make the news public as they explored the scientific and strategic repercussions of Russia's leap to atomic parity. Finally, on 22 September, America, Britain and Canada simultaneously told the world of the Soviet explosion. As Philby was no doubt keeping Moscow in touch, the Russians had an intriguing opportunity to watch the West's step-by-step assessment of their new power. It should be added, however, that Kim could tell the Russians only the highlights of the top-level Anglo-American debate because his cipher clerks handled only the cabled traffic. Technical documents, both scientific and military, went by bag and he would not have had access to them. The damage he could do was therefore to some extent limited.

Hardly had the shock waves of the bomb itself subsided than the President and his closest advisers were racked by the hideous dilemma of whether or not to trump the Russian ace by pressing ahead with the construction of the 'superbomb' –

the hydrogen bomb. For Truman the decision to make the H-bomb was an even more difficult one than that of using the first A-bomb on an inhabited city without warning. In the case of Hiroshima, he was bolstered with positive advice from his senior scientists: opposing views did not get through to him. But in the hectic H-bomb debate of the winter 1949–50, both sides of the argument were put before him, and his only comfort was the hope that this terrible weapon would prove impossible to produce. In the end, when he decided in favour of the bomb in January 1950, the simple argument which over-rode all other considerations, strategic, scientific or moral, was that if the Russians had built an A-bomb, they could probably one day build an H-bomb. Anything they did, the Americans had to do as well.

What could Kim have learned of all this? Even though Britain was a privileged ally, she had had since the 1946 Mac-Mahon Act no ready access to American military secrets of this importance. As recently as July 1949 Truman had pro-posed reviving the wartime sharing of atomic information with the British, but opposition in the Senate had killed the scheme on the grounds that British security was deficient. Since British scientists had signally contributed to the invention of the A-bomb, frustration in London was very great and held in check only by the hope that the Americans would be persuaded to change their minds. However, even if vital technical details were withheld, London learned a good deal of the arguments in the H-bomb debate, and Kim no doubt saw to it that Russia's knowledge did not lag far behind.

It is arguable that not for many years would a British official again be in a position to learn as much as he did about Ameri-can military secrets. From then on the climate for the exchange of information tended to become harsher rather than laxer, and when Burgess and Maclean disappeared in 1951 and Philby fell under suspicion, the Americans clammed up almost totally. The Russian A-bomb had another, less expected, effect on Anglo-American intelligence relations. In the immediate post-war years the chief achievement of the SIS was to help British leaders keep their heads about the Russians when the Ameri-

cans were losing theirs. In the late 1940s, at the time of the
Berlin and Czechoslovak crises, for example, the Americans
were ill-informed about Soviet strength in Europe and were
therefore liable to make dangerous political judgements. Britain
in contrast had successfully penetrated Eastern Europe and
had first-class intelligence on the deployment of Russian
forces. British ability to produce a detailed order of battle kept
her American allies from doing anything daft. But the explosion of the Russians' first atomic weapon in 1949 immediately
downgraded such ground knowledge of troop movements.
What now mattered were global strategic estimates – estimates
which the Americans were better equipped to produce themselves. Thereafter there was to be no question as to who was
the junior partner.

Keeping abreast of America's emergence as a super-power
was a full-time occupation: the sheer reporting job was
colossal. Kim's days were crowded with meetings, briefings,
dictating reports, sifting the mass of material thrown up by one
international crisis after another, channelling a flood of top-
secret traffic to his overworked cipher clerks for transmission
to London. There were conferences with OPC to plot the
Albanian operation, sessions with James Angleton and his
colleagues at OSO to co-ordinate Anglo-American penetration
of European Communist movements, long painstaking hours
with the FBI. As the American intelligence bureaucracy grew
daily bigger, more powerful and more menacing, so the days
of British parity, let alone tutelage, began to seem very distant
indeed. Kim's prestige as chief British representative inevitably
declined with this shift in the balance of power during his years
in Washington. Battling for access to American secrets – on
Britain's behalf as much as on Russia's – he suffered from a
further handicap. Britain's once flawless reputation for security
which had already taken a sharp knock in 1946 with Alan
Nunn May's arrest was now again suspect – and again in the
all-important field of atomic weaponry. America was in a mood
to blame all her reverses on traitors in her midst, but there
were some real grounds for grievance behind the hysteria. The
two cases then under most pressing FBI investigation both

seemed to point to a weak British link in the chain. There was first the still baffling leak from the British Embassy in Washington and, even more alarming, further evidence uncovered by the FBI in the summer of 1949 that yet another Russian spy had been at work in a wartime American atomic establishment. The suggestion was that, as in the case of Nunn May, the culprit was a British rather than an American scientist. Little wonder then that when Klaus Fuchs was arrested in January 1950, only four months after the Soviet A-bomb blast, the Americans attributed the Russian success to his treachery, and from then on chose to play their atomic cards very close to their chest.

Fuchs was a Russian spy whom Philby could not save. The case was too far advanced by the time he reached the scene and he could do nothing but stand by helplessly in Washington while his colleague, Peter Dwyer, relentlessly drove the case to its conclusion. Like Burgess, Maclean, Nunn May and Philby himself, the German-born Klaus Fuchs was an anti-fascist of the 1930s who had fled from Hitler in 1933, only to be interned without much ceremony in England in May 1940 as an enemy alien. On his release he joined a British wartime research team on the atom bomb, moving in due course first to New York and then to Los Alamos, New Mexico. It was when he had been safely back at Harwell for three years that the FBI's fresh evidence brought him and other America-based wartime British scientists under suspicion.

At this point in the investigation someone remembered Britain's interception five years earlier of secret intelligence traffic between New York and Moscow. Once again it was to make a decisive contribution. Just enough of the coded exchanges had been cracked for the British to learn the seemingly trivial fact that a Russian spy had a sister at an American university. Only when the search narrowed to Los Alamos, and to the small group of scientists who could have told the Russians about the bomb, was it recalled that one of them, Fuchs, had had a sister called Kristel studying in the States.

What later emerged was that Fuchs had carried his secrets to a courier, Harry Gold, who in turn had carried them to Yakovlev, a Soviet intelligence officer working under the cover of the Soviet Consulate General in New York. Fuchs gave Gold details of the American plutonium bomb – its size (a vital point), what it contained, how it was constructed, and how it was detonated by means of an implosion lens. Once Fuchs had been arrested the trail led to Gold, and then to an American traitor at Los Alamos, David Greenglass (who had passed to the Russians an actual drawing of the implosion lens) and finally to the Rosenbergs. This Soviet spy network had helped to rob America of her nuclear monopoly. Watching its step-by-step dismantling under his very nose put tremendous strain on Kim's nerve. How long would it be before his own clandestine contacts were uncovered?

As in Turkey the insecurity of his position took its toll on Kim's life with his family. All things considered the household had pulled itself together pretty well after the disastrous Turkish episode and, at least for the first few months in Washington, had presented a viable front. This senior official, his very English wife, his large family and his secretary lived in bohemian disorder – a way of life less anomalous then, only four years after the war, than it might appear to official Washington today. Their ramshackle, spacious, two-storeyed house at 4100 Nebraska Avenue seemed with its classical portico quite elegant from the front, but at the back the untidy garden fell away steeply into woods and rough ground. Although it stood only a few yards off a busy avenue, it gave an appearance of isolation and of darkness and gloom in its inner recesses. The children slept upstairs and it was not unusual for one or another of them to stray downstairs stark naked in the middle of a party.

There were a lot of parties. At the start, at slightly besotted, seemingly light-hearted evenings, Kim would bang out popular tunes on the piano. Aileen, still very thin and fragile, appealed to Americans because of her sense of humour and lack of stuffiness. She drank, too, although less obsessively than Kim. As an American friend of the time recalls, 'The furnishings were sparse: Kim exhibited a noteworthy disregard for the décor of his life. Luxury *chez* Philby was a full martini pitcher and several bottles of whisky; it mattered not a whit who served them or from what one drank.'[1] But as 1950 wore on visible cracks began to appear in this tolerable façade. When Kim made a duty trip to London that year, acquaintances and former colleagues who had not seen him for two or three years were shocked by the deterioration in his appearance. One of them recalls: 'The evidence of heavy drinking on his face was clear. I had an overpowering feeling that he was going to pieces.' Visitors in Washington also began to remark on the unusually heavy drinking, and the birth of a fifth child, Harry, who suffered from convulsions, seemed to inflict on Aileen a burden she could hardly carry. One member or another of this complicated household seemed always to be ill.

Then, for the second time in three years, Guy Burgess imposed his anarchic presence on the family and precipitated tragedy. In August 1950 poor Aileen wrote a despairing letter to the Sporels in Istanbul, the friends who had taken them in: 'Who do you think has arrived? Guy Burgess. I know him only too well. He will never leave our house.' The Foreign Office had appointed Burgess to the Washington Embassy as a Second Secretary, apparently on the grounds that his oddities would be less conspicuous in a large mission. He had spent the previous three years in London, at first in the office of the Minister of State, Hector McNeil, latterly in the Far Eastern Department. On a holiday in Tangier he had been heard talking with wild indiscretion in a bar by an alert member of the local SIS station. Astonishingly, as it may now seem, his transfer to Washington (of course without transfer to Branch A) was considered to be a punishment for this misdemeanour. Fearing they would suffer the worst of the punishment, members of the embassy staff who knew something of Burgess resisted his appointment, but to no avail, and after his name had been buckpassed round the offices for a time, he was eventually detailed to Middle East affairs, a subject of which he knew nothing. Before leaving London Burgess went up to Cambridge to dine with his old tutor, F. A. Simpson, but it was not a happy occasion: Burgess was sick all over the carpet, and he had with

1. James McCargar, a personal communication to the authors.

him a 'very common fellow'. In Washington he appears to have done little more than clip press cuttings, but his lowly position was offset by his prestigious contacts. When Anthony Eden came to Washington, Burgess took him sightseeing, and later made much play of a bottle of Kentucky Gentleman bourbon which Eden had given him.

Burgess took it for granted that the Philbys would put him up, at least at the start, and, in spite of Aileen's opposition, Kim complied. Was this the fatal slip which was to bring Kim under immediate suspicion when Burgess fled with Maclean? In his book Philby admits having debated the point with himself for years, but there were cogent reasons for his actions at the time. He felt safer having Burgess close at hand where he could exert some control over him, or at any rate keep a wary eye on his extravagances, rather than have him roaming wildly and at will round Washington.

Burgess was an archetypal security risk, garrulous, drunken, homosexual. As in London, so in Washington he chased boys relentlessly and publicly (although he often escaped notice as the Americans were bad at spotting British homosexuals); however J. Edgar Hoover once complained to Colonel Vivian that Burgess avoided arrest by using Embassy cars in his lecherous pursuit. He made no pretence to like most of the Americans he met, but took pleasure in parading his utter contempt for the whole pyramid of values, attitudes and courtesies of the American way of life. He had a natural superciliousness, a shop-worn hangover of his Cambridge élitism, which Americans found extremely offensive. But however indiscreet, Burgess had managed for years to keep secret his Russian allegiance: politically his slate was clean; perhaps his lack of social caution was a compensation for this restraint. In this domain he pushed his luck to the limit. He survived because behind the squalid, food-stained front there were still flashes of the old brilliance and wit and an apparent commitment to serious issues which won respect. Arriving in Washington at the height of the nuclear debate, he affected a deep interest in atomic warfare to the point of being obsessed by mushroom clouds (a frequent motif of his doodles). He really thought he was working for peace.

Within a very short time the tone of the Philby household was set by Guy, or at least subtly altered. The thin skin of respectability began to dissolve laying bare the tell-tale deviancy. He brought to the surface a hatred of America until then concealed. Aileen started running down everything to do with the country, but from a basis of prejudice and ignorance. To visitors she seemed no longer to connect. Burgess's influence over Kim was more radical. It was as if he had been able to regain something of the ascendancy that at Cambridge the dazzling Apostle exerted over the timid Westminster schoolboy. Kim insisted on taking Burgess everywhere and making much of their friendship, in the hopeless endeavour of persuading the Americans to like Guy as much as he seemed to. He was attempting to control Burgess but instead was swept along in his dangerous wake.

The association damaged Kim's position with his professional American counterparts. One evening the Philbys gave a party at which a senior FBI man was guest of honour – one of J. E.'s boys, as Kim would say. The drawing-room on Nebraska Avenue was thick with American intelligence and security men and their ladies. The wife of the guest of honour was as formidable as her husband, with a face distinguished by an unusually long jaw. Halfway through the evening Burgess, in duffle-coat and tousled hair, obviously intoxicated, made a noisy entrance.

Approaching the lady in question with raised arms, he exclaimed, 'How extraordinary to see the face I've been doodling all my life!'

'Oh do draw me,' she simpered. Burgess had a small reputation as an artist.

He did. A few deft strokes produced a savage caricature. Deeply insulted, the lady demanded to be taken home. A mass exit followed of the FBI contingent. Aileen was distraught at the collapse of her party, but those who remained spent the rest of the night tossing back half-tumblers of whisky. Kim, tieless and jacketless, displaying a pair of scarlet braces, fell in tears on the settee. Next morning one of the guests who had been too drunk to drive himself home the night before came to collect his car. Hearing voices upstairs he went up to find Kim and Guy in bed together drinking champagne. They had already been down to the Embassy but not being able to work had come back.[1]

Inevitably there was gossip, and Kim's relations with his colleagues, very good at the start of his tour, now became rather unhappy. He seemed less sure of himself. His standing was falling. Some of the men whose traffic went through his communications network began to wonder how such confidential material could be entrusted to such a drunk. It was as if Burgess, slovenly, down-at-heel, a social misfit, lurching around Washington in a huge Lincoln in frequent contravention of the traffic laws, were dragging him down to his own erratic level. Colonel Vivian, then SIS Security Inspector, visited America and told Kim he thought it very unsuitable for Burgess to live with him. 'Kim replied that Burgess was a great nuisance to him, and that he had told him to get out. In fact he said that Burgess's mother had come to Washington to find her son a flat. It was a very plausible story.'[2]

It has been argued that Kim's Washington appointment was to put the seal on his upward climb to the very summit of the SIS, that, had it not been for the Burgess and Maclean affair, Kim would one day have been Chief, that he was being groomed for leadership. The truth is that on arrival in Washington he was several rungs from the top, possibly one of a dozen men who might eventually be competing for the directorship, but that even before Burgess and Maclean fled his behaviour had robbed him of such prospects. Adverse reports on him had reached London barring him from further promotion, at least for the time being. What escaped notice then was that this wild behaviour was not merely the result of Burgess's influence, but was a symptom, as to a milder extent in Turkey, of

1. Dr Wilfrid Mann, a personal communication to the authors.
2. The late Col. Valentine Vivian, a personal communication to the authors.

fear. The case of the 1945 Embassy leak which Kim was straining every nerve to follow was moving to its denouement.

Maclean, after his crack-up in Cairo in May 1950, had been recalled to London for convalescence and, on being passed medically fit, had, in the humane British manner, been appointed head of the FO's American Department in October. But the net was closing in. The file on the 1944–5 Embassy spy – code-named Homer as the intercepts had shown – had been gradually growing, revealing the high quality of the intelligence passed to Moscow, and it would surely be only a matter of time before Homer was identified as a senior diplomat and the finger pointed at Maclean. The Russians were determined to bring him to safety, but not before they got their pound of flesh. He was too well placed an operator at that vital moment in American–Soviet relations to be retired prematurely. In order to keep him operational the Russians would long have hidden his peril from him, although towards the end they may have warned him to be extra-careful, thus adding to the nervous strain he was already suffering. He may not have known that Kim was working for him in Washington – or even that Kim was in Soviet employ at all.

In readiness for the inevitable moment of Maclean's being identified an escape plan was prepared, meticulously worked out by Kim and his Russian contact at lonely meetings outside Washington. In it Burgess was to play a key role. Kim was ordered to make Guy 'conscious' and to instruct him in what he must do. Plans for Kim's own escape were also drawn up: if Burgess bungled his task the trail would by association immediately lead to Kim and he might have to get out in a hurry.

However, things were not yet so desperate. There was at that time no properly organized system of comprehensive and thorough reporting on members of the Foreign Service. It took the Burgess and Maclean affair to make the service adopt one. Kim's two-year tour of duty was to run out in the early autumn of 1951, and he had calculated with his Russian friends that Maclean's escape should therefore be engineered by mid-1951 while he himself could still exercise some control over the case. So early in the year, with the escape plans made, Kim set about constructing himself a shelter against the storm to come. The best way to escape guilt by association was surely to help crack the case, to contribute a key document to the file which would stand there on the record in his defence. Two Russian sources – the GRU agent,[1] Water Krivitsky, in 1937 and Konstantin Volkov, the luckless defector in Turkey in 1946 – had both spoken of Russian spies in British government service. Krivitsky had even specified the recruitment by Soviet intelligence of an expensively educated young man of good family, won to the cause by the anti-fascist struggle of the early 1930s. In a memo to Headquarters Kim suggested that the bulky file on Homer should be matched with this evidence and a search begun for this sort of gentleman spy. Had anyone meeting Krivitsky's specifications served in Washington at the time of the 1944–5 security leak? In fact, unknown to Kim, the Foreign Office had recognized the importance of Krivitsky's evidence as early as 1949, and this line of approach had thrown up a long list of suspects including not only Donald Maclean but such later diplomats of distinction as Roger Makins, Paul Gore-Booth and Michael Wright. What was lacking was evidence to pinpoint one of them.

His contribution made, Kim set Maclean's escape plan in motion. The game dictated that Maclean, perhaps already under MI5 surveillance, should at no time break his cover by making contact with a Russian agent, and so communication would have to be made with him some other way. The unpredictable Burgess was this other way. He was to be the courier. Was this his moment of fulfilment, the summit of his service to the Soviet Union? Burgess was not as insane a choice for this delicate mission as might appear: the problem being to furnish this courier with a self-sustaining reason for the journey to London, his very unfitness for a Foreign Office career and his outrageous personal conduct were mobilized for the job. Clearly he had worn official patience so thin that it needed only one more little scandal to snap it. With

1. *Glavnoye Razvedovatelnoye Upravleniye* (Chief Intelligence Directorate), the Soviet military intelligence service.

considerable skill and daring Burgess, in his Lincoln, contrived to get himself booked for speeding three times in one day. He was recalled to London.

His task, carefully drilled into him by Philby, was to check the escape plan with the Russians in London, and then pay an official call on Maclean in the Foreign Office – there would be nothing remarkable in a man just back from a US posting calling on the head of the American Department, already his acquaintance. He was to pass across Maclean's desk a slip of paper with the time and place of a future rendezvous. At their second meeting, this time a more private one, Burgess was to outline to Maclean the mechanism of his flight. Burgess was then to fade out of the picture and sink back into the not disagreeable pleasures which London could offer.

What Philby and Burgess may not have known was that a tiny, insignificant detail in the London file on the Embassy leak was to focus attention on Maclean far sooner than either of them had calculated. The 1945 intercepts, fragmentary as they were, had yielded the information that the Embassy source delivered his secrets to the Soviet Consulate General in New York *twice a week*. As it happened, Donald Maclean and his wife, Melinda, led separate lives when they went to America in 1944 – he in Washington and she in a New York flat with her mother. Twice a week he used to visit her there. It was the perfect alibi for his clandestine work. This was the giveaway on which a clever mind in London stumbled.

The enemy was closing in on Maclean and still Burgess, unaware of the desperate need for haste, had not paid the vital first call. He was dallying with a lover, and it was Kim again, gnawing his nails to the quick in America, who had to remind him of his mission. Characteristically Burgess had left his car in the Embassy car park. Seizing on this pretext Kim wrote that if he did not act at once it would be too late – the Lincoln would go to the scrap-heap. Burgess carried out his mission in the very nick of time. On the very morning of the escape, Friday, 25 May 1951, Herbert Morrison, Secretary of State for Foreign Affairs, gave MI5 the go-ahead to call Maclean in for interrogation. But Burgess was unpredictable to the last.

From fear, from bravado, from irreverent indiscipline, he went too. As a courier he had succeeded, but as a cut-out man he was a disaster. Philby, his host and friend, was now deep in trouble.

News of Burgess and Maclean's flight reached the Embassy in Washington in an overnight, Most Immediate, cable to the MI5 representative, Geoffrey Patterson. But as Patterson's secretary was on leave, Kim's secretary was woken at three a.m. to help decode the message. Out of affection for him she let him sleep undisturbed until morning. In fact he already knew from Patterson of the cable's arrival but had decided it would be prudent to show no great interest in its contents. Next morning, reaching the Embassy at his usual hour, he called in to see Patterson, ready to pretend dismay at the news of Maclean's disappearance. But when he learned that Burgess too had fled, leaving him horribly exposed, his horror was unfeigned.

13 The Recidivist

Guilt unproven but suspicion remaining.

— MI5 ON KIM PHILBY, 1952

Burgess's indiscipline in fleeing with Maclean left Kim's life in ruins. Almost at one stroke it destroyed his overt career with British intelligence, his covert career with Soviet intelligence and his marriage with Aileen, relegating him for the next five years to a shabby limbo of semi-employment and doubtful reputation. But he survived. He was still relatively young, only thirty-nine when the blow fell, and he had qualities of intellectual and moral self-reliance, a dogged patience in adversity, an indifference to the comforts of life, which saw him through. Above all, there never was enough evidence to convict him of espionage and complete his destruction – and he knew it.

The termination of his overt and covert careers was almost a matter of routine. From the moment he was compromised he was useless to the Russians. The best service they could render him was to sever all contact, immediately and totally, and leave him absolutely alone. He had already had a taste of the loneliness of the spy when rejected by his masters. But this time he had to face the prospect that the rejection could be for life, that the Centre might never again make contact with the leper he had become. On the very day London cabled the news of Burgess and Maclean's disappearance, Kim used his lunch hour to bury his spy camera and tripod in a wood outside Washington, thus formally putting an end to his work for Russia.

As for Kim's liaison work with the FBI and the CIA, this was wound up almost as speedily. The telegram from London had instructed Geoffrey Patterson, the MI5 man at the Embassy, to pass on the bad news to the FBI, and Kim accompanied Patterson on this shaming mission to FBI headquarters that same morning. Over the next few days there were further meetings on the case with the FBI, with Hoover himself, and with senior officers of the CIA. But for the Americans too Philby was now unclean, and even before he was recalled to London a week later, all working contact with him had been ended by US government order.

After the atom spies Nunn May and Fuchs, the flight of Burgess and Maclean was the third body-blow American security had suffered on account of the British. Where their privileged allies across the Atlantic were concerned, tempers were understandably frayed. The Americans felt that their whole atomic programme had been betrayed – largely by foreigners – and God only knew what further damage the 'missing diplomats' would now do them. Burgess had been intensely disliked in Washington and Kim's association with him was now recalled and resented. The fact that Kim's personal standing with the American agencies had been falling over the previous few months did not help. In the FBI he had an influential enemy in the man whose wife Burgess had insulted at the party, and still more dangerously James Angleton of the CIA was gunning for him. Angleton's doubts about British security, formed in the last phase of the war over the *Rote Kapelle* case, now hardened into a suspicion focusing on Philby. In the absence of evidence, it was no more than a strong hunch, but given America's then current preoccupation with Communist treachery, a hunch was enough.

All this resulted in Washington's taking a very stern line with London: General Walter Bedell Smith, the Director who had whipped the CIA into effectiveness, was not prepared to give the British the benefit of the doubt where vital American interests were at stake. He wrote a tough, angry letter to Sir Stewart Menzies, making it clear that Philby had to leave America. No American was ever going to sit at a conference table with him again. Bedell Smith's letter stopped short of recrimination: after all, America too had her traitors; but it was nevertheless a great shock that such a sophisticated and experienced service as the British could have been taken for such a ride. All links in the chain would now have to be ruthlessly tested, a great probe set in motion of all possible contacts with Burgess and Maclean, right back to the 1930's, and far greater attention would have to be paid to the personal conduct of intelligence officers. As Allen Dulles, then Bedell Smith's deputy, has put it: 'Philby was living with Burgess in a pig-pen and nobody noticed it.'[1] The British felt no temptation to argue and Kim was immediately summoned to London, leaving Aileen to pack up house and bring the children home as best she could in an atmosphere of calamity and glacial ostracism.

Anglo-American discussion of the B and M disappearance took place at the highest security level. On 11 June Sir Percy Sillitoe, the MI5 chief, flew to Washington for consultations with Hoover, Bedell Smith and Dulles, and, as the latter recalled, pronounced the case 'a real shocker'. The British position *vis-à-vis* the Americans could not have been weaker; desperate for access to American secrets and defensive about the series of major security lapses, the best they could do was go about the necessary purge with all possible grace. It was a matter of distasteful routine. No one disputed that Philby, touched with the suspicion of being a Soviet agent, had to go – and he did.

But, for a variety of reasons, some personal, some a reflection of the uneasy climate of Anglo-American relations at the time, the SIS in London did not entirely share Washington's strong presumption of his guilt. As Broadway saw it at the moment of his recall, their senior man had been booted unceremoniously out of the United States simply because he had taken in, befriended (and admittedly lived it up with) the now missing Burgess. This was the main, if not at this early stage the only, item in the anti-Kim dossier: MI5 investigation of his career had only just begun and, in any event, his sharing a house with Burgess could be interpreted in his defence. It was hardly conceivable that he would have done so, had he and Burgess been clandestinely linked. Moreover, his perfectly genuine horror at learning the news of Burgess and Maclean's escape had deceived his closest and most observant associates. In retrospect, it was indeed fortunate for Kim that

1. The late Allen Dulles, a personal communication to the authors.

his allegedly tainting association with Burgess, which the Americans made so much of, was examined and dismissed as trivial in London before it could be supported by other evidence. The upshot of that first hectic week was that he returned to headquarters less as a culprit than as a man hard done by, a victim of American high-handedness.

From the start his demeanour counted strongly in his favour. 'I'm no good to you now, and never will be again,' were his first, self-sacrificial words to his chief, Sir Stewart Menzies. 'I'll put in my resignation. I think you'd better let me go.'[1] Once again it was the upright junior officer speaking, ready to suffer for the good of the service, volunteering to throw up his career to save his superiors from embarrassment. As Colonel Vivian recalled, 'He was rather taking in that way.' So Kim was not sacked, he resigned; psychologically he had won the first round. The investigation into his background was of course to go on and was to uncover things that could not convincingly be explained away, but a man's character cannot be destroyed overnight. In spite of the unfortunate drinking, Kim's ten years' service in the SIS had won him a fine reputation. It was not so much his talent as an intelligence officer that had impressed his colleagues, but rather that he appeared the personification of integrity. He seemed to embody the very British virtues of low-keyed, understated moral excellence, and this image, noteworthy in a world of men whose profession was cynicism, now did him sterling service. There were other factors working for him. To many people he appeared a casualty of the McCarthyite hysteria which was then sweeping Washington and which in Britain seemed exaggerated and despicable. There was a strong streak of anti-Americanism in the British establishment at the time, made up of pique at America's overpowering strength, genuine concern at American bellicosity in the Far East, and an undertow of cultural antipathy. The more the Americans damned Philby, the more the British instinct was to give him the benefit of the doubt.

1. The late Col. Valentine Vivian, a personal communication to the authors.

With all that is now known, it seems scarcely credible that Kim was not soon identified as the chief culprit. But it should be remembered that at the time he was by no means the only suspect. The revelation of treachery among senior, impeccably British, diplomats of the 1930s vintage raised a daunting spectre for the security service. Who else of that generation was affected? For the first time the anti-Fascist left-wingery of the 1930s was combed for possible security risks, with C-E officers no doubt sifting through back numbers of *Granta* and membership lists of the Cambridge University Socialist Society. The vetting ranged far and wide, and not only in government service, drawing into the net friends, acquaintances and even casual contacts of the missing pair. In the SIS, where the search for an accomplice was most intense, at least one other resignation apart from Philby's was accepted. If there had to be a Third Man who tipped off Burgess and Maclean, as the press speculated, there were other candidates for the role. Moreover, however vigorously the SIS conducted its internal spring-cleaning, it was only human that with its reputation already under fierce attack, it should hope that the probe would unearth no more skeletons. But of course the main reason Kim escaped arrest and trial was that his repeated interrogations yielded no positive proof of guilt.

His first grilling, on the day of his return, was by Dick White, by this time a very senior official of MI5 and soon to replace Sillitoe as chief. Although never close friends Philby and White had been wartime colleagues in the days when Kim's Section Five (d) was feeding B Division of MI5 with advance information of operations mounted against Britain from the Abwehr base in Spain. They respected each other but there was an element of rivalry in their relationship which ended only with Kim's final uncovering and flight in 1963. There is a story, possibly apocryphal, that from Moscow Philby sent White a message: 'You have won the first round; I shall win the second.' But what second contest he could have had in mind is still obscure.

White's interrogations, tentative circlings round a potential suspect, were followed five months later, in November 1951, by a more formal interview with Helenus Milmo, K.C., a former MI5 lawyer who was then conducting a judicial inquiry into the Burgess and Maclean affair. Milmo lost his temper and Kim had recourse to his stammer. At the end of three hours he had given nothing away. From Milmo Philby was passed on for a more leisurely and thorough questioning to William Skardon, an ex-policeman whose high reputation as an MI5 inquisitor had been enhanced by his deft and devastating handling of Klaus Fuchs. But even Skardon made no noticeable dent in Kim's defences, a fact which became evident from his final, almost formal, session early in 1952 with the new SIS chief, Sir John Sinclair. On the whole his ex-colleagues in SIS still thought him innocent and ill-served; but in MI5 opinion was veering round to the view that the Americans had been right after all.

None of the interviews was much more than shadow-boxing, as by the very nature of the case both sides were compelled to caution. Kim's discretion needs no explanation. But his questioners were equally discreet: their wish to make him talk was matched by their need to keep from him how much they already knew or did not know. Thus they could not always afford to set out their evidence against him, such as it was. But the fact that there was little hard evidence on the files showed that in such key posts as Turkey and the US, he had not been routinely watched by British counter-intelligence, as he would have been in the CIA, for instance, where all operations were subject to C-E control as a matter of common practice.

Naturally enough the inquiries began with the B and M affair: how had Maclean known that the net was closing round him? How had Burgess known? Had Philby told Burgess, and Burgess told Maclean? Philby categorically denied having so much as mentioned the Maclean investigation to Burgess, advancing instead a hypothesis of his own. According to this interpretation, Maclean in London guesses his peril when he finds himself under surveillance and notices that top-secret papers are being withheld from him – as indeed was the case in the days before his escape. But not daring to break cover in order to call on his Russian contact for help, he can do nothing to save himself. At this critical juncture Burgess walks in unexpectedly from America and rescues him from his dilemma. Not being himself under surveillance he conveys Maclean's SOS to his own Russian contact and makes the arrangements for the escape. One of the merits of this theory was that it fitted the known facts: Burgess had in fact hired the getaway car in which he picked up Maclean in the country and drove him to the Channel steamer at Southampton. More important, Scotland Yard's Special Branch, used by MI5 to shadow Maclean, confessed to having been caught red-handed.[1] This was warning enough; there was no need for a tip-off, no need for a Third Man.

When the inquiries came to focus on one of the most damaging incidents in Kim's own career – the Volkov affair – he benefited, as has been seen, from a similar let-out. The fact that British officials in Turkey had mentioned Volkov's name over the telephone, and that their conversations were surely tapped, provided an explanation without reference to any other British leak for Volkov's liquidation by the Russians. Other shadows on his intelligence career, such as the mysterious disappearance of the cable from Germany in the *Rote Kapelle* case, were too slight to incriminate him. In any event, against such suspicions stood much favourable evidence. If Maclean had got away, Nunn May and Fuchs, of whose step-by-step pursuit Kim was aware, had not. His memo to headquarters on the Embassy leak, recalling Krivitsky's allegations, had after all contributed to the pinpointing of Maclean. Moreover, he had done the British competent service: in Turkey, for example, Operation Spyglass had seemed a useful anti-Soviet initiative. As the probe pushed further back into his life, it uncovered little that was damaging. Unlike Burgess and Maclean, there was no record of his ever having joined the Cambridge Communist cell – or indeed the Party at all. Litzi, a

1. The late Col. Valentine Vivian, a personal communication to the authors.

known Communist, was a problem, but he had disarmed suspicion by the frank and open way in which he had volunteered information about this youthful escapade.

There were two sticky moments in his interrogations which must have left black question-marks on his dossier. The first concerned his freelance trip to Franco's Spain early in 1937, some months before *The Times* took him on. What was the motive for this journey? How had it been financed? Was he the 'young British journalist' Krivitsky said had been sent to spy on Franco by Soviet intelligence? Philby's explanation was that he had sold his books and records – uncheckable transactions – to get himself to Spain in a bid to break into Fleet Street. The second, more serious, piece of circumstantial evidence, thrown at him by Milmo, had been provided by the tireless monitors of the GC and CS. Could Philby explain why two days after Volkov's appeal for asylum reached London in 1945, there had been a sharp jump in the volume of Soviet intelligence radio traffic between London and Moscow, followed by a similar jump in communications between Moscow and Istanbul? Could he also explain why, four years later, the lines between London and Moscow were equally busy shortly after his briefing on the Washington Embassy leak? Philby's only possible response was to be as puzzled as his interrogator.

The interrogators, Milmo, Skardon, and most significantly the future chief, Dick White, believed him guilty, but could not prove it. Menzies tended to think him innocent, but wanting a quiet life with MI5 accepted a verdict on Philby of 'guilt unproven but suspicion remaining'. Sinclair, Menzies' successor, was at this time and probably for long after emotionally committed to a belief in Philby's innocence. On letting him go the still friendly SIS gave him a modest golden handshake of £2,000 down and a promise of another £2,000 in half-yearly instalments of £500. So Philby escaped the worst. He was not brought to trial, as no sufficient body of legal evidence could be assembled against him. This was as he had calculated, a gamble based on his long experience of counter-espionage and his understanding of the enemy's mind. But if he kept his freedom, he lost his honour. The shining moral armour, his main asset throughout his life, was tarnished for ever.

Kim always knew how to rise to a professional challenge. However drunk the night before, he could when the occasion demanded clear his fuddled brain and quell his queasy stomach to give an impression of control and precision. He was a tidy, efficient person, known never to miss an appointment or mislay a document. In his many interrogations he had put up an effective performance, appearing as anxious to establish the truth as his questioners, modest, steady voiced and helpful, but never lowering his guard for a moment. He paid for this achievement with an off-duty collapse dwarfing any of his previous binges. Night after night he would return from London to his house at Heronsgate, in Hertfordshire, almost insensible with drink and demanding more. His eldest daughter, Josephine, then about ten years old and very impressionable, remembers her father falling downstairs and having to be put to bed.[1]

Life at Heronsgate was intensely unhappy. The house was a mean little bungalow called Sunbox, rather like a Victorian lodge-keeper's cottage, which Kim had rented for his family on their return from Washington in the summer of 1951. Kim painted it up, mowed the grass and settled Aileen there. Then he more or less left her. Abandoned by most of their friends, with money short and the future bleak, he and Aileen could no longer live tolerably together. Under the impact of Burgess and Maclean their marriage had gone to pieces. Kim started an affair with Connie, fortyish and in government service in London, and he would quite often not bother to come home at all. When he did turn up he was very depressed, almost suicidal, while Aileen, who had found out about his other woman, seemed a pathetic, tortured figure. In an atmosphere of constant tension, their once friendly bickering sometimes

1. Mrs Melanie Learoyd, Josephine's aunt, a personal communication to the authors.

turned into violent rows, even in public. Dining one night with some of their last remaining friends, their tempers flared and Kim, stumbling out to his car in a drunken fury, smashed the windscreen with his fist. Aileen immediately got in and drove off, leaving him to make his way home on foot.[1]

But there was more fear than defiance in Aileen's attitude to him. The obscure, half-formulated terrors which had nagged her in Turkey now, in the collapse of their lives, came to obsess her. We cannot know whether at this stage she consciously put to herself the hideous thought that Kim might really be a traitor; but gripped by the other, very actual, fear that he might leave her, she would do anything to hold his attention, even to the extent of mentioning the unmentionable. When their friends dined at Heronsgate one night, she blurted out her nightmare: 'I know you're the Third Man!' It was laughed off, but such taunts were nails in Aileen's coffin. She tortured him in a way that his gentlemanly interrogators of MI5 could not approach. She made him hate her.

Early in 1952, when his interrogation ended, Kim set about trying to find a job, but in a rather desultory fashion. In his present mood he was not very employable, however, and nor were his funds so tight as to drive him to take anything that offered. Some of his old wartime friends who thought he had been grossly victimized now tried to help him. A Covent Garden fruit importer, a contact from the days of the Iberian Section, offered him a job in Spain. Kim went to Madrid for a few weeks, perhaps hoping to pick up some pre-war journalistic threads – and incidentally calling on his royalist mistress, Frances Doble. But he was soon back in London and on the market. He turned down a job in advertising. His father introduced him to Mitchell Cotts, the City traders and shippers who had bought St John out in Arabia. That too came to nothing. Bickham Sweet-Escott, the executive ace of wartime SOE who had returned to peacetime merchant banking, arranged for Kim to be interviewed by Shell with a view to a Middle East post. Kim was short-listed, but once again the job

1. Mrs Patricia Collins, a personal communication to the authors.

fell through. There had, it appeared, been an official intervention at a very high level to prevent his recruitment. It was evident that MI5 had not lost interest in him. For a time he came to rest in a small trading company with offices in Cannon Street, run by a Lebanese, where for a little under a year, from mid-1952 to mid-1953, he made a half-hearted attempt to be a businessman. Then he reverted to writing, offering to produce for the publisher André Deutsch his own version of the Burgess and Maclean affair. Deutsch was enthusiastic and, between April 1954 and March 1955, advanced £600 in monthly instalments of £40 or, later, £60, but the book never materialized; the advance was eventually repaid by a friend. Finally, in August 1954, a Foreign Office man who had known him in Turkey got him a hack job at under £15 a week on the *Fleet Street Letter*, a newsletter specializing in diplomatic stories.

Kim probably touched bottom in mid-1953. His SIS gratuity was running out and he had discovered no congenial way of making money. There was no solace in his home and family. MI5's hostility seemed as resolute as ever and the goodwill of even his most patient friends was wearing thin. For two years he had heard no word from his Russian masters. Stalin had died and his security chief, Lavrenti Beria, had fallen in his wake, leaving every Soviet intelligence officer and agent, in one service or another, at home or abroad, trembling for his future. Kim's loneliness and insecurity were intense. He had no way of knowing if his ordeal would ever end. Was he to remain in the cold for ever, wearing away his life in petty jobs, always short of a fiver, struggling to bring up his children? A CIA officer, Kim's opposite number in the ill-starred Albanian adventure of a couple of years earlier, came to London and thought of looking up his old friend. Sounding dismal over the telephone, Aileen gave him a London number where Kim could be contacted. He was persuaded to come round for a drink. Seedy and haggard, he betrayed the embarrassment of a man, now down and out, who had once held an important and powerful position.

Aileen's rich mother, Mrs Alleyne, then intervened to rescue her daughter from the miseries of Heronsgate. She bought her a large Edwardian house, Leylands, in Crowborough,[1] a dormitory town on the Kent–Sussex border favoured by retired Indian civil servants. Mrs Alleyne thought to do well, but in fact she put Aileen, already at the end of her tether, in a far from cheerful place. There was nothing for a woman like Aileen to do in Crowborough. She had no local roots, knew nobody, and was not visited by her neighbours. The house, at the end of a dank lane, was closely hemmed in by a neglected shrubbery of rhododendrons. Beyond were funereal cypress trees and beyond them a vast wild garden of about two-and-a-half acres, where the traces of an overgrown tennis court and a bowling green could be discerned. The interior furnishings were mean: cream walls, fake furniture, and on the stairs thin Axminster rather than best Wilton. Cheerless and cold, it would have taken a dozen servants to make the place comfortable. The only pleasant and civilized room was at the top of the house which commanded a view of Ashdown Forest. This Kim commandeered for his rare visits, installing there a fine stand-up Victorian desk and his books. He would occasionally come down at weekends to see the children, but rather than sleep under the same roof as Aileen, would pitch a tent in the garden. By this time he had pretty well left Aileen for good, and was living in London either alone or with Connie.

When he did come down to Crowborough he did a lot of cooking and looked after the children. If they cut themselves playing in the wild shrubbery, he would put on the sticking plaster, but as he was rather squeamish at the sight of blood, he tended to put it on not very accurately. Aileen, alone most of the time in this mausoleum with five children to look after, beset by money troubles and worried out of her mind about Kim and her own future, seemed neurotically incapable of keeping the household going. She would squander the house-

1. We are grateful to Mrs Molly Izzard for an account of life at Leylands.

keeping money or the school fees. From time to time her mother came down to help her out, but Aileen could not constantly appeal to her to meet the gaps in the family budget. Already Mrs Alleyne had put a private detective on Kim's tail in London to find out how much money he was spending on his other woman: she did not want to continue supporting his legitimate household if money was being siphoned off on the side.

Aileen no longer tried to hold on to Kim. Neglected, she was like a wild woman, unwashed and frantic-eyed. She once crashed her car into a shop-window in Crowborough. She was more than once in hospital. She developed a bad abscess on her thumb which isolated her still further as she could no longer drive. She seemed to be giving up hope of life. Above all she was increasingly filled with fantasies of spies and secret villainy. One day in a hysterical moment she said to a friend, 'I couldn't bear the children to go to Russia!' But it was unclear whether this outburst reflected any real knowledge or was merely an emotional reaction to the publicity Kim was given in the press in 1955.

At about this time Mrs Hazel Sporel, the Philbys' hospitable friend in Istanbul, happened to meet Kim in London and suggested that her own daughter, Fayhan, might like to visit Josephine, her childhood friend, at Crowborough. Kim would not hear of it. 'Don't ever send Fayhan there,' he said, 'Aileen is very ill and has been to a psychiatrist. The doctor says she has something in her which makes her want to hurt most the people she loves most. That was why she tried to set fire to your house in Turkey. And that's why she sent a telegram to the Foreign Office saying I was the "Third Man".'[1] Kim had always said his wife was incompetent. Now he had to make her out to be mad. Her accusations, founded or not, were too damaging. If she had guessed the truth he must have wanted to destroy her, and to abandon her was a way of doing it. Certainly it did not seem to bother him that in his absence she was drinking herself to death.

1. Mrs Hazel Sporel, a personal communication to the authors.

In December of 1957, after struggling on for four years, Aileen died of abandonment. She had caught Asian 'flu and had gone to convalesce with Kim's sister, Helena, at nearby Rustington. The Christmas holidays were approaching when the children would be returning from school, so Aileen would often drive across to Crowborough to potter about the empty house and make preparations for their arrival. One night she decided to sleep there, and the next morning, 15 December, she was found dead in bed by her daughter Josephine. There was a hint that she might have taken her own life but the coroner's verdict was that she had died of heart failure due to influenza. There was no evidence of an overdose of drugs. 'She can't even die in an uncomplicated way,' Kim complained unfeelingly, 'it has to be all crumbed up with problems.'[1]

He was by that time in Beirut working as a journalist but he took three weeks' leave and returned to England for the funeral. He found the house in great disorder and the children very disturbed. With great efficiency he took control, cooking the Christmas dinner, teaching the children games and running the house virtually single-handed. Leylands was put on the market, the garden sold off for building land, and what money was left after settling £600 or £700 of domestic bills was put in trust for the children. 'I never want to see the place again,' Kim said.

Philby's name was first mentioned in the House of Commons on 25 October 1955. Over the four years since Burgess and Maclean had disappeared, questions about them and about the whole subject of Foreign Office security had been asked from time to time in Parliament, and the affair had been aired with more or less imagination in books and newspaper articles. The missing diplomats had left a dent in the complacency of British upper-middle-class life, by showing that the imposing front of government service could conceal some pretty scandalous goings on.

'Would the Foreign Secretary,' George Wigg asked in the House, 'institute inquiries into the suggestion made in a Sun-

1. Mrs Molly Izzard, a personal communication to the authors.

day newspaper that there is widespread sexual perversion in the Foreign Office ...?'

'I can only say that perhaps I have not been long enough at the Foreign Office to express an opinion,' replied Herbert Morrison.[1]

There was a good deal more of thrust and parry at this level, but as late as the autumn of 1955 the general public, including Members of Parliament, knew practically nothing about the case. The interrogations, the purges, the remaining suspicions, the damage to Anglo–American intelligence relations – all these were known only to a small group of insiders. From the start there had been speculation that Burgess and Maclean were tipped off by a Third Man, but no names had been publicly mentioned, and Kim, wrestling with his family difficulties, was as anonymous as any drop-out from any job.

Then a story published in the *People* one Sunday in September 1955 forced the government to take the public a little further into its confidence. The newspaper story was by Vladimir Petrov, a former intelligence officer in the Soviet Embassy in Canberra, who had defected to the Australians in the spring of 1954. The bombshell dropped by Petrov that Sunday morning was that Burgess and Maclean were not just failures on the run, or even merely homosexual lovers, as had been suggested, but were long-term Soviet agents recruited in their youth at Cambridge and spying for the enemy ever since. They had fled to escape arrest. The Foreign Office confirmed the truth of these points and promised a full statement, which was published in the form of a White Paper on 23 September. It admitted that Maclean must have known he was under suspicion, either because he noticed that secret papers were not reaching him any more, or because he realized that he was being followed or because he was warned. Otherwise the White Paper gave very little away. When it was issued, Parliament was in recess, but a debate was promised after the House reassembled on 25 October 1955. On that first day of the session Lieutenant-Colonel Marcus Lipton, Labour M.P. for Brixton, reflecting the general impatience with the govern-

1. *Hansard* parliamentary report, 11 June 1951.

ment's secretiveness and apparent inaction, opened the attack with a direct reference to Philby:

'Has the Prime Minister made up his mind to cover up at all costs the dubious third-man activities of Mr Harold Philby who was First Secretary at the Washington Embassy a little time ago, and is he determined to stifle all discussion on the very great matters which were evaded in the wretched White Paper, which is an insult to the intelligence of the country?'[1]

Marcus Lipton had taken a close interest in the Burgess and Maclean case since the beginning and had set himself up as a scourge of the government on this issue. In 1955 alone he had already tabled questions in the House three times. He explains this preoccupation by his early conviction that Burgess and Maclean could not have acted alone.

They must have had some other contact, someone in the know. When one narrowed down the field, one was left with a comparatively small number of possible associates. A process of elimination led me to Philby.

One or two journalistic friends of mine assured me that they believed him to be the Third Man and this served to confirm my own feelings. An article by a British journalist appeared in the American press making the same allegation.

A little while later another journalist friend told me that he had been walking down Whitehall one day with a man in MI5 when suddenly his companion, pointing to a passer-by said, 'That's Kim Philby, that's the Third Man'.

This incident seemed to me to add considerable substance to my suspicions. I learned that reports on Philby had been submitted by the lower echelons of MI5 to the top. But no action had followed. I determined to raise the matter in the House.[2]

In this casual way, as a result of journalistic gossip working on one man's sense of duty and with no apparent trace of a scheming counter-espionage hand in the affair, the rehabilitation of Kim Philby began. In the weeks immediately preceding Lipton's question in the House, Fleet Street had been buzzing with renewed speculation about the Third Man and,

1. *The Times* parliamentary report, 26 October 1955.
2. Lieut.-Col. Marcus Lipton, M.P., a personal communication to the authors.

as a result of a leak somewhere in the system, Philby's name was being whispered about. But no newspaper in Britain dared to print it for fear of libel. This did not however prevent news reporters nosing around Crowborough, stopping Kim's children outside the house, and generally ferreting around for a break. Acting like a man whose patience was sorely tried, Kim made contact with the SIS to say that he could not long delay speaking out.

It was a bold move. It was vital for him to find out whether the authorities were playing cat and mouse with him. Had his name been deliberately leaked to the press to tempt him to break cover and make a run for it? Had MI5 got fresh evidence against him which they wanted to cap with an attempted escape? He was soon reassured. An interview with SIS convinced him that, although his file was still open, the security authorities still did not have enough on him to bring him to court. The SIS concern appeared to be that he should say nothing to the press which might embarrass the government before the forthcoming parliamentary debate on the B and M White Paper. They asked him to surrender his passport, fearing that the inevitable publicity might drive him abroad. Cooperative as always, Kim complied.

He now felt confident enough to counter-attack and carefully laid his plans. When Lipton named him in the House, he abandoned his family in Crowborough and his mistress in Highgate, and went to ground to await the denouement in his familiar haven – his mother's flat in Drayton Gardens. He had a fortnight to wait.

His judgement of the state of his dossier was confirmed by the House of Commons debate on 7 November. Harold Macmillan, then Foreign Secretary, assured the House that no evidence had been found that Mr Philby, a former temporary first secretary in the Washington Embassy, was responsible for warning Burgess or Maclean. He had, he said, no reason to conclude that Mr Philby had at any time betrayed the interests of his country or to identify him with the 'so-called Third Man, if indeed there was one'.

Armed with this high-level testimonial of his innocence,

Kim went into the attack by summoning a press conference at his mother's flat for the morning after the debate. He knew that Fleet Street's accolade was as important as the official clearance if he were truly to emerge into reputable daylight again. It was a carefully planned and triumphantly executed performance. Philby, looking spruce and young, his stutter conquered, dominated the gathering like an accomplished politician, his even good humour in answering questions or blocking indiscreet ones only giving way to a touch of anger when he challenged Colonel Lipton to repeat his charges outside the House. He opened the press conference by presenting copies of a prepared statement. It was a model of hypocrisy. For three reasons he had refrained from speaking out earlier, he said. First, he was bound by the Official Secrets Act not to disclose information derived from his official position; secondly, he had no means of knowing whether words of his, perhaps lifted from context or even garbled, might not prejudice the government in its conduct of international affairs; finally, 'the efficiency of our security services can only be reduced by publicity given to their organization, personnel and techniques'. Then the journalists put their questions. 'An imprudent association' with Burgess in Washington, Philby admitted, had led directly to his resignation from the Foreign Office. Burgess's political views were 'all over the place' and he never knew he was a Communist. Burgess did drink, but 'his behaviour was not disgraceful in any sense of the word known to me', and in any event he was not prepared to indulge in mud-slinging. 'There are fair-weather friends and foul-weather friends, and I prefer to belong to the second category.' As for Maclean, he was only a shadow on his memory. He himself had always been on the left, he frankly acknowledged, but 'I have never been a Communist ... The last time I spoke to a Communist, knowing he was one, was in 1934.'

Most journalists there were won round. Most believed him to have been unfairly maligned, and thereafter left him in peace. They had no means of appreciating how bold was his effrontery. By killing the worst allegations against him, the

Macmillan clearance allowed him to embroider on his innocence with impunity. There were dozens of people in London who knew he was lying when he claimed not to have spoken knowingly to a Communist since 1934: he had after all only parted from his Communist wife Litzi in 1936, a fact known to many British and Central European left-wingers. But whatever lie he uttered would not be contradicted now. The unfortunate Lipton unreservedly withdrew his charges, thus making his contribution to the general exculpation of Kim Philby.

My evidence was insubstantial. Although I knew the name of the security officer who had pointed Philby out in the street, I could not produce it. It would have ruined the man's career. Members of MI5 had strict orders not to make contact with politicians. So when it came to a showdown my legal advisers counselled me to retract.

Moreover I was shouted down in the House. Within the Labour Party, many members considered Philby a progressive left-wing influence in the Foreign Office, as he was clearly not part of the old guard. Their instinct was to protect him.

The head of MI5, Sir Roger Hollis, asked to see me, in a letter from a box number in Whitehall. I replied saying I didn't like going to a box number and that perhaps he had better come and see me. We talked in the Central Lobby of the House of Commons in full public view. Of course he wanted to know my evidence but I could not give it.[1]

So Philby had a clean bill of health. It looked as if, lacking the legal evidence necessary for a prosecution, the authorities had had no alternative but to exonerate him when forced by Lipton's intervention to pronounce publicly on his case. But a quite different interpretation of these events is possible. Was not Macmillan's statement in Parliament a shade too categorical? His whitewashing was so nearly complete that it gave no hint of the still-open file and the continuing suspicion. It may be that for the purpose of an ongoing counter-espionage investigation, Philby had to be given maximum reassurance. Marcus Lipton's evidence suggests very strongly that the sequence of events which led to Kim's clearance was deliber-

1. Lieut.-Col. Marcus Lipton, M.P., a personal communication to the authors.

ately triggered off by MI5, and it is indeed hard to believe that the exchange in the street between the MI5 man and the journalist, which prompted Lipton to name Philby publicly, was not carefully stage-managed. On this hypothesis, Sir Roger Hollis called on the innocent Lipton in order to verify for himself that the ploy had worked and that Lipton, his unconscious task done, would now leave well alone. If this interpretation is correct, Kim walked straight into a trap, and his confident handling of the press conference was exactly what MI5 was hoping for. In this battle of wits both Kim and his watchful enemies in British security may have thought they had got the upper hand.

In two brief months, from mid-September to mid-November 1955, Kim's life changed. The suspected traitor could walk upright again. The explosion of publicity which he had so skilfully exploited had been an ordeal as nerve-straining as his long interrogations. A wrong move at any time might have destroyed his carefully rebuilt image and forced him to flee. But now he was safe – or was he? Within a week of his press conference he received a letter from Jim Lees, his old, ex-miner, Cambridge friend whom he had not seen for more than a decade – one of the people who could know he was lying. 'I've been shattered by internal events,' Lees wrote, referring to his ulcers. 'I hear you've been shattered by external events.' He went on to invite Kim to visit him in Nottingham where he held a university lectureship, and Kim accepted by return of post, announcing his imminent arrival. He stayed several days, no doubt thoroughly exploring in the manner of the skilled counter-espionage officer that he was, what Lees knew, what he suspected, and what if anything he intended to do with his information. After surviving so many perils, how galling to be brought down by an almost forgotten friendship!

It was a thoroughly boozy visit. In those days Kim liked gin, a taste he shared with his mother. (Visitors to her Drayton Gardens flat in the 1950s would be astonished to see this large, thickset, red-haired woman reach in mid-sentence for a gin bottle on the floor beside her easy chair, pour herself a stiff drink in a tumbler and swallow it neat.) Politely Lees asked after her. 'She's quite happy on two bottles a day,' Kim replied. When Lees asked for news of the Communist Litzi, Kim said with callous indifference, 'She's probably gone on the streets.' They discussed Burgess. 'I don't believe Guy was a bloody agent at all,' Lees said, but Kim disagreed, seeming at pains to demonstrate that Burgess was guilty. With a straight face he claimed the American authorities had discovered that Guy's sun-lamp could be used as a radio transmitter. Kim seemed anxious to establish not only that Guy was a Soviet secret agent, but also an uncontrollable drunk. In Washington, he said, Guy kept a bottle of bourbon in his car, another in his desk, and a third by his bedside, drinking all three in a day. He used to come downstairs in the morning shaking like a dog: 'Fetch me a drink, Kim,' he would gabble, 'fetch me a drink.'[1]

Kim left Nottingham confident that he had nothing to fear from Lees. His early Marxism which he had shared with Lees had been buried once and for all beneath the convincing persona of a man of conscience swept into hush-hush government service by the war, and later to fall victim through no fault of his own to an old Cambridge crony who had gone bad. A breach in his defences had been plugged.

Kim was clearly on the way back up, but full recovery from a crash such as he had suffered takes time. Confidence has to be rebuilt, the dust must be allowed to settle, and time permitted to blur the hard edges of unanswered questions. Very shortly after his public clearance he had a stroke of good fortune. His four years in the cold had left him broke, far from well and demoralized. He needed a rest cure and he got it. A friend from his Turkish days, W. E. D. Allen, who had served as Press Counsellor in the Ankara Embassy, heard of his plight and remembering his literary talent, invited him to come to Ireland to give him a hand in writing the history of his family firm, David Allen's, whose centenary was to be celebrated in 1957. Kim arrived in Cappagh, County Waterford, in January 1956, and stayed for six months, working hard, climbing in the hills and sending postcards to his children almost every day. He returned to London in July 1956 retuned for service.

1. Jim Lees, a personal communication to the authors.

Even before Kim left County Waterford plans had been made for his future. With different degrees of secrecy both the British and the Russians had already made contact with him again, both judging at much the same moment that their man was sufficiently recovered to go back to work. Like a recidivist returning to his old habits, Kim was sucked back into the intelligence world, the world he knew best. But however real his recovery he re-entered the system at a more lowly, more hazardous level. Previously he had been a commander, an initiator of operations, an inside man, a senior SIS officer under KGB control, trusted by both sides. Now he was an outsider not fully in the confidence of either service, but useful to both because inhabiting the shadowy frontier area between them. Previously he had run agents, now he was an agent being run, one of those lonely figures used by rival services to maintain hostile contact with each other. Such a position puts great pressures on a man because he provides the battlefield in this subtle war, never certain whether he is using others or being used. Kim's next six years were not tranquil.

His cover was provided by the *Observer* and the *Economist* who, unaware of these complexities, appointed him their 'stringer' in the Middle East on a joint annual retainer of £500. In addition he was paid expenses and a fee for articles published at the rate of thirty shillings per hundred words. Four years earlier, in 1952, on Malcolm Muggeridge's suggestion, Philby had written to the Editor of the *Observer*, David Astor, to ask for a job, and had even written a couple of pieces from Spain for the paper's syndicated foreign news service. This was a useful background when, in 1956, the Foreign Office informally asked Astor if he had a place for an ex-journalist with a high reputation who needed a helping hand.

The SIS has been much criticized for taking Kim back on its books in 1956. It has been said that his friends in the service were sorry for him, shielded him, and bided their time until the moment when they could re-employ him. It has even been alleged that Kim wormed his way back into the confidence of British intelligence – a remarkable double trick after his earlier penetration and fall – to give the Russians an unexpected bonus of six more years of work. This was his own proud boast, and there was no doubt some truth in it. From this argument British intelligence emerges as exceptionally humane, but also as credulous and soft-headed. But the situation was not quite so simple. Kim was not the first, nor the last, serving officer to fall under suspicion. In a profession such as his, fears of double loyalties are endemic, as it is the business of rival services to penetrate each other. So a suspected man poses a dilemma: security demands that relations with him be severed, but the need for controlled contact with the enemy tempts counter-espionage to keep in touch with him. In Kim's case the urge to help an old and valued employee was inseparable from the wish to trap him into confession, if he had anything to confess. The only way to achieve the second was to try the first. In fact British intelligence still needed Kim. More important than punishing him, if indeed he could be proved guilty, was the necessity to complete the files and close the case. If he was a Soviet agent what exactly had he passed to the Russians and when? Only when these gaps had been filled in could the Russians' secret knowledge be fully neutralized; and only by keeping Kim in play could such missing information be arrived at. It was a gamble, but the alternative was continued ignorance. So, within the service some wanted genuinely to help him because they thought him ill-used while others watched and waited and nursed their doubts, well aware that his file was still open and the matter of his innocence or guilt not finally established.

Such was the climate in which 'C', Sir John Sinclair, eased open the back door for Philby with the greatest secrecy. The intention of some was to give him a leg up, of others to insert him into the intelligence circuit in the hope of counter-espionage returns, putting him where (if he were guilty) he might damn himself and where (whether he were guilty or not) he might even be useful to the British with intelligence on Arab affairs.

Under this equivocal British sponsorship Kim appeared diffidently in Beirut in August 1956.

14   The Beachcomber

For the second time in his life Kim was sent into the field as a
probationer. On much the same informal basis as twenty years
earlier the Russians had directed him to Spain at the start of
the Civil War, so now British intelligence posted him to
Lebanon. He was not taken back on the SIS books or properly
integrated into the organization; rather his role was to be that
of an outside informant on a retainer. Before he left London
he was briefed by two senior SIS officers who explained to him
that he was being re-engaged for reasons of simple justice as
his friends were genuinely sorry for him. But because of the
shadow over his name, because his total innocence had not
been irrefutably established, he would be given no Communist targets. That is to say, it would be no part of his duties
for the SIS in the Middle East to make contact with the
Russians, the Chinese, the Eastern Europeans or indeed any of
their local sympathizers. Although Kim did not know it, this
was a reservation which the SIS Chief, Sir John Sinclair, had
personally insisted upon; but Kim must inevitably have wondered if his re-recruitment was an act of pure philanthropy.
To play a suspect pawn against the enemy is a classic intelligence operation which, like other classics, has its conventions
– conventions understood by all the players. Whatever assur-
ances he might be given Kim had to weigh the probability that
the Beirut assignment was a further probe into his case. Warned
off Communist targets, he was directed to Arab matters,
specifically to President Nasser's interventions outside Egypt
and to internal developments in Saudi Arabia, a country with
which Britain was then in dispute over the Buraimi Oasis and
with which it had no relations: it was thought that his family
connections with Arabia would yield intelligence dividends.

But apart from such general expressions of interest and some background Foreign Office papers which he was given to read, Kim was taken no further into SIS confidence. His briefing was hardly more extensive than a serious foreign correspondent might expect. Limited though it was, the new link was effected with extreme secrecy. Within the SIS only a few men knew about it and it was arranged that he was at the start to be run personally by the Beirut station commander, without SIS officers in neighbouring Arab countries being informed. (Inevitably as time passed this ruling was relaxed.) Some twelve months later when the arrangements seemed to be working satisfactorily, Kim's status as a contact man was confirmed and he was given a larger salary. The occasion was a visit to Beirut by the SIS man responsible for the Middle East who settled the terms with him over an amicable lunch at the Costabelle, a quiet, self-respecting French restaurant overlooking the sea. His brief remained the same: he was to continue producing for British intelligence material on Arab affairs. But his work was frankly marginal. Thus passed his first years in Lebanon, a relatively unclouded, stable plateau, before the pressures of his dangerous progress built up again.

By a fortunate chance of history Kim's appearance in the Middle East to swell the foreign press corps attracted no attention whatsoever. He reached Beirut just a few weeks before the Suez crisis exploded when, with the eyes of the world focused on the area, extra journalists were flying in every day. No doubt one or two men in the British, American and Soviet embassies awaited his arrival with interest, but to the great mass of foreigners in Beirut – let alone Arabs – he was of no special significance. His name had been briefly mentioned in the House of Commons a year earlier in connection with the Burgess and Maclean affair, but only to be immediately cleared. And who cared anyway? Who in Lebanon had more than a dim recollection of the 'Missing Diplomats' themselves? The Middle East has a way of living within its own boundaries, absorbed in the constant drama of its internal tensions to the neglect of everything not directly relevant to them. The dramas of Philby's own career were totally unknown.

His arrival coincided with the opening of Nasser's great decade, from Suez in 1956 to the Six-Day War of 1967. With the seizure of the Canal Company, Nasser gave notice to the world that Arab nationalism had come of age and was ready to challenge the old tutelary powers. He himself was transformed from a local military dictator into a charismatic leader of all the Arabs. He seemed to have struck a great blow for subject peoples everywhere. Every major event which Kim was to write about in those crowded years – the Communist threat to Syria in 1957 and the Eisenhower Doctrine; the Syrian–Egyptian union of 1958; the overthrow of the Iraqi monarchy and the subsequent pressures on King Hussein of Jordan; the Lebanese civil war; Nasser's quarrel with Khrushchev in 1959 and his break with the Syrian Baath leaders; the collapse of the United Arab Republic in 1961; the war in the Yemen – all these profound transformations in some measure owed their existence to the massive fact of the Egyptian leader. Rarely did Kim's dispatches reflect this powerfully unfolding pattern. He shared the liberal sympathy for the aspiration of Arab nationalism – rather more clearly in private conversation than in his public journalism – but he never transcended his limitations. He wrote with careful deliberation in a tone sometimes more suited to a diplomatic communication than a newspaper report. The excitement escaped. He was judicious in analysing the news, rather than first with it. Above all, he saw the Middle East essentially in terms of Great Power interests – were the Russians gaining ground? Had the Americans blundered? What pieces could Britain pick up? – rather than in terms of the all-important stresses and strains within the family of Arab states. As a whole his work in those years shows no scoops, few flashes of insight, little sense of history being made. Where he did shine was in his consistently elegant prose and in the humorous point he gave to little, out-of-the-way vignettes of Arab life. But on balance he seemed satisfied with getting by.

Admittedly the newsprint shortage still afflicting Britain in the late 1950s left him little space to develop his themes, even had he wanted to. But the fact that for weeks at a time nothing from him would appear indicated pretty clearly that journalism was not an engrossing preoccupation. However, he cared enough about his reputation not to wish his name to be associated with trivial subjects, inventing for the purpose the pseudonym of Charles Garner. When Ronald Harker, editor of the *Observer*'s syndicated news service, wrote to ask him for a story on Arabian slave-girls, Kim wrote back, 'You ask me hard things. I will try to meet your request, but the piece will have to be attributed to the unfortunate Charles Garner.' He was in many ways the answer to an editor's prayer – always filing on time, never failing to respond to a cable, his copy never too long, always clean and easy to sub.

In Beirut he soon established himself as a personage of a sort, a rather washed-up, somewhat old-fashioned Englishman, hampered by a stammer, drinking more than was good for him and yet compelling a certain respect. The heavily marked face, the literary prose style, the humane, rather pessimistic judgements pointed to a mind shaped in the Europe of the 1930s, strikingly out of place in the Middle East. He was not one of those Englishmen who fall in love with Arabs. The call of the desert and the freedom of bedouin life which had so attracted his father left him quite unmoved. He saw only ignorance, corruption and the boredom of a denuded landscape, while the warm, vital, showy life of Beirut seemed to have no greater appeal for him. Most foreigners in his position quickly get hooked on the daily drama of Arab politics; Kim did not. He knew what was going on but quite simply did not seem to care much about it. Perhaps for the first time in his life he was a spectator – and a minor one at that – rather than an active participant in the political situation around him. In this Arab context what marked him out from others was not any achievement of his own but the fact that he was St John Philby's son.

When Kim first arrived in Beirut in 1956, his father, then aged seventy-one, was living in the Lebanese mountains, an impatient exile from Arabia. His troubles had started with the death in 1953 of his old friend and patron King Ibn Saud. With his protection removed, St John's influence at court had waned and he did not endear himself to the younger Saudi princes by

Philby

his testy criticism of waste and mismanagement. Breaking point was reached when his company Sharqieh secured a contract for a British firm to build a palace and harem for a member of the royal family. The project was a fiasco: the prince kept insisting on features not in the original design, the British contractor withdrew, the work was incompetently done (on one occasion the U-bend of a lavatory broke through the ceiling of a banqueting hall), and Sharqieh, taken before the courts by the prince, was ordered to complete the palace. It cost a quarter of a million pounds and was never paid for. After this rumpus, St John was told to leave the country and did so, taking with him the Arab wife whom Ibn Saud had given him and the two small sons he had had by her.

This was the household Kim joined as a lodger in the Lebanese village of Ajaltun above Beirut. St John's white stone house, commanding a fine view of the mountains, was called Mahalla Jamil – 'a beautiful place'. And it was a beautiful place. Coming up from the sweltering heat of a Beirut September, the pure mountain air was a benediction. On the flank of the hills facing out to sea, there was a great feeling of space and undisturbed silence, but the neat village and its crisp, well-tended orchards put everything on a human, gentle scale. Above all there was the generous Mediterranean light, so different from the dank gloom of Crowborough and its dripping shrubberies. Here was a place to eat well, sleep long, and recover from anxiety – or at least diffidently to begin rebuilding a shattered life. Kim took a ground-floor room in his father's house, and there embarked on a rather sober, monkish existence, reading a lot and spending the evenings in conversation with St John. A couple of days each week were spent in Beirut where he picked up stories and cabled them to London.

For a man of Kim's understated nature, there must have been strains in sharing a house with his colourful father. This was probably the first time since his prep school days that he had spent so long under the same roof as St John. They got on well, appreciating each other's different gifts, but it must sometimes have been a trying experience. St John had adapted himself to Arab life, to its chaos, noise and uneven tempo, in a way Kim never could. Known universally as 'the Hajji' – one who has made the pilgrimage to Mecca – the old boy was at his ease in Ajaltun. Done up in a white suit, he would stroll with great dignity down the village street, undismayed by the noise of children, his own and others, but distributing clips across the ear as seemed necessary. On the veranda of his house he would sit in a deckchair wearing gym-shoes, often with the laces undone, no socks, old flannel trousers and a short-sleeved shirt open at the neck. When it grew chill he would throw around his shoulders a brown woollen *abaya*, or bedouin cloak.

What Kim found hard to adjust to was his stepmother, Rosie, one of two 'slave-girls' presented to St John in the late 1940s, the other of whom he sent home to her family. Rosie was a Baluchi whose family, originating in Sind, had moved to the Buraimi Oasis in northern Arabia where she was born. After the birth of her first son, Fahd, who died in infancy, she was known formally as Umm Fahd, 'the mother of Fahd'. She had two other sons, Khalid and Faris, much loved by their father who at Ajaltun took in hand their education, translating for them into Arabic each evening such BBC children's serials as *Dick Barton*. Rosie never appeared when St John received visitors nor accompanied him to social functions, while he in turn hardly mentioned her unless to refer occasionally to 'the mother of my children'. She stayed in the house, slopping around in carpet slippers and stuffing the children with candy. She wore European clothes and liked to paint her nails. It was a low-class, somewhat raucous Arab household, but the Hajji did not seem to mind. Sometimes he would intervene to impose order with a clout on her behind. Once she complained in the village of such high-handed treatment, and some irate villagers threw stones at the house. The Mukhtar, or mayor, of Ajaltun gave a banquet of reconciliation. Kim could not understand how his father put up with it all. Something in his middle-class background prevented him from swallowing it, some childhood memory of nannies and well-ordered nurseries in India. In spite of his leftist ideals, his instincts in such matters were in the end tinged by old-fashioned colonialism. One day the

Hajji remarked on how similar little Khalid was to Kim as a child: Kim did not warm to the remark.

In late 1956 the Hajji made his peace with the Saudi royal family and took Rosie and the two boys back to Arabia. But Kim, for reasons of economy and discretion, continued to live alone in the village, making only occasional appearances in the hotels and bars of Beirut. It was as if he were lowering a toe carefully into the water to test its temperature. Survival, and nothing more ambitious, seemed at this early stage his principal objective. He could not afford the self-assertion or the vigorous search for contacts of an ordinary newspaperman arriving in an unfamiliar city. The delicate nature of his covert duties for both the British and the Russians forced him to move cautiously; but in any event his resilience seemed low. At forty-five he was already touched by middle age. But life up in the mountains was lonely. He missed his children and his private life remained depressingly unwarmed by friends or affection. Visitors to Ajaltun noticed a great collection of empty bottles under the kitchen sink. It was in this period of deprivation that he started a love affair with Eleanor Brewer, the wife of Sam Pope Brewer, Middle East correspondent of the *New York Times*.

Eleanor was an American, a couple of years younger than Kim, who had lived much abroad since the war. A small daughter to care for and an interest in sculpture were not enough to make her marriage happy. She was a tall, composed, gentle-voiced woman whose years in Europe and South America had given her a top-dressing of cosmopolitan know-how; but underneath she was still a simple, decent, unintellectual girl from Seattle who had picked up surprisingly little information about the world and neither understood politics nor cared much about them. From their first casual meeting in September 1956 in the bar of the St George Hotel – the classic place of rendezvous for foreign journalists in Beirut – Kim and Eleanor took warmly to each other, started seeing each other frequently, even making secret assignations in out-of-the-way cafés or in apartments lent to them by Eleanor's friends. Kim was invited to spend Christmas 1956 with the

Brewers. When Brewer was away on assignments the lovers would spend whole days together, travelling cheaply about the country and picnicking in the mountains. When Kim eventually took a small flat in town to be nearer Eleanor, she helped him decorate it.

Theirs was an old-fashioned courtship, marked by an almost daily exchange of notes, letters, *billets-doux*. Kim's side of this correspondence confirms the picture of him as a lonely man craving tenderness, now finding sudden relief in an outpouring of sentiment – even sentimentality. Once, on the eve of a trip that was to take him out of Beirut for three weeks, Kim answered a sad note from Eleanor.

... I, too, feel very near to tears, though it is silly. Such a short time; what are three weeks, after all? The answer is, I suppose, that there are weeks and weeks, and some of them much longer than others. Reckoning it up quickly, I think it must be nearly 900 weeks since I was *anything like* so happy as I am now. So you see how long I waited for you without knowing you. And you, my love, must have been nearly as long without real happiness; (we can forget the counterfeit article – the 'good times' coming with the Martinis!) ...[1]

He inundated her with a flood of honey. He pledged the utmost commitment and seemed to bare his soul. The effect was often that of a romantic novelette, with only an occasional note of banter creeping in. If his figure of 900 weeks is to be taken seriously, he would admit to no real happiness later than 1939 – the year before his embroilment as a double agent. The affair developed and took solid hold of them, and Kim urged Eleanor to seek a divorce although the chance of their marrying seemed remote. Then in December 1957 events came to their rescue. To Kim's unconcealed relief, his wife, Aileen, died in Crowborough, and he was free to propose to Eleanor. There were other deaths that year in both their families. Kim's mother, Dora, died in London a few months after the death of Eleanor's mother in Seattle. Eleanor went to America to put her father in an old people's home and to get the Mexican

1. A letter written in 1957, quoted in Eleanor Philby, *The Spy I Loved* (London, 1968), pp. 34, 35.

divorce she needed to marry Kim. Secure in the knowledge that a new life was at last about to begin, Kim waited not too impatiently for her return nearly a year later, in the autumn of 1958. They set up house together and shortly afterwards, on 24 January 1959, legalized their union at Holborn Register Office in London. She was forty-five and he forty-seven. 'This is love with a capital L,' Kim told a friend. 'We shall take a house in the mountains: she will paint; I will write; peace and stability at last.'

That journey to London was a landmark in Kim's rehabilitation. Now, almost eight years after the Burgess and Maclean affair had destroyed both his career and his marriage to Aileen, he could be seen in his old circles without unspoken constraints. The cloud of suspicion appeared to have lifted. If, as he no doubt suspected, he had been sent to Beirut as a pawn in a power game between rival secret services, it was not proving to be a very dangerous game. Like the old pro he was, he had got by with minimum performance. No one appeared to be gunning for him. He could afford to live normally. At a family house party at Littlehampton that Christmas, Eleanor was for the first time introduced to his five children. He took her on an extended sentimental journey round his favourite London pubs. With characteristic decency, he called on Mrs Alleyne, his former mother-in-law, to inform her of his plans to remarry – parking Eleanor meanwhile at the foot of the Albert Memorial. His friends opened their arms to him – among them, the two witnesses at the wedding, Jack Ivens, Kim's wartime associate in the intelligence contest with the Abwehr, and Tim Milne, whose Secret Service career had for so long paralleled his own and who had stood by him through thick and thin.

In the progress back to normality, he had above all Eleanor, his third wife and fifth woman to date. They were an assorted collection, Kim's women, with apparently little in common, except that they all, in turn, mattered to him, and that they were ultimately sacrificed – together with his own feelings and peace of mind – to the harsh demands of his secret life: Litzi, the Communist *militante*; Frances Doble, the exiled London socialite; Aileen, the unnerved and tormented product of the English counties; Connie, the shadowy civil servant who befriended him in the bad days; and now Eleanor whose principal contribution to his sense of security lay in her total innocence of the ugly underside of politics. For much of their married life in Beirut, Kim and Eleanor lived in a comfortable, but quite modest, top-floor apartment in the rue Kantari, whose main feature was a semi-circular living-room giving on to a terrace with fine views of the mountains. A tiny lift, like two coffins put together, meandered up the building. With bright rugs and printed cotton hangings Eleanor made a more substantial home than the rather makeshift arrangements he had known before they married. Favourite possessions of his, like an old Spanish table and a collection of his father's works, had been shipped out from Crowborough (and were later to follow him to Moscow). There was no doubt of his happiness and it was a happiness of a very domestic sort. They were very gentle and attentive to each other, and he used to boast of the fact that Eleanor had bought him everything he wore. He made the early morning tea, enjoyed cooking and was good at it, liked the company of children and spent long evenings teaching Eleanor's daughter, Annie, to recite the kings and queens of England and other useful accomplishments such as French. His own children were sent out from England in rotation. They found a household of pets, including at different times birds, fish, a puppy, a mouse called Wilbur and one year a fox cub, Jackie, whom Kim spent weeks house-training, before writing an adoring piece about her for *Country Life*: 'For just over two months Jackie has been learning how to live with human beings, just as we have been learning how to live with a fox. The results from our viewpoint (and, I think, from hers) have been almost wholly satisfactory.'

Rather than joining the cocktail party routine Kim preferred to stay at home, reading history (or thrillers), doing *The Times* crossword puzzle which he prided himself on completing in nineteen minutes flat, or listening to music. Scarcely a day went by without his taking Eleanor down to the Normandy Hotel for a lunchtime beer or cocktail and to pick up his mail. Some-

times he took her farther afield – to Persia, to the Empty
Quarter of Arabia, or up the Nile. And once a year they went
back to England. Returning from one such visit in early 1961,
Kim casually suggested that Berne would be a good place to
break the journey. To Eleanor's surprise he turned out to know
the town well; but he never told her that it was to a clinic there
that, a dozen years earlier, he had brought the ailing Aileen
from Turkey, and that she had convalesced in the home of the
local SIS man. It was this old friend from Berne who, in mid-
1960, was appointed to Beirut as SIS station commander –
and Kim's boss.

His arrival was undoubtedly a turning point in Kim's Beirut
career. Until then both the British and the Russians had
patiently allowed him to settle in and get acquainted with his
parish. In no very arduous fashion he had carved out a modest
niche for himself in the community of well-informed
foreigners suspected rightly or wrongly of having intelligence
connections. This community consisted of a score or so of men
whose ostensible jobs as businessmen, bankers, university professors, consultants for foreign companies and so forth, did
not wholly account for their insiders' preoccupation with Arab
politics. They were for the most part men in their forties and
fifties, veterans of the Second World War and generally considered to be principals in some clandestine line of country.
Kim was to be seen in their company, dining quietly in a
restaurant or chatting on the fringe of a reception or cocktail
party.

By 1960 pressure was mounting in the SIS for some further
action on Kim's case. If the Philby enigma, recognized as one
of the most dangerous puzzles in the history of the service,
were ever to be solved, now was the moment to do it. In the
British intelligence community Kim's most dangerous opponent had from the moment his case broke in 1951 been Dick
White, the counter-espionage maestro who was to rise to head
MI5. If, as seems highly likely, MI5 secretly master-minded
Kim's rehabilitation in 1955, White must have been the directing brain. Events were to ensure that he remained in control

of the operation. In the autumn of 1956 White was transferred from MI5 to take command of SIS in the wake of the Commander Crabbe fiasco – the political row caused by the disappearance under a Russian cruiser in Portsmouth harbour, during the visit of Khrushchev and Bulganin, of a British underwater sabotage expert. Rightly or wrongly the SIS was blamed for political ineptitude, a weakness which was cured by giving the service a tough new chief and greater Foreign Office control.

In his new job White was well placed to give a push to the Philby investigation, although for three years he appeared to let it lie, no doubt to lull Kim into a sense of security. Then in 1960 he seems to have decided to press for results, and responsibility for providing them fell to the new station commander in Lebanon, ironically one of Kim's most ardent defenders. His opinion carried some weight because, owing to the accident of his having joined the SIS before its wartime expansion, he seemed a senior figure. Charles (this is not his real name) was a very experienced intelligence officer, about fifty when he was posted to Beirut, who since 1945 had been largely concerned with the anti-Soviet intelligence conflict in Europe. He had known Kim since the war and indeed had worked under him when Kim was head of Section Five and he himself the counter-espionage man in Istanbul.

The son of the headmaster of one of the great English public schools, Charles's top-drawer image was confirmed by his enthusiastic membership of White's. He was a thin, spare man with a reputation as a shrewd operator whose quick humorous glance behind round glasses gave a clue to his sardonic mind. In manner and dress he suggested an Oxbridge don at one of the smarter colleges, but with a touch of worldly ruthlessness not always evident in academic life. Foreigners liked him, appreciating his bonhomie and his fund of *risqué* stories. He got on particularly well with Americans. The formal ladylike figure of his wife in the background contributed to the feeling that British intelligence in Beirut was being directed by a gentleman. From the moment of his arrival he saw a lot of Kim, appearing to treat him as his personal adviser on the bewildering politics of the area. As a non-intellectual he was clearly impressed by Kim's cultivated mind, though no admirer of Kim's beachcombing life-style. They met at least a couple of times a week for long talks. It was an old friendship resumed under new conditions.

Charles must have put Kim to work, setting him targets, sending him on trips, requesting reports which were then combed over in conversation. The technique was, it seems, a simple one: it involved forcing Kim out of the safety of inactivity to see whether his greater participation in the British intelligence effort would tempt the Russians into making contact with him. This meant sharing some confidences with him to test whether the bait would land the fish of a Soviet connection – not that there was any great hope of actually catching him red-handed with a Russian; rather items of information would be fed to him and counter-intelligence alerted to see where they surfaced. It was a game Kim could not refuse to play whatever the cost to his nerves. Of course he could not be sure beyond doubt that he was being investigated, although he must have thought it possible; but Charles's whole effort and demeanour, his whole panoply of trust, were designed to persuade Kim that he was not. Charles had, after all, long been one of his most ardent defenders within the service, and Kim knew it, so he combined, in a sense, all the trust and reassurance the service could offer – as well as the outside chance that he was there to trap Kim if he could. In their long-drawn-out probing of each other Kim tried to persuade himself that he was winning. 'I like Charles,' he used to tell Eleanor, 'but he's not very bright.' He must have been further reassured by the unsuspicious behaviour of the junior men in British intelligence whom he came across: Kim had been given a clean bill of health in the House and put back on the payroll; that was good enough for them. What Kim could not have known was just where he stood on the spectrum spanning trust and suspicion in the higher echelons, nor who in the SIS – MI5 leadership now believed him innocent and who did not. He could not have known exactly where in the service the operation involving him was mounted or who was privy to it. If he were being trusted and watched simultaneously, who was doing the trusting and who the watching? Such uncertainty is more than a hazard of such operations, it is an essential prerequisite of them. Here was a situation calculated to reawaken the anxiety slumbering just below the surface of Kim's life.

In the months before Charles's arrival Kim travelled and wrote little. Only six reports by him appeared in the *Observer* in the first nine months of 1960. But under pressure from Charles to produce more intelligence, his journalistic productivity also picked up and from late 1960 to the end of his career as a foreign correspondent he travelled to, and sent dispatches from, many parts of the Middle East, including Saudi Arabia, Egypt, Jordan, Kuwait and Yemen. In July 1962, when he was feeling increasingly hounded, he yet managed to produce a first-rate analysis of Nasser's régime on its tenth anniversary, which won him the congratulations of the editor for 'a most distinguished piece of reporting' and a bonus of forty-five guineas. The *Economist* were less satisfied with his coverage, and John Midgley, then Foreign Editor, who had known him in Berlin in 1933, wrote to him reprovingly. With facile contrition Kim wrote back, 'Let's try a *neue beginnen*,' an allusion to the German socialists' stubborn resistance to Hitler. Midgley felt it struck a false note. He was no more impressed when he visited Kim on his home ground in late 1960. Kim and Eleanor were waiting for him at Beirut airport and, evidently seeking to demonstrate that he was a good man to be met by, Kim seized Midgley's passport and waved it peremptorily under the nose of a Lebanese official. The effect was counter-productive: they were last through the barrier. Another small incident later in his visit underlined what Midgley took to be echoes of latent colonialism in Kim's attitude to Arabs. Calling on a local dignitary, they found the iron gate locked, and Kim called to an Arab boy to open it. Impishly the boy pointed to a small door by the gate which was already open. 'But it's this gate I want opened!' thundered Kim, shaking the railings. Arab intellectuals and other local friends could counter with evidence that his heart was firmly in the radical camp. Thus he clearly appreciated the company of such a man as Professor Walid Khalidi, of the American University of Beirut, a leading critic of the British record in Palestine and eloquent advocate of Arab Palestinian rights. With Indian journalists such as Willy Lazarus in Cairo and Godfrey Jansen in Beirut, Kim shared a detestation of imperialism and a sympathy for the Third World underdog.

Over the years from September 1956 to January 1963, Kim made a steady £2,000 to £2,500 a year from both the *Observer* and the *Economist* in salary and expenses. This was very far from princely for a man in his position, and clearly not nearly enough to meet the costs of his children in English boarding schools, his household in Beirut, his far-flung trips around the Middle East, his and Eleanor's generous consumption of alcohol. With a touch of self-righteousness, he had early made his case to the *Observer* for a rise (which he got):

There is no need for me to stay at a plush hotel. But I reckon that bed and board cannot be managed much under £2 a day ... You will have noticed perhaps that I have not made any claim in respect of entertainment so far ... The trouble begins when one forgathers with the chers collègues and finds it necessary to finance a round or two of Scotch, or get the reputation of being a mean stinker which is neither nice nor helpful.

All in all, I should say that an extra £500 p a would make all the difference. At the same time I would not want to press the matter, as I don't regard freedom from financial anxiety as a right to which all men are entitled!

It may not have been evident to his employers that he had other sources of income. One late December day in Beirut he dazzled Eleanor by producing ten $100 bills and scattering them about the room. 'Oh boy,' he exclaimed, 'This is going to make our Christmas!'

Whether the Russians or, as Eleanor believed, the British were responsible for this agreeable bonus, the dollars were a sign of the growing encroachments of intelligence on his hitherto peaceful life. It was unfortunate that at a time when he needed all his reserves of strength, two events took place which shook his confidence. The first was the death of his father at the age of seventy-five on 30 September 1960. To the end St John's appetite for life was unimpaired. Only a month earlier he had travelled to Moscow to attend the World Congress of Orientalists where after the daily sessions he was out every night visiting Russian scholars in the city. On the long train journey back to London a fellow delegate noticed that he did ample justice to the vodka and Crimean wines on sale in the restaurant car, and pretended surprise at finding such tastes in a professed Muslim. 'Can't get the stuff in Riyadh,' retorted the unperturbed Hajji, 'so I'm making the most of it now.' While the Soviet trial of Gary Powers, the American U-2 pilot shot down over Russia, was relayed remorselessly through the train's loudspeakers, St John talked about his old enthusiasm, cricket: he was looking forward to taking Kim's sons to Lords when he reached London. On his way home to Arabia he stopped in Beirut where he was wined and dined by Kim and Eleanor and a host of other friends and admirers. The morning after a particularly festive evening he suffered a heart attack in his room at the St George's Hotel and died that afternoon. Kim and Eleanor gave him a Muslim funeral at the Bashura cemetery above the city, inscribing on his tombstone the words 'Greatest of Arabian Explorers'. Kim's obituary in the *Observer* on 2 October was as elegant and almost as brief.

St John's death set Kim off on a prolonged drinking bout. Far more than most men of middle age he appeared affected by the loss of his father, and it was several days before he came round sufficiently to answer the letters of sympathy pouring in. Throughout his life Kim prided himself on the integrity of his moral positions. He convinced himself that what others called treason was selfless devotion to a glorious cause. In a very different way his father too had broken with the English establishment, pursued a lifelong course of dissent, and yet had remained admirable – and indeed widely admired. It was as if the father, by these achievements, had reinforced the moral posture of the son, giving his seal of approval, though unwittingly, to Kim's own dissent. 'If he had lived a little longer to learn the truth [about his son's espionage], he would have been thunderstruck, but by no means disapproving,' Kim has claimed, as if citing higher authority in support of his case. With his father gone, he had to shoulder his own responsibility.

Kim found himself involved in two practical problems after his father's death, the dispersal of St John's papers and the future welfare of his two sons by Umm Fahd. The elder boy, Khalid, wrote Kim a letter 'containing the thought-provoking phrase that God and myself are all they have left'. Kim's solution was to unload both problems on to the broad shoulders of Aramco, the Arabian American Oil Company, for one of whose founder companies St John Philby had won a concession in Arabia. But Kim could not escape a journey to Riyadh to rescue his father's papers and library which within hours of the old man's death had been seized by the palace. He spent a fruitless week arguing with officials, then wrote a last plea to the king. The result was an immediate authorization to take everything away. Instead of shipping the lot to Beirut, he had the books loosely packed and addressed to George Rentz, the Aramco official at Dhahran whom St John had appointed his literary executor. There they were stored for some months before their sale to Aramco was agreed, after some haggling, for a sum of $10,000. On St John's instructions, the money was earmarked for the education of his two young sons. Kim never met his half-brothers again.

Hardly had he dealt with these problems than he suffered a second, and possibly even more shaking, body-blow with the arrest in April 1961 of the Soviet spy George Blake. This able agent is thought to have been trapped by the careful analysis of the 'product' supplied both by a defector and by a double-agent. The exploitation of the latter source may serve as an illustration of a successful counter-espionage operation. An exceptionally alert British C-E officer noticed in a report from an agent he had 'turned' against the Russians a tiny item of secondary information which he thought he had seen before. On checking the files he located the self-same item in a two-year-old report by Blake. The presumption was that Blake had passed it to the Russians from whom it was now making its way back. And so the evidence against him grew. On a pretext he was recalled to London from Lebanon, where he had been studying Arabic in the British-run centre at Shemlan, and given a savage sentence of forty-two years in prison – rather than the 'standard' fourteen years maximum he and the Russians had expected; instead of sentencing Blake on all the convictions together, the judge gave him separate maximum terms on three different charges, the sentences to run consecutively. Kim did not fear exposure from Blake's arrest – the two men were operated separately by the Russians and knew nothing of each other's double role; but the success of British counter-espionage and the vindictiveness of British justice must have startled him.

By 1962 Kim's jousting with Charles was approaching its showdown. Occasionally anxiety betrayed him into signs of muddle or disturbance. It was his habit never to accept invitations for Wednesday nights. One day a friend said teasingly, 'I know all about your Wednesday nights.' He seemed visibly upset. Another time he vehemently denied all knowledge of an Armenian restaurant called *Vrej* (Revenge) where he had once got very drunk. Could this have been a place of clandestine rendezvous? For the first time Kim was making stupid blunders, pointers to his imminent crack-up. Visiting Beirut in April 1962 an acquaintance from his past was struck by his deterioration. F. W. D. Deakin, a fellow Westminster schoolboy who after brilliant wartime exploits in German-occupied Yugoslavia had become the first Warden of St Antony's College, Oxford, had arrived off Beirut together with Winston Churchill on board Aristotle Onassis's yacht. He spent a long evening with Kim and remembers how reluctant Kim was to leave, how anxious to cling to someone familiar, how near to collapse.

15 Endgame

> Those who were caught by the great illusion of
> our time, and have lived through its intellec-
> tual and moral debauch, either give themselves
> up to a new addiction of the opposite type, or
> are condemned to pay with a lifelong hangover.
>
> ARTHUR KOESTLER, *The God That Failed*

All his adult life Kim Philby took refuge in alcohol from
situations of psychological stress. Many men drink and for just
this reason, but in Kim's case the remedy, like the reason, was
beyond normal experience. The story of his life strongly suggests that he did not take like a duck to water to being a double
agent. He had no natural gift for living dangerously, no zest
for taking risks. He was a man shaped for a quiet domestic life,
a gentle, affectionate, rather unambitious person for whom
contentment lay in books, music, looking after pets and trying
his hand at cooking. Instead, a decision taken in youth and
stubbornly held to had let him in for unimagined anguish.
Throughout his life as a spy he suffered attacks of nerves so
painful that the insensibility brought about by gargantuan
quantities of alcohol seemed to offer the only relief. He started
drinking in Spain, on his first major assignment as a Russian
agent, and thereafter he never let up.

Drink was not a haven from the fears of espionage alone: all
the emotional crises of his life, the deaths of his mother and of
his father or accidents befalling his children were occasions for
drinking himself unconscious. His women were forever having
to pick him up off the floor, undress him and put him to bed.
But at least the griefs of his life as son and father could be
talked about as well as drowned in whisky. What made the
Russian connection such a burden was that he was doomed to
bear it in silence and alone, enjoying only such rare moments
of relief as clandestine contacts with his Soviet handlers
afforded. Other spies have testified to the profound psycho-

logical need to discuss with another person the details of their secret existence. And so from an early age Kim developed a habit of heavy drinking, which served the purpose not only of helping him forget, but of keeping his mouth shut. The remarkable feature of his drinking bouts was that by seemingly blocking out a part of his mind, they made him a lesser, instead of a greater, security risk. Never when drunk did he give himself away, or even hint with the muddled portentousness of an habitual drunk that there was more to him than appeared. He was strictly speaking an off-duty drinker, able to climb back to full professionalism the morning after.

His drinking in Beirut repeated a pattern already evident in Turkey and in Washington: what started as a high level of convivial consumption plunged, when the going got tough, into bottomless wells of alcoholic gloom. He knew how destructive this habit was, and felt guilty about it, defensively nicknaming alcohol 'snakebite' and repeatedly promising to lay off the poison. One Sunday Kim and Eleanor decided to picnic with another couple at Tabarja, a small rocky bay a few miles north of Beirut. Before setting out the Philbys announced that they wanted to stop at the Normandy Hotel to pick up Kim's mail. Reluctantly the others agreed, but barely had the car stopped when Kim and Eleanor made a dash for the bar. It was a while before they could be induced to continue the journey. At Tabarja Kim went back and forth to a little Arab café above the beach to buy miniature bottles of whisky, emptying in all about forty. By sundown he and Eleanor were falling over the rocks and his arms and knees were bleeding. She would pick him up and set him on his feet giggling and laughing. For much of the time they seemed happy drunks, bruised and scarred by a hundred falls against the furniture. On occasions, however, liquor brought out less agreeable sides of Kim's character. He was not by nature a violent man, but given a few drinks in the Beirut years he often revealed a bullying streak. It would be heralded by a strange sort of buzzing noise, a hum which developed into a chant, until he suddenly reached out to grab a girl's wrist or ankle and twist it violently. He was an adept at Chinese Fire, the child's trick which consists in gripping a wrist in both fists and wringing the skin in opposite directions. Someone would have to come to the aid of the victim, but Eleanor was never subjected to such attacks.

Almost every acquaintance from that time has a story to tell of his moments of drunken violence. The Indian journalist, Willy Lazarus, often his host in Cairo, remembers Kim, after a heavy evening, grappling with him in the middle of the night, shouting, 'Where's Eleanor? You've hidden her somewhere!' and tearing the apartment apart in his search. After such an outburst he would collapse, go on the wagon for three or four days, and recover. On a journalistic trip with Eleanor early in 1962, this time to Teheran, his host was awakened by the crash of falling furniture in the guest room and by a storm of angry voices. In a lull could be heard the unmistakable sound of Kim making water on the tiled floor, an event confirmed the next morning. But his friends forgave these occasional lapses, so considerate and full of delicate attentions was he when sober. The cruel pressures of his double life made this fundamentally gentle person do violence to his nature, like a suspect who leaps to his death from the window of his prison to escape his torturers.

In the first week of September 1962 Kim took Eleanor, her daughter Annie and his own son Harry for a few days' sight-seeing in Jordan in the relative cool of the late summer. For reasons he did not explain he returned to Lebanon a day early, leaving the family to follow him home. When Eleanor reached the flat in the rue Kantari the next evening, she found Kim slumped on the terrace, deeply depressed and barely coherent from drink. Here once more were the signals of a personal crisis: clearly some calamity had befallen him since she had last seen him two days earlier. 'Jackie's dead,' he mumbled. Eleanor gathered that their pet fox, to which Kim was very much attached, had fallen, or been pushed, to its death from the parapet of the terrace. Fond as they were of the animal she found Kim's misery excessive; but he had no other explanation to offer. Unlike earlier crises, this one was not resolved, and Kim's gloom did not lift, nor his recourse to alcohol slacken.

Ever since he was nearly betrayed by Krivitsky in 1937 and by Volkov in 1946, Kim must have been haunted by the fear that someone on the Russian side would successfully defect and give him away. It must be assumed from the evidence of his behaviour that on that day in September word had reached him to confirm his fears. Anatoli Dolnytsin was a senior Russian KGB officer serving under diplomatic cover in the Ottawa embassy of an Eastern European country. In January or February 1962 he defected and was taken for safety across the frontier into the United States. After some six months' interrogation by the American secret service, he was passed to Britain where the information he gave on KGB knowledge of British secrets pointed conclusively to a spy in the SIS in the years up to 1951. Dolnytsin appears not to have known the spy's identity, but his evidence filled in the gaps in the case against Kim. This defection not only put Kim in danger of retaliation by the SIS, but it destroyed the basis of the subtle contest that his critics in the service had been waging with him for the past couple of years. The British could no longer pretend to consider Kim innocent or to attempt to play him against the Russians. After Dolnytsin they knew that the Russians knew that they knew about Philby. The pawn had to be removed from the board. The game was up.

The question was: who was to do the removing and how? While Moscow perfected an escape plan there were intense consultations in Whitehall as to what could be done about Kim. Assassination was presumably ruled out: Kim had no more British secrets to be protected by his death, revenge was an unworthy motive, and there must have been reluctance to take a step that might trigger off an even more violent Soviet reaction. Ever since the Commander Crabbe affair in 1956 had brought the SIS under tighter ministerial control, bold initiatives of this nature had required clearance at a high political level. And as intelligence officers often have reason to note, politicians develop very delicate moral sensibilities when the risks of failure are great. If these arguments weighed heavily against assassination, they could equally be invoked against kidnapping. It was simply impractical: the SIS were not equipped to carry out such tasks in Lebanon. Moreover the service preferred information to retribution. In spite of Dolnytsin's revelations, they still hoped to secure from Kim a clear admission of guilt together with as much detail as possible about the dates, techniques and scope of his activities as a Soviet agent. Only in this way could they estimate precisely the damage he had done and close their files. Rightly or wrongly, the view was taken that he was more likely to talk while still at large than languishing in a prison cell in Britain. The SIS wanted the information more than they wanted the man, whose trial anyway could only bring unfavourable publicity on themselves.

So it was decided that Kim should be confronted with the fresh and damning evidence against him, in the hope that with nothing to lose he could be tricked or cajoled or simply tempted into filling in the detail. The man chosen for this interesting assignment was Charles, whose old friendship with Kim would, it was hoped, loosen his tongue. Charles had left his post in Beirut that summer on the completion of his tour of duty and his successor in Lebanon had not kept up the intimate and regular contact which Kim had had with Charles. At the same time other British intelligence officers were advised to be discreet in their dealings with Kim.

Of course Kim had no way of knowing how the British were reacting and what action, if any, they would take against him. But with the example of George Blake's sentence before him, he must have had few illusions about what to expect in England if he were caught. Quite apart from the rigours of prison for the rest of his life, his whole establishment-formed soul must have cringed at the prospect of public obloquy. For a man whose self-image had leaned so heavily on an appearance of total integrity, the contempt his exposure would earn him, the humiliation, the shock to his family, were too much to be borne. It was one thing to boast about his exploits from the safety of Moscow; it would have been quite another to defend them from the dock. So, not for the first time in his life, he suffered that autumn in Beirut from all the terrors of Hades.

He was an ordinary man trapped in an extraordinary situation, and not surprisingly he sought relief where he had always found it.

An event then took place, far away in the south-eastern corner of Arabia, which roused him from his now almost continual drinking. In late September the old Imam of the Yemen, a fiercely repressive tribal and theocratic ruler who had kept his backward country cut off from the outside world, died and was succeeded by his more liberal son. Almost immediately the young Imam was overthrown by a revolution. Its impact was like an electric shock through the Arab world, causing kings to tremble and radicals to rejoice. It seemed as if the flame lit by Nasser had at last set feudal Arabia alight and would sweep across the whole peninsula. Kim was a member of the first party of Western journalists to visit the Yemeni capital of Sanaa in mid-October and witness the populace cheering the new revolutionary régime. Dropping his reserve, he joined in. From Sanaa the journalists flew to Saudi Arabia where they met Prince Faisal, the effective ruler of his country (although he had not yet taken over as King from his brother Saud). 'From what I hear you are not on our side, Mr Philby,' the prince said to St John's son. Kim's answer is unrecorded.

Naturally the Saudis supported the deposed Imam, and escorted the journalists across the frontier into northern Yemen where loyal tribesmen were preparing to launch a counter-revolution. Kim returned to Beirut confident that the revolution had little to fear from such comic-opera enemies. A month later he paid a second, briefer visit to republican Yemen which served only to confirm his judgement. The civil war in Yemen was perhaps the only event which provoked Kim into taking sides in his career as a foreign correspondent. Perhaps the conjunction of an uprising by the people with the downfall of a reactionary dynasty in his father's old stamping ground was too much for him to resist.

On both his journeys to Yemen in those last few weeks of 1962 Kim passed through Aden, then still a British territory. Had they wished to do so, the British authorities could presumably have arrested him there. Apparently they still judged that a confrontation in conditions less restrictive than a prison cell would yield better results.

Shortly before Christmas Charles returned to Beirut to resume the interrogation shelved ten years earlier. Then the verdict had been 'guilt unproven but suspicion remaining'; now, with Dolnytsin's evidence, the guilt was proved, the suspicion confirmed, but for the purposes of 'damage assessment' – the meticulous balance sheet drawn up after the uncovering of a spy – a full confession was required from the culprit. In particular, nothing was known about Kim's channels of communication with his Soviet handlers at any stage in his career. In Turkey, for example, Kim's travelling about the country must have made contact easy; but how did he manage it in London and Washington where, on certain crucial occasions such as the Volkov affair, the Russian atom bomb explosion, the agreement on the escape plan for Maclean, speedy and secure communications in volume were essential? So skilful was he that he had never been detected breaking cover. He owed his downfall to the blunders of others.

Kim and Charles had perhaps half-a-dozen meetings. What the feelings of the two men were, how their delicate business was broached, what ground was covered, are not known; but it requires little imagination to evoke the drama and poignancy of these encounters. Faced with the strength of the case against him, Kim could no longer stall. It is known that he formally confessed to having been a life-long Soviet agent, to having warned Maclean through Burgess, but as for the rest, the precious detail of how, when and where remained tantalizingly vague although he is said to have admitted to meeting his Soviet contact in Beirut, a Counsellor at the Soviet Embassy, once a month, and to filling the Russians in as to Western intelligence targets and personnel in the Middle East. While Charles tried to pin him down to the nuts and bolts of the thing, he seized the opportunity of these conversations to justify his treachery in a long philosophical apologia, ranging from the failure of the democracies to cope with fascism in the thirties to the inherent irresponsibility of post-war American power. It is thought he pleaded that he was a man of politics, that his life had been dedicated to an idea and shaped by a morality, a world view above vulgar calculations of gain, self-interest or personal security. Now with his life at risk his chief concern was to prove an ideological point.

Charles, it seems, was not unimpressed. An ideological traitor, hooked early and with the guts to stick to his convictions, deserved some respect, however much one disapproved of him and however total and ruthless one's hostility to his position. But a *leitmotif* of Kim's defence was self-righteousness, a certainty that he was right and an anxiety to persuade others of it. Pondering this, Charles became convinced that the key to the enigma of Kim's character was a sort of moral egotism, the vanity of a man who could not bear to be wrong. This conclusion may have suggested to Charles and his advisers a line of approach. Was not Kim perhaps another Klaus Fuchs, a traitor whose need to justify himself could, in the right circumstances of unrestrained liberty, be cleverly exploited to loosen his tongue?

There is a further twist to the affair which must be considered. In the counter-espionage operation started in 1955, the objectives had been, first, to attempt to play Kim back against the Russians; and second, when Dolnytsin's defection made this no longer possible, to secure as full a confession as possible. But were there further advantages to be wrung from Kim's betrayal? It seems inconceivable that Charles should not have been instructed to horse-trade with Philby, to offer him safety from British retaliation in exchange for a small shift of loyalty from Russia back to his native land. In other words, they must, at this late hour, have tried to turn him. No other explanation fully accounts for the failure to arrest him in the British colony of Aden, the fact that he was left undisturbed in Beirut, the slow, gentlemanly pace of the progress to the climax.

Kim was left to brood on the options open to him over Christmas, Charles returned to SIS headquarters in London to report, and the two men agreed to resume their somewhat leisurely conversation in the New Year. The view in London seems to have been that their quarry was clearly under strain, was drinking more than was good for him, but was apparently prepared to cooperate if given time. He might even be enjoying the luxury of self-explanation, of speaking at last in his true voice.

As great an interest in the dialogue between Kim and Charles was felt by Kim's Russian masters, who had, however, considerably less enthusiasm than the British for its continuance. Just as the British needed to know what Kim had done for the Russians, so the Russians needed to know how much of their secret knowledge Dolnytsin had betrayed. The way the British showed their hand would provide the best clues, and therefore Kim was not whisked to safety as soon as Dolnytsin defected. Instead he was kept *in situ*, was eventually told of his exposed position but left to stew in it until Charles turned up with the proof the Russians wanted. Beyond this point there was little profit in waiting. They had to be sure that Kim would give away less than he learned.

The longer Kim's dangerous dialogue with the British went on, the less the Russians must have liked it. They must have been well aware that the British would try to turn him, and the inviolability that Kim appeared to enjoy must have made them wonder if the British had had some measure of success. Could this renegade Englishman be expected to be a loyal Russian to the core of his being? Can a leopard change its spots? Whether or not Kim succumbed to British blandishments, the doubt planted in Russian minds that he might have was enough to make sure that Kim would be a sort of prisoner for the rest of his life.

It must be assumed that one of the first things Kim did on arrival in Lebanon, as a matter of routine, was to prepare with his Soviet friends a plan of escape. From the autumn of 1962, and even more urgently from the moment of Charles's reappearance in Beirut, he must have begged them to put it into effect. The Russians, who are known to go to some pains to protect their men in order to maintain the morale and prestige of their secret service, must have been conscious that he could not long resist the terrors he was suffering – they were not to know, after all, that the British had decided against assassination or kidnapping. And so the KGB informed him that, to forestall any such unpleasant surprises, he was to be taken, very soon, to safety. Bolstered by this knowledge he must have persuaded Charles that he would be more forthcoming at their next meetings. He laid out false trails to indicate that he had no intentions of disappearing. For example, on 29 December 1962 he wrote at length to the editor of the *Observer* about his plans for the coming year, requesting, surely somewhat prematurely, permission to spend some time in England the following September. Presumably he took it that the security service might check his movements with the *Observer*. Two days later, on 1 January 1963, his fifty-first birthday, his nerve cracked.

Tired out by the interrogations, by the fears of the ordeal which he might have to face in England if he failed to get away, even by his trips to Yemen, Kim was by Christmas ready to throw in the sponge. He sat at home drinking moodily, refusing to leave the house, turning down one end-year invitation after another, driving Eleanor to distraction by his unwillingness to tell her what was on his mind. They saw the New Year in, alone, at home, over a bottle of champagne. So weak was his condition that to celebrate his birthday the next day Eleanor planned nothing more ambitious than a lunch-time drink for a few people, but in the afternoon they were persuaded to call in on an all-day New Year party given by some American friends near by. With great difficulty Eleanor got Kim home. In the bathroom he lost his balance and fell against the radiator, splitting his head open. As he tried to get up, he fell again, opening his head a second time. The bathroom was covered in blood. Frantically Eleanor picked him up, somehow dragged him to his bed, and attempted to stop the blood flowing. Then she called a doctor, who after repeated unsuccessful attempts to get the protesting Kim into the lift, finally carried him off to be stitched up at the emergency ward of the American University Hospital. This accident was the nearest Kim had come in over twenty years to losing control.

He was still in bed a week later when, on 6 January, the

secretary of the new SIS station commander at the British Embassy telephoned to call him to a meeting. He declined, suspecting no doubt that he might leave the meeting a prisoner. Bedridden and bandaged, he spun out his convalescence, waiting with growing desperation for the Russian signal. His newspaper employers in London had no inkling of these dramatic developments. On 16 January John Thompson, the *Observer*'s news editor, cabled Beirut:

interested taut piece friday afternoon whats happening kuwait stop alternatively whats happening syria should this seem you harder news query space tight with common marketeering this week thus possibly kuwait can wait please advise

Professional to the end, Kim replied the following day:

syria apparently teacup storm therefore kuwait probably timelier stop will cable as requested philby

On Saturday, 19 January, Kim filed his last piece from Beirut – a minor story, and indeed about Kuwait.

Four days later, on the night of Wednesday, the 23rd, he disappeared. It was a night of violent winds and lashing rain such as Beirut experiences three or four times a winter. The Philbys had accepted an invitation to dine that evening with Glen Balfour-Paul, a British diplomat, and his wife. In late afternoon, with only his raincoat to protect him against the downpour, Kim left the rue Kantari flat on an unexplained errand and at about 6 p.m. telephoned home to say he would join Eleanor at the Balfour-Pauls' house about eight o'clock. He was never seen in Lebanon again.

Much later in Moscow Kim told Eleanor that he had worn out a pair of shoes escaping from Beirut, which led her to suppose that he had left the country on foot. This was just credible. The mountain frontier between Lebanon and Syria to the east is notoriously difficult to police. Smugglers, fugitives from justice or political oppression, mere shepherds cross it regularly by one or other of the tracks which avoid the tarred highway and the frontier posts. Like many Englishmen in Lebanon Kim was fond of walking and knew the terrain well, a knowledge strikingly demonstrated on one occasion to a British radio engineer who had come to Lebanon to build a communications network. Accompanying the prospecting party in the frontier area, Kim was able to tell them that a certain stony path would lead them to Syria. Sure enough, after a long scramble they eventually found themselves across the border. When they sought to return to Lebanon they had trouble persuading the Syrian frontier police to let them leave a country which their passports indicated they had never entered.

But the truth of Kim's escape was probably less adventurous. The Lebanese mountains on a nasty night in late January are no place for a middle-aged man in poor shape, and it is most unlikely that the Russians would have exposed their veteran agent to such an ordeal. Although they appear to have left his retrieval to the eleventh hour, they had plenty of time to plan it. The most plausible explanation of his movements is that he threw off any surveillance, entered the port area with Russian documents, and boarded the Russian freighter *Dolmatova* which weighed anchor about midnight without loading her cargo. His complaint to Eleanor of wear and tear to his shoe-leather was no doubt his way of saying that he had done a lot of walking through the streets of Beirut to make sure he was not being followed.

He was out, leaving behind him a certain disarray whose ripples were to widen until the full enormity of the Philby story reached the public domain.

The first victim was the innocent, unpolitical Eleanor who from one day to the next lost her husband, her security and her happiness and found herself playing a major role in a hideous melodrama. For a couple of days she did not even know whether Kim were alive or dead; perhaps he had fallen drunk into the sea; and when mysterious messages arrived from unspecified addresses, in her anguish and uncertainty she did not know what credence to give them. But gradually, as the months passed, she came reluctantly to acknowledge that she had married a Russian spy – now safe in his chosen country –

only to be faced with the further dilemma of whether she should join him there.

As for Kim's long contest with the SIS, it is a moot point who took the honours, such as they were. He escaped British justice. He gave counter-espionage little reward for hanging on his tail for a decade. And yet the steady and humane harassment to which he was subjected did in the end force him to break cover and flee. His file, at least as an agent at large in the West, could be closed once and for all. The SIS may have lost their quarry, they may have gleaned little information from him, but they secured the admission of guilt they wanted: the outcome was by no means dishonourable. At least the SIS could claim with some justice that the whole tussle had caused the Russian service to extend and expose itself as much as they had themselves. To quote only one example, Eleanor later identified from photographs provided by her British questioners a Soviet agent who had once called at their house. More subtly, the delicate mixture of trust and watchfulness with which the British had handled Philby since 1951 robbed the Russians of *total* confidence in their agent. If the British could not be sure he was guilty, they could not be sure he was loyal. Was he a double, or a triple, agent? It is a question which no doubt someone in Moscow still puzzles over.

The final stages of the affair were certainly messy, suggesting a panic-stricken improvisation at odds with Soviet intelligence's reputation for efficiency. Kim's whole getaway was ill-managed. Was it necessary to indulge in the melodrama of the missed dinner party and the frantic wife? Could not Kim have left the country on one of his routine journalistic trips as soon as it was evident that the game was up? A dozen years earlier Donald Maclean's flight to safety had also been left to the dangerous last minute and committed, furthermore, to the unsteady hands of the barely controllable Burgess. George Blake in turn was kept *in situ* even when his position was endangered by a Soviet defector. All three cases illustrate the ruthlessness of the Russian service in pushing their men to the limit, although they may also be adduced as evidence for the Russians' ultimate loyalty to their agents. After all, Blake was sprung from a British jail with dazzling efficiency while Maclean and Philby lived to enjoy what pleasures Moscow has to offer. Perhaps the messiness of their respective escapes is the inevitable consequence of the Russians seeking to strike too fine a balance between the need to get their pound of flesh and the equal need to protect their men. Spies, like everyone else, have in due course to retire – but rather sooner than in most professions. Some spymasters believe that seven years is just about the maximum period of effectiveness for a secret agent, a pattern rather strikingly borne out by the careers of these three: Kim and Maclean made their contributions to Russia between 1944 and 1951, with Kim putting in a second, if scarcely valuable stretch between 1956 and 1963; while George Blake's span of effective espionage lasted from 1953 to 1960. The spy has much to contend with: leaks from his own side, the inexorable pursuit of the opposition's counter-espionage, not to mention the wear and tear to his own nervous system.

On the British side Kim's exposure and escape left a lot of raw nerves. Men who had worked with him and respected him, brother officers as well as technicians who at various stages of his career had advised him on operations, felt betrayed – and none more than those who had stood by him after 1951. A defection from the family hits an intelligence service in its entrails: it arouses doubts and inhibitions, it makes recruitment difficult, it discourages outsiders with specialist information from approaching the service. But the shock was also salutary. The conjunction of the Blake and Philby cases gave a further impetus to the strengthening of the always important counter-espionage side of the SIS – which now absorbs, it is thought, about a quarter of the total force.

Today's service is very different from the one Kim joined in the war. It is more professional, more secure, but also less ambitious and less autonomous. There are some countries, notably America, in which the intelligence community has a direct hand in the making of national policy, but Britain is not among them. Her secret service, now renamed DI6, is firmly under the thumb of the Foreign Office, a servant of the Foreign

Secretary and his diplomatists rather than a truly independent organization freewheeling round international politics. All its important initiatives need a politician's signature, a singularly inhibiting state of affairs. This gelding of Britain's spies was presided over by Kim's old opponent, Sir Richard Goldsmith White, and consolidated by his successor Sir John Rennie, a career Foreign Office official who headed the service from 1966 until his retirement in 1973. It must be assumed that just as Britain's status has shrunk from world power to EEC member, so the targets of her secret service have in turn dwindled to focus on Europe.

As for the crucial matter of relations with the already very powerful American services, it may be said that the ending of the Philby affair caused little or no damage. For insiders in both countries it was no more than the winding up of an old case, rather than the shock of a new one. In any event, the American record was itself not spotless. They too had had their traitors, such as Bernon Mitchell and William Martin of the National Security Agency who in 1960 did great damage to the whole American code-breaking effort.

The SIS kept its Philby secret strictly to itself, leaving his journalistic employers to puzzle over their lost correspondent. The *Observer* and the *Economist* got little help from Kim's newspaper colleagues in Beirut, equally at a loss to explain his mysterious disappearance but reluctant to throw the first stone accusing him of a political defection: in the circumstances it seemed to them more plausible that he had stolen a march on them in a crisis spot like the Yemen, or was simply coming out of an alcoholic coma in some clinic. Bewildered cables between Fleet Street and Beirut failed to make sense of Kim's absence. But in the first week of February, the Baath Party in Iraq overthrew General Kassem, the revolution had to be covered, and Kim was replaced. On 3 March, about six weeks after his flight, the *Observer* publicly acknowledged it did not know what had become of its Middle East expert.

Rumours of his whereabouts came thick and fast to contradict each other. He was in Ethiopia; he was in southern Sudan; he was in Kurdistan, or dead; he was in Cairo, where on 1 March a fond cable to Eleanor, signed 'H. Philby', was handed in at the post office, by an Arab for what ferreting reporters later discovered was a two-shilling tip. His disappearance was raised in a question in the House of Commons on 20 March: the Lord Privy Seal, Mr Edward Heath, would not speculate but reassured the House that 'since Mr Philby resigned from the Foreign Service in 1951, twelve years ago, he has had no access of any kind to any official information'. (The government was soon to eat its words.) The following day Colonel Tawfiq Jalbut, chief of Lebanese security, issued a warrant for Kim's arrest on a charge of illegal departure. On 3 June the Moscow *Izvestia* (displaying an unexpected sense of humour) reported him serving as an adviser in the Yemen – with the royalist forces!

Then, at the end of June 1963, the truth came out. The American magazine, *Newsweek*, clearly tipped off by a CIA source and undeterred by fears of a British libel action, scooped the world with the blunt affirmation that Philby was the Third Man, that he had been recruited as a Communist agent as early as 1936, and that he was now probably safe in Russia. *Newsweek* fanned the story into an international security scandal with its questions: Why had Harold Macmillan cleared Philby in spite of American warnings? Why had the Foreign Office foisted him on British newspapers in 1956? Had he been protected by the Old Boy Net? Could the United States trust Britain to keep their secrets?

The British Government reacted with an immediate statement confirming the bare bones of *Newsweek*'s story: Mr Harold Philby was indeed the Third Man in the Burgess and Maclean case, and he was now thought to be behind the Iron Curtain. After so tantalizingly scant an admission, Mr Heath could not escape further close questioning in the days that followed. In particular M.Ps pressed the government to explain how the Foreign Office had come to recommend Philby to the *Observer* five years after they had sacked him for security reasons. In his answer Mr Heath came as near as the authorities have ever done, then or since, to admitting to a counter-espionage operation: 'He was recommended because

Philby

it was thought not unreasonable – *and indeed wise* – at that time that Mr Philby should be in employment.'[1] Twice in the House that day, 8 July, Mr Heath stressed the 'wisdom' of Kim's re-employment as a journalist, but without of course saying in what sense it could be so described.

Clearly this public probing of so delicate a situation was worrying the intelligence and security services. In mid-July the Prime Minister, Mr Macmillan, privately briefed the Labour leaders, Harold Wilson and George Brown, and secured their agreement to bring the curtain down on the Philby debate. For four years the curtain stayed down until in the autumn of 1967 the rivalry between two British Sunday papers, the *Observer* and the *Sunday Times,* hauled it up once more, revealing not only a wealth of detail about the life and times of the superspy but also many long-cherished secrets of the British service he had served so ill. For Kim in Moscow this blaze of publicity was a sort of posthumous triumph.

Meanwhile, on 30 July 1963, the Supreme Soviet had granted him political asylum and Soviet citizenship.

1. *The Times* parliamentary report, 9 July 1963. Authors' italics.

16 Russian Pensioner

> You choose your side once and for all – of
> course it may be the wrong side, only history
> can tell that!
>
> GRAHAM GREENE, *The Confidential Agent*

So, after long years in the field, Kim Philby retired to Moscow.
The Soviet citizenship that he had in effect applied for in the
mid-1930s was now a reality, providing security, giving his
future certainty as well as limits, shaping the everyday detail of
his life. He took to Russia pretty well. In many ways his experience was that of any stranger settling in a foreign city, but
with the knowledge that he was there for good supplying an
added motive to make a go of it. Freed from the deforming
pressures of the chase, his methodical nature took over once
more and he set about solving the problems presented by the
Russian capital with all the system of the high-class civil
servant he was. From the moment of his arrival he worked
steadily at the language, spurred on by his old passion for the
Russian classics, which he now has the pleasure of being able
to read in the original. As steadily he taught himself the map
of the sprawling city on long regular walks: his sense of place,
always good, has been deliberately cultivated throughout his
life by excursions on foot.

His is a home-based life[1] whose pleasures are those of
domesticity, leisure and retirement. With something of an old
age pensioner's fondness for little routines, he fills his days
with reading, shopping for food and cooking it, and regular
visits to opera and ballet whose choice is pondered over at the
start of each season and the tickets purchased after mature
deliberation. His Moscow flat houses three thousand books or
more, constantly added to with packets of new publications
arriving from Bowes & Bowes of Cambridge or direct from

1. We are indebted to the late Mrs Eleanor Philby for much information about Kim's life in Moscow.

publishers in England and America. Mainly it is pretty solid reading that he buys – four-volume histories of Russia or Nabokov's translation of Pushkin's *Eugene Onegin*; but he also indulges his taste for thrillers, books on animals, and P. G. Wodehouse, whose extravaganzas have him giggling helplessly in bed long after lights out. He keeps up with the news from abroad, having a more than layman's interest in it. On daily trips to the post office he collects copies of the *Washington Post* and the *International Herald Tribune*, *Time* and *The Times*, and of course *Le Monde*. Food is his chief non-intellectual hobby and at home he spends long hours over the stove, perfecting a ratatouille or a piperade or, more ambitiously, a *veau à la moutarde* or a *crabe au gratin*. He has taken to making his own large winter stocks of jam and chutney – 'fun when it comes out right and infuriating when it doesn't'. His love of animals is expended on a cageful of canaries whose fertility, however, has been on occasions embarrassing, obliging Kim to pass on to his friends in the KGB some of the surplus population. Like other men of his age, he is concerned about his health. When he first arrived in the Soviet Union, in January 1963, he was physically fragile, near the end of his tether, broken down by worry and alcohol. But the Russians have looked after him well and after a few spells in hospital, release from anxiety, plenty of good Russian food and enforced temperateness (not without a few lapses), have made him better able to survive the bronchial colds which afflict him in the winter. His face and figure have sagged somewhat but his appearance suggests not so much deterioration as comfortable and relaxed middle age.

But this pensioner of the Soviet state is not totally retired. His first months in Russia were a concentrated period of 'debriefing' getting down on paper and on tape just about everything he knew about the West which might have an intelligence value. From then on he has served as a KGB consultant, writing papers or making himself available at home for questioning on the issues that crop up. Such a career offers no prospect of advancement, and his expertise about Western intelligence matters must be considered a wasting asset. He is therefore seeking less to climb a ladder than to stand still, giving what satisfaction he can. This he does. His bureaucratic gifts, once recognized in the SIS, are now wholly at the service of the Russians. In particular, he is clearly a valued adviser in both the offensive and defensive operations which the Russians run against Britain. Sometimes he is wheeled out to deal a public blow at his 'old friends', as when, in October 1971, he retaliated to the mass-expulsion of 105 Russians from Britain by naming in the pages of *Izvestia* a number of alleged British intelligence officers and agents. In addition he has continued to write for publication from time to time – both journalism and books. In 1965 he polished the text of *Spy*, the memoirs of Konon Molody, alias Gordon Lonsdale, the Russian spy who penetrated the Portland Naval Base in England. (Lonsdale was arrested and convicted in 1961, but was exchanged three years later for Greville Wynne, the SIS contact with the Soviet defector Oleg Penkovsky.) Then, in 1968, the publicity given to his story in the Western press presented Kim with a golden opportunity to put his own gloss on his career and, at the same time and more seriously, to tear down what was left of the curtain of secrecy shrouding the workings of British intelligence. This he achieved with a good deal of elegance in his book, *My Silent War*. It was a very personal piece of propaganda, but effective: it must be counted his last major operation against Britain and certainly earned him his retirement pension. To compensate him for the loss of his OBE, withdrawn by the British government on 10 August 1965 – and for his expulsion from the Athenaeum – the Soviet state awarded him the Order of the Red Banner, a decoration in which as a loyal and steadfast servant of Soviet Russia he takes great pride. There is no doubt that the VIP treatment he is accorded and the evident approbation of his masters matter to him.

But even when his satisfactions, professional and domestic, are taken into consideration, Kim's life in Moscow must be judged a rather cheerless one. It is a life almost without companionship. His circle of acquaintances appears to be rigidly restricted to his housekeeper who comes in daily, a handful of his fellow officers in the KGB, two or three other ageing defectors from the West, and one or two trusted Muscovites: in all, under a dozen people. He makes a point of avoiding contact with Western journalists and if taken by surprise in a restaurant or at the Conservatoire, will counter their advances with a stony 'I don't speak English', delivered in Russian. But is life so different for a Soviet defector seeking safe obscurity in Britain or America? – especially a defector from that holy of secret holies, the intelligence service? Solitariness is to some extent dictated by his situation but, fortunately for him, his character, tastes and training all equip him to support it tolerably well. Once a year, usually in the summer, one or other of his sons or daughters comes to visit him.

There were two men in the Russian capital in 1963 who had been waiting for Kim for twelve years. One, Mark P. Fraser, otherwise Donald Maclean, owed him a debt of gratitude for his eleventh-hour escape to safety; the other, Jim Andreyevitch Eliot, otherwise the impulsive Guy Burgess, owed him an explanation, if not an apology, for bringing Kim to the brink of destruction by his unplanned flight from Britain. But the passage of years had blunted the sharp edge of Guy's guilty conscience as well as Kim's resentment, and there is little doubt that the two friends were eagerly looking forward to a reunion. No satisfaction that Moscow offered could have matched the intense interest and pleasure of such a meeting. But they were never to have time to enjoy it. For six months after his arrival in Russia Kim was kept strictly incommunicado and too busy for anything but work. When he was finally allowed to see his friend, Guy was dying in the Botkin Hospital.

Guy's life in Russia could have served Kim as a model of how not to behave. In the drab conformity of Moscow, he was as irreverently conspicuous as a drop-out at a board meeting. The Russians are immensely loyal to anyone who has worked for them and to anyone they think is basically a friend, but Burgess must have sorely tried their patience and they were at a loss to know what to do with him. The average Soviet government servant could have no inkling of the society which had spawned a phenomenon like Burgess. He in turn detested the bureaucratic, KGB side of Soviet life. With Maclean as a correct figure in the background, he burst upon the expatriate Moscow scene in 1956, after the pair had spent several dreary years on ice in the provincial obscurity of Kuybyshev, some five hundred miles east of Moscow. They had arrived in the Soviet Union in 1951 on the eve of Stalin's last purge, but in the more liberal Khrushchev era, Burgess's oddities at last found a metropolitan setting.[1]

In Moscow he lived with a Russian boyfriend, Tolya, a factory-hand in his twenties who played the accordion and was said to come from Tolstoy's village. Burgess claimed to have found Tolya himself. He used to say that it was either a question of the KGB providing him with a boyfriend or of his fending for himself; so he had gone out on the streets one night and come back with Tolya. They used to quarrel a good deal, when Burgess would explode into execrable pidgin Russian: he had no gift for languages. They shared a two-room flat in a huge apartment block, where some quite important people lived, near the Novodevichy Monastery, eating their meals off old blue and white Tsarist china (which Burgess said he would return to the Soviet state on his death). For the most part they had to be content with a diet of local produce, washed down by inferior Armenian cognac, but whenever Burgess had any foreign exchange he would order a case of luxury food and drink from Copenhagen. The case would be left standing open in the flat and Guy and his friends would help themselves from it as though it were a schoolboy's tuck-box. At the top of his bed was a magnificent carved head-piece, once the property of Stendhal – or so he claimed. Books and newspapers were stacked to the ceilings.

In his last years Burgess was to be seen around Moscow very shabbily dressed in a 1940s double-breasted suit, spotted with

1. We are indebted to Mark Frankland, a correspondent of the *Observer*, for information about Burgess's life in Moscow.

ash and cigarette burns, or in a huge, very stained, camel-hair coat dating from the same epoch. Invariably he wore an Old Etonian tie and, in his buttonhole, his Soviet decoration, the Order of the Red Banner. 'I always find it helps in restaurants,' he would say with a dismissive wave of the hand. Right to the end he was very conscious of being an Apostle, a member of that glittering Cambridge coterie which in the thirties had so valued his gifts of fluency, wit and intellectual self-confidence. In spite of his vaunted internationalism and his escapades in the Soviet service, he was in essence a product of a very restricted, very protected, very English society. In Moscow he was a fish out of water.

Unlike Kim or Donald Maclean, Burgess just was not a Russophile. He really only cared about England and his talk almost always came round to it: it was as if his conversation was fixed for ever when he left home. In his work for the Foreign Translations Publishing House he was always trying to get the Russians to publish E. M. Forster (an old Apostle); but the Russians were not enthusiastic. In Russia as in the West, Burgess was never more than semi-employed: projects for translations, some advice on English-language propaganda, were all that the Russians could find for him to do.

He was very lonely, and from the beginning grasped eagerly at links with his English past, soaking up the English papers daily and avidly listening to the overseas service of the BBC. From Moscow he used to telephone his stockbroker (for this scourge of capitalism still had a small portfolio of Rolls-Royce and gold shares), and even, from time to time, a friend of his in Hertfordshire, Peter Pollock, to ask for a hamper of choice food. The village postmistress would come galloping across the fields calling, 'Mr Pollock, it's Mr Burgess for you in Moscow!' Sometimes his overtures were rebuffed: in February 1956 Guy offered his fee for a statement in the *Sunday Express* to the Royal National Lifeboat Institution. Patriotically the RNLI declined it. Repeatedly he insisted that he had not taken out Soviet citizenship, but was still a British subject (a status recognized by the British government which, designating him a

non-resident in November 1957, allowed him to transfer dividends tax-free to Moscow for the rest of his life). He used to fall
into the arms of the very rare Old Etonian or Cambridge friend
visiting Russia and would seek out Western journalists, sometimes even gate-crashing their parties in his need for contact.
A recurrent theme of his conversation on these occasions was
his longing to go back to Britain for a holiday and his fear
about what would happen if he did. Sometimes he seemed to
think the British would prosecute him, because the 'stupid'
White Paper had called him a Soviet agent; sometimes, with
a touch of bravado, he would boast, 'They would never dare
to do anything to me – I could spill the beans about so many
people. I have many friends in high places.' Haunting the few
hotels and restaurants where he might expect to meet British
visitors, he was sorrowfully surprised at how little he was recognized.

In his last year or two he would admit, with a hint of
desperation, both that he had hardening arteries ('I think it was
Churchill who said nobody does any good work who has not
had hardening of the arteries,') and, more indiscreetly, that 'it
comes to everybody to feel he has made a mistake: I'm a
socialist, not a Communist'. He came increasingly to live on
drugs and drink, neither doing much good to his ill-treated
heart and stomach. So unpredictable did his social behaviour
become that even the two or three friends he had left were
nervous about inviting him to meals. As the end approached
he lay about in bed, asking for Alka Seltzer and protesting
about the daily injection that his Russian doctors insisted upon.
He was a sad and dreadful sight.

Late in August 1963, aged fifty-two, he died in hospital of
heart disease, and was cremated in Moscow while a brass band
played the *Internationale*. Maclean, with whom he had been on
bad terms for several years, delivered a funeral oration, describing Guy as a 'gifted and courageous man who devoted his
life to the cause of making a better world'. A KGB colleague
added a few words in Russian. Kim, the man he called his
most faithful friend, was not there. Burgess's last wishes,

scrawled on a scrap of paper found in his flat, were that a good chunk of his estate in England, £2,000 out of just over £6,000, should go to Kim, who in turn passed the money over to his children. As Burgess might have wished, his ashes were buried in England, in the churchyard at West Meon, Hampshire, the village where his family had once lived.

So ended a life which had for so long and so profoundly marked Kim's own. In a way Burgess's death, by blotting out a nostalgic past, may perhaps have helped Kim settle into Soviet life. But, as he was painfully to discover, there was one other human bond to be severed before Russia could fully claim him. Eleanor, his wife, was still very much alive and at loose out there in the West. From the moment of his flight from Lebanon he and his KGB friends wrestled with the problem of what to do about her.

It had been a good marriage and Kim, newly arrived in Russia, alone and in poor health, very much wanted it to continue. For circumstances outside his control he had disappeared from her life in a manner calculated to cause her mental anguish. But as soon as he could show his consideration and concern, he did so, in a series of notes and letters, delivered to Eleanor in Beirut by more or less clandestine means, and all urging her to join him. The principal obstacle to this plan was that she had not known he was a Soviet agent, and he could only guess how she would react to the shock of the truth. In the event the shock was too great. It was unrealistic of the KGB planners to expect that this simple, unpolitical, not very practical woman would have the skill and guile necessary to elude the clutches of the press, of Western intelligence agencies and the Lebanese police, and herd herself and the two children in her charge (one without a passport or travel document) unnoticed on to a Czechoslovak Airlines plane to Prague. These were her instructions from Kim. Their cloak-and-dagger fanciness was not calculated to reassure: she had to write the date of her flight in chalk upon the wall of an alley near her house, or, if in trouble, scrawl a cross. Not surprisingly, Eleanor chose a cross, whereupon she was visited by a Russian agent, eager to help her, but it was too late: she had already confessed all, or almost all, to Kim's so recent colleagues in British intelligence who insisted on spiriting her off to London (not, however, before they had maliciously chalked up a fictitious date on the wall, bringing Kim to Prague airport for a fruitless three-day vigil).

And so the British won the first round, but Kim won the second. He continued to write her loving letters, persuading her of his need for her, and in September 1963, with the help of the Soviet Embassy in London, she joined him in Moscow after an eight-month separation. But she brought him more embarrassment than comfort. Her gaze was fixed on their relationship, his on the challenge of adaptation to new surroundings, an enterprise for which she showed little talent or enthusiasm. She was a hopeless linguist, she feared and suffered from the cold, the drab austerities of the Soviet scene appalled her, as did the painfully restricted social life they were compelled to lead. Virtually their only friends were Donald Maclean and his American-born wife, Melinda, who after a dozen years in Russia had accommodated themselves to the monotony of an expatriate's existence. For Eleanor, Communism, the workers' state, Kim's lifelong sacrifice – all these were overshadowed by her struggle to remember the Russian word for cabbage. She did her best to create a home for Kim, but her insensitivity to his situation must have offended him. So when, nine months after her arrival, she insisted on paying a visit to America to see her daughter, he consented, although he, the Macleans and the KGB in general were understandably worried about what she might reveal to the world outside. It was finally decided that she could say anything she liked, except to give away Kim's Russian name and Moscow address.

In one of those emotional reversals so characteristic of human beings, Kim started to miss her as soon as she had left. It was in his nature to be kind and reassuring, and to express his concern in sentimental terms. Naturally enough he also wanted to retain some control over this unwitting 'spy' he had sent out into the hostile West. Thus a further series of tender

letters flowed from his typewriter, relating the little incidents of
his domestic life, expressing his loneliness in her absence, requesting her to send him lots of new books but also rubber
bands, ballpoint pens and pickling spice. Increasingly, his
letters showed that he was thrown on the company of the
Macleans, taking Melinda to concerts or on shopping expeditions when Donald was busy with the affairs of his publishing house, going with them on trips, spending weekends at
their country dacha.

These messages from Kim sustained Eleanor in her inevitable tussle with the American authorities – they confiscated her
passport for nearly five months – and brought her back to
Moscow in November 1964. Her return was a mistake. All the
old incompatibilities were there, magnified by her absence and
by the fact that she was still a stumbling novice in a life that
Kim had learned to lead. Moreover she discovered that he was
unfaithful to her. He had started an affair with Melinda
Maclean and did not seem prepared to give her up. He never
told Eleanor she had to go, but froze her out by neglect. Out-
raged, bewildered, she left Moscow for the last time in May
1965, tearfully parting with Kim in a hospital where he was
getting over his annual bout of pneumonia and the crippling
alcoholic blind in which he had sought relief from the
emotional triangle. Never an unfeeling man, Kim could not
easily rob Eleanor of her chance of happiness, but with his
usual discipline he submitted to the inevitable. A woman who
treated the KGB as a tourist agency, expecting to come and go
as she pleased across the Iron Curtain, was not a suitable wife
for the Soviet Union's greatest English spy. With a gallant
gesture paid by cynicism to innocence, the KGB saw Eleanor
off at the airport with tulips. A recidivist in marriage as in
other things, Kim has twice set up house since then: with
Melinda Maclean (who in 1976 left Russia and went home to
the United States) and, in 1970, with Nina, a Russian woman
twenty years his junior, with whom, as far as is known, he still
lives.

After leaving Moscow, Eleanor lived for only three more

years, a rather touching person, who tried to express her ambivalent feelings for her husband in a book, *Kim Philby: The Spy I Loved*, with the proceeds of which she bought a house in northern California where she died.

Kim survived. On one level his life has been an exercise in survival in the face of danger. For nearly thirty years he carried the risks of betraying his own nation-state in the service of another, living daily with fear, knowing himself a sort of fugitive, and yet emerging from the ordeal exhausted but intact enough in mind and body to find a new and dignified equilibrium in Moscow. But if he had done no more than physically survive, his career would have only the straightforward interest of an adventure story. What distinguishes Philby from other political deviants, from the venal, the indiscreet, the self-deluded, the weak in flesh or spirit, from the whole post-war rag-bag of defection and spying, is that he compels us to recognize his moral identity. His survival is more than physical. At the end of his story we are confronted with a personality rescued by moral considerations rather than destroyed by the pressures, however harsh, of his work. Like him or not, praise him or blame him, one cannot deny that his is a cultivated, even a humane, sensibility whose values, at least in non-political areas, are ours. Within the boundaries allowed him in Moscow, his life has an attractive rigour and fastidiousness. Equally respectable are the steadiness and integrity of his political positions, his readiness to assume continued responsibility for decisions taken in early manhood, the stoical submission of the self. His is a philosophy of discipline rather than self-indulgence.

Herein perhaps lies the secret of the hold he has on our attention, a pointer to the enigma he poses. How could a man who so convincingly displays such virtues have done the things he did? How could the carefully nurtured product of English upper-middle-class excellence, reared in and marked by a tradition of integrity and public service, have sent men to their deaths, have betrayed family, friends, colleagues and country?

How can a man of his sophistication excuse the repressive record of the Soviet state and hope to be accepted as morally serious by his critics in the West?

As his story shows, part of the answer is that Philby did what he had to do. He had no choice. Unlike other left-wing intellectuals of his generation, he could not, as an agent of the Russian secret service, afford to waver in his commitment to the Communism he had embraced so young. The penalties for defection were too great. Once embarked, he had to act, and he and others to suffer for it. But the crude instinct for survival was reinforced by a self-righteousness which is an expression of precisely those moral characteristics which so distinguish him. He acted as he did throughout his life, not only in self-defence but because he convinced himself that he was right: he could not countenance the thought that his moral position was full of holes. It was his very submission to an ideal which allowed him the freedom from ordinary moral restraints required by a successful penetration agent. That he paid for his ideological convictions in shattered health suggests that he did not inherit his father's iron nerve along with his arrogance. He was a brave man, all the more so as he was not physically equipped for the job he set himself.

There is a third part to the answer. From the start Philby fell under the spell of a machine, as much as of a set of ideas. His ordered and careful nature responded to the lure of belonging to a powerful organization. An insight into his attitude may be gleaned from the complacent comment he makes on his own recruitment by the Russian intelligence service: 'One does not look twice at an offer of enrolment in an élite force.'[1] Evidently he continues to derive much satisfaction from his membership of that élite, as from the approbation of his superior officers. At bottom he is an organization man, a skilled bureaucrat, good staff officer material; and in the end it has been his qualities of loyalty and method which have carried him safely through the physical hardships as well as the moral minefields of his life. It is not to undervalue bureaucrats to observe that theirs are not often free-ranging spirits, constantly putting

1. Kim Philby, op. cit., p. xix.

everything in question from their own beliefs to the foundations of society.

Philby claims to be a man of politics. He does not justify
himself in terms of his professional achievements, of the *coups*
he brought off, of the counter-*coups* he sabotaged, or of the
momentary triumph of the Soviet service which he represented.
Rather, he demands that his career be viewed in world
historical terms, as a contribution to the shaping of a Communist future. Granted he has suffered in his person some of
the great turmoils of the twentieth century, and as such lived
for and in politics more than most men. But it could also be
maintained against him that only once in his life did he make
a truly political decision – and that at an age when his judgement can hardly have been fully mature. Thereafter he could
be no more than a cog, at times an important one, in an
executive machine, serving a policy which he had no hand in
determining. This is a sacrifice, among so many others, which
the practitioners of the politics of espionage are called upon to
make.

17 Epilogue

> In the intelligence world, you can never believe
> your ciphers are broken or your friend is a
> traitor.
>
> A SECRET SERVANT

In the five years since we wrote this book, the Philby phenomenon has refused to go away and be forgotten. It is, heaven
knows, a long quarter of a century and more since Burgess and
Maclean fled to Russia, and fifteen years since Philby joined
them. Yet his shadow still haunts the corridors of Whitehall,
and in particular the minds of men of his generation, senior
civil servants retired or close to retirement. The theme of the
gentleman-traitor who betrayed the establishment of which he
was a member has also proved of undiminished fascination to
the public at large. It has inspired a play on the West End stage,
a television drama, a feature film now in preparation, and tireless investigations by press sleuths in pursuit of a possible
'Fourth Man'.

Philby was the Third Man, and as such performed a role
which this book has documented. The Fourth Man is an invention of the media, a label variously and loosely used to mean
either a master-recruiter for the Russian intelligence service in
Cambridge in the 1930s, or an insider who protected Philby
after 1951, or, more generally, a yet undiscovered agent in the
top ranks of a British government department. The very im-
precision of the phrase has spread much confusion, heightened
the aura of covert threat, and done its bit to keep the legend of
the defectors alive.

One ghost at least can now be surely laid. There was no
Soviet spy-master masquerading as an honest Englishman in
Cambridge before the war, signing up undergraduates to a
lifetime of clandestinity. That is not how recruitment to the
Russian service was done. As we have shown, the 'red thirties'
created at British universities a great pool of young people

who fell in love with the Soviet ideal and longed to transplant it in British soil. Equally there were on the do-gooding left in London, Cambridge and elsewhere a number of talent-spotters, rather older people, some English, some émigrés, in touch with the British Communist Party, or the Comintern, or one of the numerous front organizations which flourished at the time. We have named some of the more likely of them. The talent-spotter would volunteer the names of promising youngsters to his contacts, whereupon the professionals at the Russian Embassy took over, separating the wheat from the chaff, and themselves managing the transition underground of a handful of recruits. The talent-spotters, and indeed the British party, would in all probability remain in ignorance of these developments.

In June 1977 *The Times* rashly advanced the name of Mr Donald Beves, an amiable and gregarious fellow of King's College, Cambridge, from 1924 until his death in 1961, as the 'Fourth Man', suspected of a 'key role in changing Cambridge undergraduates into agents'. Unable to advance a scrap of evidence in support of the allegation, *The Times* was subsequently forced to retract it and apologize. Among the fatuities of the story was the confusion between talent-spotter and recruiter. In any event, Beves was neither.

The real significance of *The Times* story is that it was a public expression (although ill-founded) of the continuing confidential security inquiry in Whitehall. The possibility of there being a number of 'Fourth Men', in the sense of still active Soviet agents, is taken very seriously. The generation born just before the First World War and shaped by the events of the 1930s is now in its sixties and being phased out of public life through retirement or death. But the phasing out is not yet complete, and the security authorities keep a wary eye on these veterans, possibly tainted by early Communism: it would be a mistake, they consider, to underrate the potential threat from the over-sixties. Men of Kim's age still in government service continue to pay for his defection in the vetting, surveillance and other vexatious harassments they must undergo.

It is one of Philby's achievements to have deflated the complacency of the British establishment. In some ways this was no doubt salutary. But Kim's demolition job also dissolved the cement of mutual trust which must bind any ruling group together. Not only the establishment of his own generation came under scrutiny, but also the one that has since displaced it, or at any rate overlapped with it, since Labour came to power in 1964. No one is any longer safe from suspicion, if not on grounds of political ideology, then from vulnerability to blackmail, through possible financial, sexual, or other misconduct. Many prominent persons have been touched by rumour, but just which have been put on the investigators' rack is not public knowledge.

It is known, however, that in recent years the security authorities have entertained suspicions about a very senior MI5 officer who retired in 1964 and is now dead – perhaps the closest they have come to identifying a potential 'Fourth Man'. Andrew Wilson, the well-informed Defence Correspondent of the *Observer*, was the first journalist to give public attention in July 1977 to this possible 'defector in place'. The cases of such high-level suspects come before a joint team drawn from both the SIS and the Security Service and chaired by a top civil servant connected with neither. This team is believed to meet every six months to review the file of the suspected MI5 man, in the hope that one day some echo from the past will establish his guilt or innocence once and for all.

Thus, in the Whitehall his defection so altered, Kim remains actual. But his old friends are also very aware of his physical actuality in Moscow and, should they be tempted to forget him, he sends them occasional tangential reminders by way of his sons and daughters or other intermediaries. Perhaps these tentative approaches are an attempt to restore contact, to re-open a dialogue across the great divide created by his actions.

Insofar as one can judge the mood in London, there is no enthusiasm for renewed contact. The bitter hostility of the early years has been softened by the passage of time, but there is no inclination to give him succour or comfort, no readiness to strike any sort of a bargain. The hard core of resentment remaining against him is due less to his treachery to his country or to the Western cause, less to the operations he brought off for the Soviet Union or the men he sent to their deaths – these were no more than casualties of war – than to his betrayal of friends. He was false, not just to the Service, but to the men inside it who, up to the very moment of his escape, refused to think him a traitor and gave him the benefit of the doubt. If the SIS is to be criticized for its management of the Philby affair, it is because it entrusted the delicate task of extracting Kim's eleventh-hour confession to such loyal friends. A confrontation which should have been clinical was instead cosy.

Beyond the upheavals he caused in the lives of men and organizations, a wider judgement of his career can now be made in the perspective which a quarter of a century gives. Setting aside the twilight years of his last decade in the West, it can now be seen that he, Maclean and Burgess were a Soviet weapon directed against the Atlantic Alliance, and in particular against the US–UK relationship. The late 1940s and early 1950s, when America lost its atomic monopoly and was swept with anti-Communist panic, brought this relationship under great strain. The gentlemen-traitors nearly managed to snap the link, undermining American faith in all things British. Curiously, it was their uncovering rather than their espionage which nearly blew the Alliance apart and, from their point of view, was their finest hour. Paradoxically again, it was the Cold War which saved the Atlantic Alliance, together with the fact that a handful of key people in Britain were as cynical and critical as the Americans of the failings of the British establishment.

There is a further conclusion about his career which is only reinforced with the passage of time. It is the pointlessness of the enterprise to which he devoted his life. Kim became a Communist because he wanted to do something about the UK, not about the USSR. Would he not have been more fulfilled, and more effective, by declaring his ideals and working overtly to realize them, rather than by becoming the agent of a police state which allowed him no independent initiative? The West he despaired of has proved more capable of change than the Socialist fatherland he embraced. He has been left stranded by events. In an era of détente and Eurocommunism, he seems something of an anachronism.

Perhaps the flaw in his life was his love of secret power, and his exercise of it a reflection of how he regarded international affairs. But the possession of secret intelligence, although titillating, is seldom critical. Its practitioners usually find themselves on the margin of history, not in its mainstream.

Index

Abdullah (k. of Jordan), 23
Abel, Colonel, 108
Abrahams, William, 94n
Adcock, Sir Frank, 187, 195
Adler, Victor, 78
Alfonso XIII (k. of Spain), 120–21
Allen, W. E. D., 281
Alleyne, Mrs, 142, 211, 272, 292
Amies, Hardy, 162
Angell, Norman, 40
Angleton, James, 214, 218–19, 245, 250, 262
Archer, Jane, 115
Armstrong, Sir William, 157
Ascherson, Neal, 111n
Astor, David, 282
Attlee, Clement, 109, 215, 225, 248
Auden, W. H., 54, 166, 214

Baldwin, Stanley, 100, 117
Balfour-Paul, Glen, 312
Barbusse, Henri, 91n
Barrington-Ward, Robin, 116, 117
Bartlett, Vernon, 96
Bauer, Otto, 78, 80, 81, 82–3, 84, 85–6, 89
Beckett, John, 168
Bedford, Duke of, 168
Benson, Sir Rex, 152
Berding, Andrew, 214
Beria, Lavrenti, 271
Bernal, John D., 52, 70

Bernasek, Richard, 84
Best, Captain S. P., 156
Beves, Donald, 334
Birch, F., 146
Black, Max, 54n
Blackburn, 48
Blake, Anthony, 57
Blake, George, 300–301, 306, 314–15
Blum, Léon, 97
Blunt, Sir Anthony, 68, 158, 172
Blunt, Wilfred Scawen, 18
Brewer, Eleanor, 290–94, 291n, 297, 298, 299, 303–4, 311, 312, 313–14, 317, 319n, 326–9
Brewer, Sam Pope, 290–91
Bridgeman, Reginald O., 51
Briscoe, Captain R. G., 48
Brooker, Bill, 162
Brooman-White, Dick, 166–7, 198
Brown, George, 318
Browne, Professor E. G., 19
Brunswick, Duke and Duchess of, 104
Bulganin, Nikolai, 295
Bullard, Sir Reader, 128, 128n
Burgess, Guy, 64–6, 68, 92, 170, 171–2, 251, 269, 285, 292, 314, 317; Philby and, 63, 65–6, 106, 129, 147–8, 159–60, 232–4, 253–60, 262–4, 266–7, 271, 277, 278, 281, 308, 322, 325–6; Communism, 95, 100, 105–6, 107, 109, 112, 147, 172, 240, 254,

341

More About Penguins
and Pelicans